JOURNEY
OF A
RAILWAY SIGNALMAN

A History of railway signalling on Merseyside and
in North-West England.

by

TONY COOK

PHOTOGRAPHS ON FRONT COVER

1 Dougie Doughty in Ditton Junction No 1 (1959) *Author.*

2 Chapel Lane Level Crossing (1987) *H.G.*

3 Author in Edge Hill power box (1986) *Author.*

PHOTOGRAPHS ON BACK COVER

Top

Train passing the Huskisson Monument at the site of the original Parkside Station. *P. Norton Collection.*

Bottom

The last steam passenger train to run on Britain's standard gauge railway on 11th August 1968.

It stopped here at Parkside in deference to William Huskisson, MP for Liverpool, who was killed on this very spot on 15th September 1830, the opening day of the Liverpool & Manchester Railway. *Author.*

A COOK BOOK

First published in the UK in 2016.

Cook Publishing.

Written, illustrated, edited and published by **Tony Cook**
in collaboration with Alan Young, Terry Callaghan and the
8D Association.

Tony Cook
29 Gaskell Crescent,
Thornton Cleveleys,
Lancashire. FY5 2TB.

Distribution rights of this book belong to
Stephen Carnes,
53 West Street,
Crewe,
Cheshire.
CW1 3HF

Telephone: 01270 485212
Email: stevecarnes156@yahoo.com

Printed by W & G Baird Ltd,
Greystone Press,
Caulside Drive,
Antrim,
Northern Ireland.
BT41 2RS

© Anthony Cook 2016
Published by Cook Publishing

British Library Cataloguing-in-Publication Data
A catalogue record for this book is available from the British Library.

ISBN: 978-1-5262-0147-8

'This beautiful book is an extraordinary record of a period in railway history and superbly illustrated. Congratulations on such an excellent piece of work.'

Michael Portillo (MP)

Foreword

I am delighted to write this foreword to Tony's book, 'Journey of a Railway Signalman'.

It is a vivid and personal account almost in diary form of his progression from signal box boy to top class signalman, and it covers events on Merseyside and the West Coast Main Line in the 80 signal boxes in which he worked. Many hundreds of signalmen will relate to this story as they progressed on a similar route.

However, this book is an indispensable historical record not only of signal boxes that have been abolished, but of some of the lines as well.

Many signal boxes controlled entrances to sidings which served factories, chemical works, collieries, local traders and other businesses, but the ongoing industrial decline made it necessary to dispense with some of them. In addition, the concept of power signalling was introduced. These changes have now been further accelerated with the introduction of those hideous signalling centres being built in office blocks throughout the country: so remote from the real world!

In my signalling career I remember the wonderful sights of a Class 8 'Austerity' steaming its way up the bank on a frosty moonlit night with 50-or-so wagons of coal to furnish the ships' bunkers on the Mersey, or a double-headed 'Class 9' roaring its way from Bidston Docks with iron ore for Shotton steel works. I remember the Up and Down night sleepers and postal trains between London and Scotland dashing through the night on the West Coast Main Line, and I have no doubt that Tony and many other people can recall them, but, regrettably, these heart-stirring moments are no more. This historical record, as well as being a personal one, is certain to prove its worth not only to railwaymen but to railway enthusiasts as a whole.

Enjoy the hidden stories unfolding in signal boxes which are so well recorded here.

Ron Couchman, formerly Area Manager for British Rail at Manchester Piccadilly.

I first crossed paths with the author of this book (Tony Cook senior) back in the summer of 1992.

I was working for British Rail as a Relief Signalman on the night shift at Astley Level Crossing signal box, whilst Tony was working as a fellow signalman operating the central panel at the neighbouring Warrington power signal box a few miles away. One of my first, and lasting, memories of him is that he would occasionally tell his colleagues stories about his own working life, the characters he met and workplaces now, sadly, long gone. I recall him telling me that during his railway career he had worked in no fewer than 80 different signal boxes throughout the North-West of England as he progressed through the signalling and operating grades.

He finally retired in the mid 1990s at the height of his railway career.

They do say that there is at least one book in all of us: well, this one is Tony's.

'This is Tony's story.' H.G.

H.G in Brewery Sidings signal box, Manchester.

CHAPTER		PAGE

INTRODUCTION

Railways have always played a significant part in my life, and there have been many uncanny incidents which were hard to understand at the time, but which I now believe were predestined rather than merely a matter of chance. I was born in the Lincolnshire town of Stamford in 1930, and I recall the train journey, at the age of four, that brings my family to the seaside town of New Brighton on the Wirral peninsula in Cheshire.

New Brighton station; our home is extreme left.

Courtesy of Liverpool Echo.

Our home stands next to the Victoria Hotel - recently gutted by a devastating fire - overlooking the wide expanse of the Mersey estuary, with the Lancashire coastline merging into the distant horizon. In the foreground runs a railway line, minuscule in comparison to the overall land and seascape. We have a large garden, and a shed full of doves at the back of the house, but I find much more interest in the almost endless procession of liners and merchant vessels steaming into, and out of, Liverpool and Birkenhead.

'RMS Titanic' and tug boats. Courtesy of Liverpool Echo.

My attention is frequently drawn to a passing electric train; but the ships have more character, almost certainly owing to the continuous spiralling smoke trails in their wake which create visual patterns of movement. By contrast the trains just resemble boxes running on rails.

It is not long after seeing **HM Submarine 'Thetis'** passing New Brighton lighthouse on its fateful voyage that my friends and I, from Christ Church School, Birkenhead, are marching down Borough Road in pairs. We are sporting giant labels pinned to our coats, each of us with a small brown cardboard box slung over our shoulders containing a contraption called a gas-mask.

HM Submarine 'Thetis' 1938.

Courtesy of Liverpool Echo.

'Where are we going?'

After first passing the white-coloured library we arrive at Woodside railway station. In No1 platform stands a train with steam and smoke rising into the semi-circular roof, forming a cloud that partially restricts the daylight. The green engine, decorated with gleaming brass work, contrasts sharply with the drab brown coaches that it will pull. A whistle sounds, and slowly the train begins its journey to an unknown destination: unknown to us, anyway!

Evacuees boarding train: 3rd September 1939.

Courtesy of Liverpool Echo.

Today is **3rd September 1939,** and war has just been declared, but this has little significance for a lad of my age. I watch the beautiful countryside pass by, listening to the 'clickety-clack' as we speed along through such stations as Ruabon, Oswestry, Abermule and Newtown. A river meanders alongside in zigzag fashion, as we travel through the mountains dotted with farmsteads and fields filled with grazing animals. The train stops; the man in the signal box gives the driver of our train a large hoop. Off we go again, only to stop a few miles further on so the driver can hand the hoop to someone on a station platform.

Train in Llanidloes Station. Courtesy of Ben Brooksbank.

After a journey of several hours we arrive at our destination. It is a place with an unpronounceable name and, to judge from the number of people on the platform compared to the modest size of the town, most of the inhabitants have turned out to welcome us.

Evacuees arriving at Llanidloes station. Photo by Author.

The town of Llanidloes, Montgomeryshire, which is to be my home for the next three years, nestles at the meeting point of four valleys. The confluence of the rivers Clwedog and Severn is in the centre of the town. The single-track railway from Builth Road, in the Wye valley, passes half-a-mile south into the Severn valley, continuing to Moat Lane Junction, near Newtown. I spend many a happy hour on Gorn Hill, overlooking the beautiful valley of the sinuous Severn, silver in colour, threading its way to infinity through the verdant fields. A small puff of brilliant white smoke against the blue background of the hills reveals the position of an approaching train, invisible from my viewpoint; the black dot grows larger, until it assumes a snake-like appearance as it wends its way up the valley from Dolwen. This spectacle, so often repeated, never ceases to fascinate me.

It is May 1941 and enemy aircraft are passing overhead on their way to Merseyside. The new home of my family, in the Harrison Drive area of the Wirral, is completely destroyed; then two weeks after the family has taken up residence in Blenheim Road, Egremont, overlooking the River Mersey, a bomb severely damages this house, forcing a further move.

In early 1943 I arrive in the Sefton Park area of Liverpool at our new home in Ferndale Road. Two hundred yards away a railway line runs past, at right angles, and it is always possible to know when a train is approaching because of the two signals that are in a direct line with the centre of the road. Unlike most boys of my age I never wished to be a train driver, though I must admit that railways now begin to occupy my thoughts.

In 1944 I start work, not on the railways, but at the British Home Stores in Lord Street, Liverpool, as a stockroom boy. After a few months I am transferred to their store in Standishgate, Wigan, which involves a train journey every day from Liverpool Exchange station to Wigan Wallgate. Opposite the latter station is a high embankment on top of which is a brick-built signal box; it stands isolated, backed by a vast expanse of sky. Its name, WIGAN NO 2, is proclaimed in concrete on its eastern facade, the name nearly as long as the signal box. While I am waiting for my train home, I sit and watch in awe as speeding trains pass this signal box, and I think secretly, 'I would like to work here.' A couple of years pass by as I carry out my menial tasks.

But I am not really happy and decide that I need a change.

Lord Street, Liverpool in 1944. BHS is to the right.

Courtesy of Liverpool Echo.

CHAPTER ONE

LADS, MEN AND SIGNALBOXES (LMS)

1947-49

EDGE HILL No 13 SIGNAL BOX

My uncle, Ozzie Wheeler, worked as a foreman on the London Midland & Scottish Railway at Wapping Bank Head. This was the site of the original passenger station, quite close to the existing one at Edge Hill, Liverpool. The cabin that his staff used was a room chiselled out of the solid sandstone in the cutting wall at the time when the railway was built. He joined the railway shortly after the Boer War and spent his entire railway career in the Edge Hill area. On many occasions he reminisces to me about his experiences, and it is no surprise when he lets me know that he wants me to follow in his footsteps. This comes to fruition when I am accepted for employment on the LMS just after the Second World War.

I leave my home in the centre of Liverpool to report to the administration offices in Picton Road, where a bridge spans a large group of railway sidings east of Edge Hill station. After the preliminary documentation is completed, the Yard Master informs me that I will be working in a signal box. Departing from the offices, he and I make our way on foot through the Park Sidings. Wagons are hurtling down the nearby tracks and colliding with those which are already stationary, catapulting coal all over the place and giving the whole area the appearance of a colliery rather than railway sidings. Continuing on, we arrive at the Park Sidings shunting cabin where the foreman is puffing on his pipe, surveying the activities around him. The Yard Master and he have a conversation regarding the workings of the yard, then exchange farewells.

We pass Exhibition Sidings, filled with loaded coal trains, and the large Littlewood's Pools building provides a backdrop to the scene. Gingerly, we step over a few tracks to reach the safety of a pathway on the perimeter of the railway. As it approaches a signal box in the distance, a train emitting a large amount of drifting smoke blots out our view momentarily but, as it clears, a sign becomes visible:

EDGE HILL No 13.

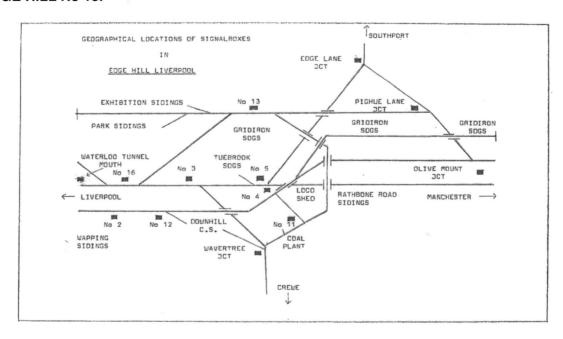

Locations of signal boxes in the Edge Hill area.

Edge Hill No 13 signal box. Photo by J A Sommerfield, courtesy of Martin Bott.

Edge Hill No 13 signal box is to be my place of work for 18 months. I am introduced to the signalman, Alf, and the box lad, John. It is their unenviable task to train me for my new position. John has received his calling-up papers and is leaving in three weeks' time to join the army.

A desk supporting a train register book stands against the back wall, halfway along the signal box. On this wall are six old telephones connected to the various signal boxes and cabins in the immediate area. Behind me the signalman is busy pushing and pulling levers of different colours, as bells ring on the instruments above the lever frame. Trains pass at regular intervals on the eight tracks outside the signal box, and a safety valve on a boiler at the nearby Automatic Telephone works blows off every so often, adding to the dissonant sounds. The first problem I encounter concerns the desk: owing to my limited height I cannot reach it. However, Alf produces a hammer and nails from a locker - which also acts as a seat, with a suitable piece of wood propped up to serve as a back rest for him - and within ten minutes he has made a small box for me to stand on.

The paintwork inside the signal box, originally cream, has a distinct grey colour; the emissions from the two coal-fired stoves that stand equidistant from the desk go some way to explain this, but the paintwork has clearly not been refreshed since before the war.

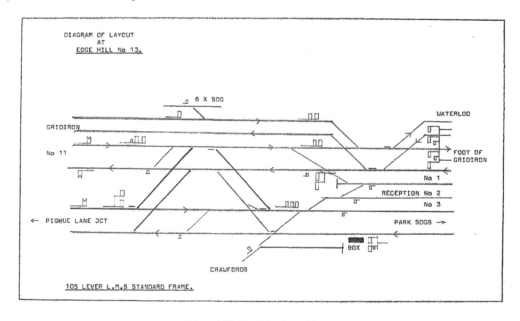

Edge Hill No 13 signal box.

Electric lights illuminate the main areas and between them, suspended from the apex of the roof, are two old fashioned glass-domed oil lamps, for emergency use only. These have been home to many spiders whose dust-covered webs still surround them. Most of the windows are decorated with black tape in a lattice-work, designed to prevent bomb blast damage; others are completely opaque, to conform to blackout regulations. An attempt has been made to scrape them clean, but with negligible success. In the corner stands a cabinet in which the signalman can take refuge during air raids, but there is nowhere for the box lad to take cover; perhaps he is expected to sit on the signalman's knee!

A box lad's duties consist of answering telephones, booking trains, stoking the fires and general cleaning; the latter task includes burnishing the lever tops with chain-mail to give them a chrome-like finish. His primary duty seems to be ensuring that the signalman has sufficient liquid refreshment to sustain him by brewing tea from the kettle which is continually boiling on one of the stoves. All railwaymen are issued with ¼-lb of tea, 2-lb sugar and a tin of 'conny-onny' (condensed milk) per month to supplement their official quota, so brews are plentiful.

The day arrives when I am issued with my first uniform. **LMS** badges adorn both lapels of the jacket and my cap, which I nonchalantly wear on my head in a cocked position. Alf gives me a 'pay to bearer' note to collect his wages from the office in Picton Road, but I am quite oblivious to the fact I have left my cap in the signal box; that is until I bump into the Yard Master - a small sprightly gentleman - only yards from my destination.

'Where's your cap, laddie?' he enquires. I tell him.

'Well, you just go back and get it, and never let me see you improperly dressed again.' Like a dog with tail between its legs, I reluctantly retrace my steps, and returning later in my full regalia I join the queue leading to the pay hut window, behind which sit two very stern-looking chaps.

'Smith, £2.5s.' shouts one, not taking his eyes off the large sheet of paper in front of him. *'Smith, £2.5s.'* booms the other, with looks to kill, as he counts the money and thrusts a hand through a small aperture to enable the recipient to collect his dues. One gets the impression that they begrudge handing it over, as if it were their own money. I hand in the note.

'Davies, £4.10s.' *'Davies, £4.10s,'* the right jab nearly dislodging my headgear.

'Number 201,' I say. *'Cook, £1.10s.'* *'Cook, £1.10s.'*

I can picture this pair at home, shouting, *'Rent, 7s.6d,'* *'Coalman 4s,'* *'Milkman 2s.6d.'* As guardian of this vast sum of money I return to the signal box where Alf, like a miser, carefully divides the notes and places them in a diary that he always carries in his waistcoat pocket. I shall see this performance repeated so many times, and it never ceases to amuse me.

Being 16 years old now, by law I can work on the night turn of duty. I am amazed at the amount of traffic in and out of Edge Hill marshalling yards. Each train is recorded in a register, and upwards of 120 freight trains pass this signal box during the night. However, the early and afternoon shifts are somewhat busier, mainly because of the local trip traffic.

In addition to the Up and Down Circular, Independent and Waterloo lines, there are three reception roads in front of the signal box which are connected with crossings and crossover roads, making a very complex junction. There are two sidings, one used by the Permanent Way Department, running onto the Down Waterloo line, whilst the other enters Messrs Crawford's private yard to the left of the signal box. All the signals are of the lower quadrant semaphore type, with the exception of two upper quadrant ones just outside the signal box, on the Up Circular line. The signals and points are connected to a pre-1943 LMS Standard Frame of some 105 levers.

4-6-0 'Claughton' No 6004, in its maroon livery, is approaching under the large signal gantry opposite the Park Sidings cabin, hauling an Edge Hill to Willesden fast freight train; Liverpool's fine Gothic Cathedral is in the distance, towering high above it. The engine, swaying from side to side, is getting to grips with the heavy load, pumping volumes of white smoke into the otherwise clear sky, giving a wonderful perspective to the overall scene. The distinctive clang at every revolution of the wheels sounds as if the big-ends have reached their last. Pungent fumes seep through the ill-fitting windows as it passes, but are soon replaced by the piquant aroma of baking biscuits emanating from Crawford's works, a few hundred yards away.

I manage to scrounge a lift on Target No 20, working to Edge Hill locomotive shed with coal. An **LMS 0-6-0 'Jinty'** engine hauls the wagons via the Up Circular line, taking the left fork at No 11 signal box, where the guard must obtain an Annett's key to unlock the ground frame points leading onto the two coal hopper roads. On one side of the hopper stands an **LMS 4-6-2 Princess Royal Pacific** in its familiar maroon livery; coaled up. The driver, dwarfed by its immense size, is oiling the motion gear prior to departure for Liverpool, when suddenly coal is released from the wagons high above with a deafening roar, accompanied by a suffocating black cloud of coal dust which completely obliterates the scene from my vantage point. The driver brushes his overalls and climbs aboard the dust-covered engine looking none too pleased, whilst the fireman, atop the **LMS 4-6-0 'Black Five'** standing on the next road, begins to fill his tender, unconcerned.

Edge Hill No 11 signal box. Photo by J A Sommerfield, courtesy of Martin Bott.

Looking down from the Coal Hopper line, Downhill Carriage Sidings lie in a large south-to-west curve from Wavertree Junction, ½-mile to the left, to Picton Road Bridge, nearly a mile in front. A shunter is busily stabling coaching stock arriving from Lime Street station, and cleaners are at the ready with their buckets and long-handled brushes. Between the locomotive shed and the carriage sidings platelayers are changing fishplates on the main line, curving in the same arc underneath the Wapping lines, and hand signalmen are positioned to warn them of approaching trains.

The signalman in Edge Hill No 4 signal box - my intended destination - views all off this activity 450yd from the north, and it is here that I have an appointment to get my hair cut. Ambling back towards No 11 signal box, along the ash-topped embankment, I am alerted by a whistle: Stopping, I raise my arm in acknowledgement as a freight train is quite close. It is hauled by a large **2-8-0 'Austerity'** locomotive, which is braking on the slight right-hand curve just before the junction, the wheel flanges squealing in resistance against the rails.

Edge Hill No 11 signal box, small in comparison to others nearby, is nevertheless extremely busy as it controls the entrance to the locomotive shed, through points on the Wapping lines, and a connection into Rathbone Road Goods Yard opposite. The Up and Down Circular lines, from Edge Hill No 13 to Wavertree Junction signal boxes, form a junction with the Wapping lines here. Situated in the 'V', the signal box looks very much like a greenhouse, there being windows on all sides, although in one corner six panes of glass are painted white to give a little privacy to the occupants.

The desk, placed by the side window, is ideally situated for locomotive spotting because it overlooks the turntable on the shed. Jack, the signalman on duty, is an avid collector of engine numbers, and a quick glance at his books proves that few have eluded him. The box lad, my younger brother Roy, has pulled the signals 'Off' for a **4-6-0 'Jubilee'** to drop onto the shed, while Jack views it through a pair of binoculars with pen at the ready. After participating in a welcome cup of tea I bid them farewell, then set off to walk along the Wapping lines towards No 4 signal box.

Rathbone Road Goods Yard consists of 11 sidings used mainly by coal distributors serving private householders in the area. It abuts the locomotive shed with its 22 roads spreading fan-like in an easterly direction, as viewed from the bridge on which I am standing. The whole area is enclosed by the Circular line embankment on the south and east sides, and a high dividing wall to the north gives it the character of an amphitheatre.

Edge Hill No 4 signal box with a London & North Western Railway Tumbler frame (the LNWR was amalgamated in 1923 with other railway companies to form the LMS) is situated in a very precarious position; it stands on the edge of a high sandstone block wall overlooking the Liverpool to Manchester main line, quadrupled between Lime Street station and Huyton Junction. It controls the Wapping Goods lines from Edge Hill No 11 to No 12 signal box, abutting Picton Road bridge, ¾-mile away down a 1 in 68 gradient.

Edge Hill No 4 signal box. Photo by J A Sommerfield, courtesy of Martin Bott.

Outside the signal box a single line (the Auxiliary), which serves as a feeder for traffic travelling up to the Top Gridiron Sidings, branches to the left over a viaduct; the main lines pass below. Contiguous, and running parallel to this single line for 200yd, then curving in an easterly direction, the Up and Down Goods lines descend a 1 in 68 gradient to Olive Mount Junction. In addition, No 4 box signals locomotives departing from the shed onto the main line underneath the Wapping lines bridge. Despite of the elevated position of the signal box the view in every direction is entirely railway-connected.

Charlie, the signalman on my turn of duty, is barber to the local railwaymen; this is his hobby. As he cuts my hair, I notice geranium plants standing on a long shelf which runs under the signal box windows, and tomato plants growing in a pot on an unused locker in a corner, adding colour to the drab surroundings. Passing below, an express in transit to Manchester, headed by **Royal Scot 4-6-0 6132 'The King's Regiment Liverpool',** has entered onto the **'Roaring Rail',** and as each coach passes, the roar increases to a crescendo, lessening as the train draws away. This phenomenon is due entirely to the bedrock formation, and it also serves as a useful barometer: a roar louder than the norm foretells rain!

The next move is an **LMS 0-8-0 'Super D'** locomotive propelling 12 wagons up the single line towards the Top Gridiron Sidings. These sidings consist of six roads, commencing at Rathbone Road overbridge and terminating on a single stop block line 25ft above Mill Lane, Wavertree. A few weeks ago one of these trains collided with the stop block at some considerable speed, causing the wagons to pile up in the middle of the lane! Luckily, no one was hurt in this incident.

Edge Hill No 3 signal box. Photo by R Stephens, courtesy of 8D Association.

Edge Hill No 5 signal box, at the west end of Picko Tunnel, signals trains on the four main lines between Olive Mount Junction and Edge Hill No 3 signal boxes. It also controls the eastern end of the 14 roads in Tuebrook Sidings, where most of the northbound trains from Edge Hill are marshalled, and the Up and Down Bootle lines through the tunnel to Edge Lane Junction. A triangle is thus formed, bordered by Olive Mount Junction, Edge Lane Junction and this signal box, which is frequently used to turn locomotives working in the northern sector of the marshalling yards. At the other end of Tuebrook Sidings stands Edge Hill No 16 signal box, adjacent to Picton Road bridge, signalling trains from the latter, and Waterloo Tunnel Mouth signal boxes. In addition it controls the exit from the Bottom Gridiron Sidings.

Edge Hill No 16 signal box. Photo by J A Sommerfield, courtesy of Martin Bott.

Two tunnels at Edge Hill deserve mention. The first, Picko Tunnel, between Edge Lane Junction and Edge Hill No 5 signal box, derives its name from Picko Lane, which no longer exists. It followed a line from Pighue Lane, near Crawford's biscuit works, to Long Lane, off Rathbone Road. The geographical features in this area are interesting, for when the Bootle Branch line opened in 1866 the track from Edge Hill No 5 signal box travelled through a small 10ft-deep sandstone cutting, bridged at Pighue Lane.

Much of Edge Hill Gridiron Sidings is formed by a man-made embankment built in 1882 on a sandstone outcrop, with a natural fall from the 80ft-high Olive Mount levelling off in the vicinity of Botanic Park; hence the need to build the brick-arched Picko Tunnel to carry the 28 Sorting Sidings of the Middle Gridiron. In addition the Circular lines were laid between Nos 11 and 13 signal boxes, passing over the Bootle Branch line and under the Gridiron, thereby creating three levels of railway, which is unusual by any standards. The southern end of the tunnel lies close to the original lane upon which Edge Hill Locomotive Shed and the junction at No 11 signal box were built. A subway, in use today to reach the locomotive shed from Long Lane, follows roughly the same course as the old Picko Lane.

The other tunnel worthy of mention - Waterloo Tunnel - is situated near to Edge Hill station. The signal box named Waterloo Tunnel Mouth is adjacent to the Up Slow line. This tunnel was hewn through solid sandstone in 1849 and it leads to Waterloo Goods Yard and Riverside station, at the Pier Head. However, the name Waterloo is misleading, because Victoria Tunnel, 2 miles long, with a 1 in 60 downward gradient and running under the city of Liverpool, precedes the ¼-mile Waterloo Tunnel, with an upward gradient, which terminates at the Lancashire & Yorkshire Railway overbridge leading to Exchange station. The tunnels are separated by 200yd of level track within a very deep brick-lined cutting, in the vicinity of Byrom Street.

Waterloo Tunnel Mouth signal box. Photo by J A Sommerfield, courtesy of Martin Bott.

Riverside station was used intensively during the Second World War by troops embarking on the ships moored nearby. Today, trains run frequently to coincide with the departure of many ocean-going liners, the famous 'Cunarders' among them.

The busiest signal box in the area is situated at the eastern end of Edge Hill station platforms. This is No 2, which employs two signalmen on each turn with a box lad assisting on the early and afternoon shifts. It signals trains on the four lines between Lime Street Station and Edge Hill No 3 signal boxes, also the Wapping Goods lines from Wapping Bank Head and Edge Hill No 12 signal box, and it has control of the carriage sidings close to the station. Of brick construction, with a pre-1943 LMS Standard Frame, it was built in the early 1940s.

It took over the workings of Edge Hill No 1 signal box in July 1947 which formerly stood in the Lime Street cutting. The line to Liverpool Lime Street station opened in 1836 but, until 1870, all trains were worked to and from Edge Hill using the stationary engine house on Edge Hill station platform. Shunting at the terminal station was carried out using horses. In 1885, widening of the large sandstone cutting was completed to enable the tracks to be quadrupled. This 1½-mile stretch of railway contains no fewer than seven tunnels and is on a 1 in 93 gradient.

Edge Hill No 2 signal box. Photographer unknown, courtesy of Tony Graham collection.

Prior to 1865-66 a level crossing existed 1½ miles east of the Crown Street terminus, where Leigh Street crossed the new railway at right angles from Botanic Park in the north to the township of Wavertree in the south. The crossing keeper's house, which survived until recent years, was situated on ground now occupied by the gas works.

Spekeland Road goods sheds, and Gullet Sidings at Edge Hill.

Courtesy of Liverpool Echo.

The building of the now nine-arch Picton Road bridge commenced in 1865 using excavated sandstone, possibly from the Lime Street cutting; but judging from the present structure, I would assume that it originally had ten arches, the missing pier being replaced by two rows of monstrous concrete columns, out of keeping with the bridge and marring its overall appearance. Leigh Street itself has passed into history, but there remains a short stretch of the cobble-stoned roadway leading to the administration offices used only by plutocratic railwaymen for parking their cars. Near the base of the southernmost pier the foundation plaque can be seen, fitted in 1865 and indicating the boundary line between the Borough of Liverpool and the Township of Wavertree. Today, however, Edge Hill and Wavertree are both within the City of Liverpool. Edge Hill No 3 signal box, worked by two signalmen on each turn, is on the other side of Picton Road bridge and diverts traffic onto the sharp curve leading up to the junction at Wavertree station.

The smallest signal box at Edge Hill is No 12, its total length being only approximately 12ft, and much less wide. It is situated directly opposite No 16 signal box, on the Down Fast line side, dwarfed by a large water tower used by train crews to fill up their locomotive tenders. It signals trains on the Wapping Goods lines and controls the western connections of Downhill Carriage

Sidings. The specially adapted Webb Sketch 80 Frame has exposed spring-loaded catch handles, similar to those found on ground frames. In spite of its diminutive size it is, nevertheless, a busy signal box.

Edge Hill No 12 signal box; No 2 is in the background.

Photographer unknown. Courtesy of Tony Graham collection.

Wavertree Junction signal box, on the southern side of Edge Hill, stands in a prominent position on a high embankment overlooking Messrs Edmondson's sweet factory. It is built entirely of wood around a large LNWR Tumbler Frame, the signals from which are a mixture of upper and lower quadrant semaphores. The Circular lines and the southern end of Downhill Carriage Sidings merge into the slow lines, whilst the Wavertree curve joins the Fast, all lines being interconnected by a double junction.

Telephonic communication is not very good in the Edge Hill area, and this signal box has no direct link with the switchboard operator at the Picton Road offices; all messages have to be relayed via No 11 signal box. My brother receives a message to pass on:

'WAVERTREE JUNCTION SIGNAL BOX IS ON FIRE!'

The switchboard operator duly advises the fire brigade, but on their arrival it turns out to be a false alarm! Some six weeks later the same message is repeated and my brother can see the flames shooting up into the night sky, but there is no way that he can convince the same operator, who was castigated for the false alarm, with the result that:

'WAVERTREE JUNCTION SIGNAL BOX IS RAZED TO THE GROUND!'

The signalman on duty at the time mends watches as a hobby, and luckily the locker in which they are stored is saved from the inferno, sparking off the story that he had started it! However, the signal box was heated by a large coke stove underneath, and the most likely cause was a spark setting the tinder-dry woodwork alight. Three weeks later the signal box is replaced with one which has an LMS Standard Frame installed.

The lines between Wavertree Junction and Sefton Park station run along a high embankment, and on its eastern side a large tract of land is visible; this is **Wavertree Playground**, locally known as the **'Mystery'**. An anonymous person donated this land to the citizens of Liverpool, (hence its nickname) on condition that it remained as a source of pleasurable pursuits. During the war, huge tree trunks were erected all over the open space to deter enemy aircraft or gliders from using it as a landing ground. In addition, barrage balloons were sited here in large numbers and in many other empty spaces throughout Merseyside.

In 1930, celebrations were held here to commemorate the centenary of the Liverpool & Manchester Railway. Among the many attractions was a circular railway erected for the benefit of the visitors. Inside the park, adjacent to Wellington Road overbridge, the embankment has been extended 50yd outwards from the railway for a length of 200yd. It is almost certain that this land, occupied at present by pigeon cotes, remains the only reminder of the auspicious occasion for which it was built as a means of access from the railway line into the park.

Hundreds of men work in the Edge Hill area, covering every grade from the Yard Master down to the humble signal box lad; but without doubt the most willing workers are six shunters, two on each shift, stationed at the Gridiron Sidings. No-one ever hears them complain, as they toil laboriously at their duties in all weather conditions, receiving only friendship and a good feed in recompense. I refer to the six shire horses, of the highest calibre, who are looked after well by their devoted handlers.

The massive Gridiron Sidings, opened in 1882, are divided into three main groups. First, there are the six Top Gridiron Reception Sidings, situated between Mill Lane and Rathbone Road. Next follow the 28-road Middle Gridiron Sorting Sidings, commencing at Rathbone Road and terminating opposite No 4 signal box. Finally there are 34 Bottom Gridiron Marshalling Sidings. All of the sidings merge at No 16 signal box.

The sidings on the northern side of the Bottom Gridiron Sidings (Exhibition Sidings) derived their name from the exhibition opened by Queen Victoria in 1861 on the site of the present Littlewood's Pools building and Liverpool Corporation's tram sheds in Edge Lane. The Queen alighted from the train in Botanic Park, a track having been laid specially for the occasion. The sandstone portals through which the train passed are still standing today and are the only visible reminder of the great exhibition.

As the shunting on the Gridiron is by gravity there is always the possibility of a train running away on the steep gradient. To avoid this eventuality, three large grab hooks are positioned at strategic points, each controlled by a shunter and a protecting signal. The signal at danger signifies that the hook, fastened to a long chain of some five tons in weight, is set at axle level. In use, the chain is dragged from its housing when the hook engages on the wheel axle, succeeding in stopping the heaviest of trains before any serious damage can be done. Resetting these mechanical wonders is achieved by using the ever-faithful horses, although at times shunting engines are utilised if the horsepower is otherwise engaged.

Bogie Bolster wagons have extremely long wheelbases, and one is being shunted on the Gridiron, but the rear set of wheels goes down a different road from the front ones. Between the two lines stands a 40ft-high lighting pole and this is cut in half as the wagon careers on until it reaches the safety provided by the drag hooks, with both sets of wheels on the same line!

During the war these marshalling yards were a prime target for enemy aircraft, and many shelters were built for railway staff in the area. Little damage was done through enemy action, though a bomb did explode in Exhibition Sidings. The surrounding district, however, received a real hammering, and probably the most serious single incident in Merseyside during the blitz occurred only ¼-mile from here when Clint Road School was hit, killing many people who were sheltering in its cellars.

I arrive back at No 13 signal box, and Alf remarks, *'It took you a long time to get a haircut.'* and, after a long pause, *'Nearly time for your next one.'* I bow my head in guilt!

Opposite the signal box, and used by the Permanent Way Department to stable their traffic, is 6x Siding. A guard's brake van is on fire here, illuminating the night sky; but fear not, help is at hand, and firemen have connected hoses to hydrants nearby and are winning the battle. Lo and behold, here comes the Waterloo to Gridiron Tripper*, travelling flat out up the heavy gradient, slicing through the hoses that have been carefully laid across the track. Thereafter the bemused onlookers can only gaze impotently at the incineration process!

[*Trippers are trains conveying traffic to local yards, usually within a radius of 15 miles, and so as to distinguish them, each is given a Target number.]

18

Two Relief Signalmen (father and son) work in this signal box on occasions, and I observe that they use different coloured chalk to mark the levers. A small plate on the front of each lever bears its number, and underneath this is a series of numbers corresponding with others in the frame, which must be pulled in the sequence shown before the actual lever required can be operated. This system is known as the sequential locking.

These two signalmen are not content with the numerical aid and have adopted the chalk method - one which I cannot decipher. The Block Bells have different sounds to distinguish them from each other, but Wal and Arthur fasten wire to the hammers, tying a small piece of paper on the end. The purpose of this novel idea is that when the bell rings the wire vibrates and the pieces of paper flutter like butterflies, indicating the source of the ring!

Every young lad is subjected to humiliating situations by their elders, like the time I started work at the British Home Stores. I was given a tea-chest full of mothballs to date-stamp! Commencing work on the railway is no exception, and the following takes place at my expense in No 13 signal box, to the great amusement of many. No 2 Home Signal on the Down Circular line reads to No 3 Starting Signal, protecting the Up and Down Waterloo lines; but No 1 lever, which is painted white, I never pull, and this puzzles me somewhat. So one day I ask Alf about its function.

'I've been waiting for you to ask me that question.' he says, adding, *'Have you noticed the locomotives with the tall chimneys?'* I nod.

'Well, they won't go under that bridge,' he advises, pointing to the Gridiron bridge passing over the Circular lines.

'So when you pull No 1 lever over, it lifts the bridge slightly, to allow sufficient head-room. There's no need to pull it for trains being hauled by "Saddlebacks" or "Super Ds",' he concludes.

This is all very well, pulling lever No 1 after No 2, but the last signal on the Up Circular line is operated by lever No 103, so I am dashing up and down the signal box like a blue-ass fly between the two, hoping that I am quick enough to avert what could lead to a chimney-less locomotive! Alf cunningly manages to keep this charade up for many weeks.

Alf, a portly gentleman, aged about 48, has worked in the Edge Hill area for many years, but the thing that fascinates me about him - apart from noticing that he is always in the horizontal position - is the way that he deftly shaves around the dimple in the centre of his chin, prior to getting relieved.

Christmas Day and, indeed, all Bank Holidays are no different from other days in the life of a working railwayman who is unable to join in the festivities to the full. Take New Year's Eve, for instance. Making my way to report for night duty in the signal box, I envy the revellers intent on enjoying themselves whilst I slave away. Two hours pass with little change, but on the stroke of midnight the ships on the River Mersey in Liverpool and Birkenhead Docks blast off their hooters. Simultaneously, the locomotives in the Edge Hill area sound their whistles, along with scores of now redundant air-raid sirens in the area. On the Gridiron the shunters play their part, expending all the out-of-date detonators, and no doubt, some in-date fog detonators, by running a wagon or shunting engine over them. The noise is unbelievable, but makes for exciting listening. At least for a few minutes one forgets being jealous.

Hogmanay may come, and Hogmanay may go, but New Year's Eve at Edge Hill is an unforgettable experience.

It may be noticed that omissions appear in the numbering of the signal boxes at Edge Hill. This is because some boxes have closed in years gone by, and Inspectors' and ground frame cabins are also numbered.

Edge Hill station.
Crown Street Tunnels to the left, Waterloo Tunnel to the right.
Courtesy of Liverpool Echo.

Southport-London coaches at Atlantic Dock Junction.
Courtesy of J A Peden.

'Super D' at Atlantic Dock Junction. Courtesy of J A Peden

To the right is a portion of the Downhill Carriage Sidings, chiefly used to stable and clean passenger coaches prior to departure to Liverpool Lime Street station terminus.

The two lines where the **'Jinty'** is standing are the Up and Down Wapping lines, commonly known as the 'Crack' to railwaymen. At the end of these lines can be seen Edge Hill No 4 (Viaduct Junction) signal box which, in addition to signalling trains onto the 'Auxiliary' line destined for the Top of the Gridiron Sidings, controls trains on the Up and Down Goods lines to Olive Mount Junction, and to No 11 signal box. It also signals trains on the Up and Down Chat Moss lines below, with a connection from Edge Hill shed to the Down Chat Moss line only. The signal box to the left is Edge Hill No 3, signalling trains to Wavertree Junction to the south and Olive Mount Junction to the east. Behind this box are Tuebrook Sidings, controlled at this end by Edge Hill No 16 and by No 5 box to the east. (No 3 box deals only with main line traffic.) Again, further left are the Bottom Gridiron Sidings, and the Middle and Top group further east which are stop-blocked high above Olive Mount signal box. In the background the factory on the left is the Automatic Telephone works and, to the right of this, Crawford's biscuit works. The express train is approaching No 2 signal box on the Down Fast line, and whilst this is adjacent to No 12 box, this actually only signals trains on the Goods lines to No 2 box.

Leaving Downhill Carriage Sidings.

Courtesy of Roy Wills.

On Edge Hill locomotive shed. Courtesy of Roy Wills.

'Super D' at Stanley. Courtesy of J A Peden.

On Edge Hill shed. (Loco passing on Wapping line.)
Courtesy of Roy Wills.

CHAPTER TWO

SIGNALMAN TRAINING

1950

PIGHUE LANE JUNCTION SIGNAL BOX

At the tender age of 18, I report to the 8th Training Regiment of the Royal Engineers (8th TRRE) in Elgin, Scotland and apply to work on the Longmoor Railway which they run. However, the hierarchy have other ideas and transfer me to the Army Air Transport Training and Development Centre (AATDC) based at RAF Abingdon, Berkshire, where I am put to work on 'Hawser' and 'Hamilcar' gliders. At least I am working in a transport environment. Later, the No 1 Training School of the Parachute Regiment is transferred to this airfield from Aldershot and I decide to volunteer to join them, but remain in the Royal Engineers. After doing my regulation eight jumps I am presented with my wings but, more important, the red beret. On being demobbed I join the 300th Airborne Squadron RETA unit in Tramway Road, Liverpool (serving a further six years as a Terrier, alternating between my signalling and army careers) and change my red beret for the mothballed black cap issued to me by the railway company three years before.

The signal box in which I am to do my training as a signalman is Pighue Lane Junction, situated at the northern periphery of the large Edge Hill marshalling yards. It is in a deep cutting between Edge Hill No 13 and Olive Mount Junction signal boxes, on the Liverpool side of Olive Mount Tunnel. The Up and Down Bootle Branch lines curve around from Edge Lane Junction signal box and form the junction just outside the tunnel mouth.

Reggie, a man of small build and in his early fifties, is renowned for his ability to train lads for this occupation, and the only reward he gets is the satisfaction that they are successful in passing out in the rules and regulations; but he does have the respect of management for his patience and voluntary role. I had worked in Edge Hill No 13 signal box on the same turn as he, so there is a certain rapport between us already, but it is up to me not to let him down.

'Rule No 1 Is Brew Up,' says Reg, pointing to the kettle conveniently steaming away on the coal-fired stove.

As we sit enjoying our refreshing beverage, I am able to take a look at the internal layout of the signal box. It consists of a 26-lever LNWR Tumbler Frame, with three block instruments on the shelf above, and three telephones on the back wall. Conduit piping, hanging from the roof, supports an electric light illuminating the junction diagram in its wooden frame, tilted forward to give a better angle of view, with a further light over the desk opposite the door. There is a very comfortable chair for the signalman, which I have commandeered from him as he is relegated to the wooden locker in the corner, away from the draught that is coming up out of the frame.

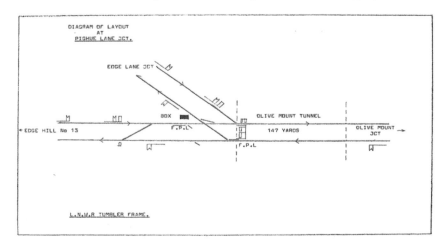

Pighue Lane Junction signal box.

One beat on the Edge Hill No 13 block instrument calls our attention. *'Sit down, Reg,'* as I rise from the locker; *'Let me answer it.'* I accept a coal train (3 beats on the bell) under Regulation 4, placing the block needle to Line Clear position, the points having already being set in their correct position and, after passing it on to Olive Mount Junction signal box, I pull No 2 lever over which clears the lower quadrant signal for the train to proceed into the tunnel.

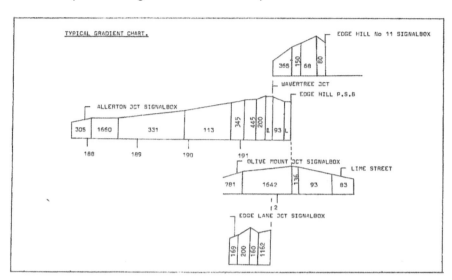

Typical signal box gradient chart.

Freight traffic is heavy here because all trains destined for the Liverpool docks pass this signal box. Train Entering Section (TES) is received from No 13, and acknowledged by 2 beats on the bell, the needle now being placed to Train on Line (TOL) position. This particular train is loaded with coal for Canada Dock and approaches on the down gradient hauled by an **LNWR 0-8-0 'Super D'** locomotive travelling tender-first. It disappears into the smoke-filled tunnel with the guard's van next to the engine, the wagons trailing, and a tail lamp thrown over the draw hook of the last one signifying that the train is complete. Train out of Section (TOS) is sent to No 13 signal box (2 pause 1) and the needle straightened to the normal position.

The purpose of this formation is to enable it to be correctly marshalled in readiness for its forward journey down the Bootle Branch line, the engine running around the train within the tunnel.

Olive Mount Tunnel; Pighue Lane Junction signal box is on the left at the end of the tunnel.
LNWR official postcard from Terry Callaghan collection.

Reggie explains the regulation appertaining to this move, which sounds fairly straightforward to me. By this time the train is travelling engine-first through the cutting towards Edge Lane Junction, having been accepted by the signalman on duty in the signal box there. An opaque cloud obscures the tunnel entrance after the train has departed, taking a long time to disperse, there being no ventilation shafts within it. At times, the volume of traffic is such as to leave it like this for hours on end; however, when clear it is possible to see trains passing through Olive Mount cutting.

Handing me a well-fingered copy of the 'Rules and Regulations for Signalmen', Reg, points out a certain paragraph and asks for my interpretation of it. The passage goes something like this:

'Where the outermost home signal is situated at least ¼-mile in rear of the next home signal, the "Is Line Clear Signal" must not be acknowledged in accordance with this regulation when the line is clear only to the latter home signal, unless fogsignalmen are on duty at the distant signal and at the outermost home signal. If, however, a fogsignalman is on duty at the distant signal only, the "Is Line Clear Signal" may be acknowledged in accordance with this regulation provided the line is clear for at least ¼-mile ahead of the home signal next in advance of the outermost home signal. If the outermost home signal for the box in advance is within that distance .. blah .. blah ..'

'I haven't got a clue,' I reply, feeling rather deflated.

'I ask all the lads the same question, but none have ever answered it correctly,' he reassures me, laughing at my embarrassment. He goes on to tell me his method of teaching and that I will have to learn the 50-or- so bell codes myself. Knowing some of them from my box lad days, within a week I have learnt the rest. We begin with the regulations on the second day, progressing daily. The first ones are relatively easy, dealing with the basic signalling principles, known collectively as the Absolute Block System.

The object of Absolute Block Signalling is to prevent more than one train being in a block section on the same line at the same time.

The block instrument from Olive Mount Junction signal box rings, offering a freight train in transit from Bolton to Edge Hill. It is helpful to the drivers to have the signals 'Off' in the tunnel because of the steep gradient up to No 13 signal box. This being done, I watch the train emerge from the tunnel, going flat out, sending a huge plume of grey smoke high into the sky; the engine is an **LMS 0-6-0 Standard Goods**, lurching on the points as it takes the rising curve. Only freight traffic is booked to run on this line, but on Grand National Day special passenger trains are run, taking the race goers to Aintree via the Bootle Branch.

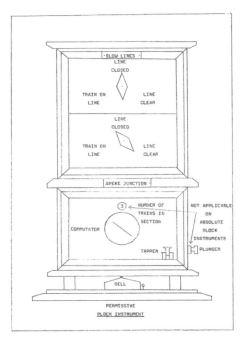

Permissive Block instrument.

Rationing is still in operation and certain commodities are in short supply, but railwaymen in the know are able to obtain black market goods, and these are distributed amongst the signal boxes in the area. I am requested to deliver a package to the signalman in Olive Mount Junction signal box. Whether it contains contraband or not I do not know, but quite possibly it does and no questions are asked! Reggie says to me:

'When you go into the tunnel, be very careful, and if you see a man dressed in a long, black frock coat, a tall hat, and leaning on a walking stick, take no notice.'

I leave the signal box in a state of apprehension and enter the tunnel, tiptoeing on the sleeper ends. I am petrified at the prospect of this spiritual confrontation, and the sensation of hidden eyes watching my every move is spine-chilling. Water dripping from the roof adds sound to the eerie gloom, but I get safely through and deliver the parcel.

Olive Mount Junction signal box is built in the confines of the extremely large cutting of the same name, isolating it from civilisation. An LNWR Tumbler Frame contains 36 working levers connected to both upper and lower quadrant semaphore signals. It signals trains on the Up and Down lines between Edge Hill Nos 4 and 5 and Pighue Lane Junction signal boxes on its west side, and Broad Green Station signal box to the east. The cutting is so deep that it blocks out a lot of light, making it necessary to illuminate the interior of the signal box artificially. It is far too busy to have a decent conversation with the signalman, so I sit and watch until it is time to leave.

Before I do, he asks me if I had seen anyone in the tunnel on my way here. I reply confidently,

'No, I didn't.'

'That's all right then; maybe you'll see someone on the way back!'

Oh, dearie, dearie me!

Originally the Olive Mount cutting was only 20ft wide, and much of the sandstone excavated went to build the 45ft-high Roby embankment further east. When the main lines were quadrupled through to Huyton Quarry and the Up and Down Goods lines from Edge Hill No 4 to Olive Mount Junction were laid, the width of the cutting was expanded to 130ft, the sandstone once more being used in the widening of the Roby embankment. An interesting feature in this cutting, opposite the tunnel entrance, is probably the only original mileage indication on the Liverpool to Manchester railway, showing 'M 28¼ Miles' (the 'M' representing Manchester), chiselled out of the sandstone rock face. Today, the route mileage commences at the Liverpool end of the line.

The only surviving milepost on the Liverpool to Manchester railway.

Britain exports coaches for use on the Egyptian State Railways, and these travel by sea from Liverpool docks. The wheel gauge is the same as this country, so they can run on our railways, but their width is too great to pass through certain tunnels safely; Olive Mount is one of these. It is necessary, therefore, to winch the body of the coaches over some 18in from centre, away from the tunnel wall. This operation causes the opposite line to be fouled and it therefore must be blocked to traffic. After reaching the other end of the tunnel, the whole process is reversed into the normal running position. In addition, the train in question must travel through the tunnel under caution.

Olive Mount Junction signal box. Photo by J A Sommerfield, courtesy of Martin Bott.

Passing Olive Mount signal box. Courtesy of Mick Langton.

Two miles away is the Stanley Abattoir, and numerous cattle trains pass here *en route* to it. Very often, as if by instinct, an animal will attempt to escape from its ultimate fate. This morning a bull manages to gain access to the line, and the signalman in Edge Lane signal box advises us that it is heading in our direction. We wait only a short time, and it appears from under Pighue Lane road bridge, 'going like the clappers'. I immediately grab the red flag, waving it furiously out of the window, but I am not surprised when it chooses to ignore it as it continues on its merry way into Olive Mount Tunnel. We later hear it has been put down near Broad Green station.

Who said *'Show a bull a Red flag'?* Uh!

Broad Green Station signal box.

Photographer unknown, courtesy of 8D Association.

Goods wagons on slow freight trains are built with grease-lubricated axle boxes which frequently catch fire if not maintained properly. The signalman in Olive Mount Junction signal box spots one on fire, but cannot stop the train so he sends us 'Stop and Examine Train' signal, (7 beats on the bell). Replacing the home signal to danger we manage to stop it outside the signal box, where the driver and guard begin to use their own water supply to extinguish the flames. However their reservoirs soon dry up so Reggie, armed with two pans of water, runs down to assist, successfully completing the operation. The train crew return to their respective ends and continue on the journey, the axle box squealing in harmony with the **Stanier 4-6-0 'Black Five'** up front.

I have now come to the end of the rules and regulations, and am ready for an oral examination by the Signalmen's Inspector. He duly arrives, and making our way along the Bootle Branch line, dodging trains as we do, he begins to fire questions at me:

'How many times does Regulation 5 come into Regulation 4?' he asks.

'Four times, sir.' 'Tell me what they are!'

Eventually the inquisition is over and we make our way back to Pighue Lane signal box, whereupon he instructs me to report to Folly Lane signal box for training.

The only problem I have is … **where is Folly Lane?**

Block instruments. Courtesy of Ray Burgess

CHAPTER THREE

BRITANNIA OVER THE WAVES

1950

FOLLY LANE SIGNAL BOX

I establish that Folly Lane signal box is in Runcorn, Cheshire - 13 miles from Liverpool - and that, during my training period, a suitable train service exists from Sefton Park station, near my home in Ferndale Road. Boarding the train I settle down, full of enthusiasm, to enjoy the journey to Runcorn where, on alighting, the foreman directs me to my first signal box, a small yellow dot about 1½ miles away at the lower end of a long, curving embankment. It is a lovely day, cumulus clouds filling the sky as far as the eye can see, and a slight north-westerly wind is strong enough to form white horses on the distant River Mersey. Walking along the top of the embankment, and looking left, there is a vast marshy area devoid of anything tangible; to the right a small row of terraced houses backs onto the railway. Just past the houses and running parallel to the line is a potholed dirt track of one vehicle width; it is edged by an undulating area overgrown with grass, weeds and wild flowers, extending to the Bridgewater Canal (an inland waterway used by barges and pleasure craft). Adjacent to this is the Manchester Ship Canal, used mainly by ocean-going vessels, and the River Mersey lies beyond. In the distance Hale lighthouse is just visible, standing on its small promontory overlooking the river on the Lancashire side.

Nearing the signal box, dwarfed by the large electric works behind it, there comes into view the Castner Kellner chemical factory at Weston Point, and an **LMS 0-6-0 350hp diesel** locomotive engaged in shunting operations.

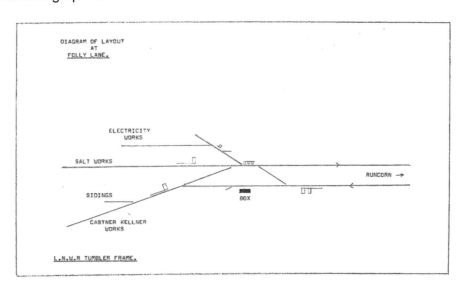

Folly Lane signal box.

The two lines from Runcorn branch into three outside of the signal box: one curves left to serve the chemical works and associated sidings; the next, via a crossover road, leads to the salt works at Runcorn docks; and the third goes into the electric works.

The signal box is very small, having an LNWR Tumbler Frame containing only 10 levers. Electrical apparatus is minimal, there being one telephone to Runcorn Station signal box and an electric light switch near the door. There is no telephonic communication to the foreman's cabin 200yd away, and to relay messages the turning on and off the light switch in the signal box causes the lights to flicker in his cabin and indicates to the occupants that the signalman needs their attention. (For obvious reasons this method of signalling is used as little as possible.)

On the stove, next to the desk, a regulation black iron kettle is steaming away, making a perfect match with the familiar LMS paintwork. Hanging from the roof, in a wooden frame, the layout diagram is just visible through the dirty glass. Some of the windows are broken, and pieces of cardboard serve as a substitute to exclude the draughts.

After one week's training I go through the rules and regulations once more with the Block Inspector who then signs the Certificate of Competence for me to work this signal box. I have attained the position of Temporary Signalman, on the fabulous wage of £4-2s-0d per week; my first turn of duty is to commence at 6am on the following Monday.

Early morning trains on the ex-LMS line from Liverpool start too late to arrive in Runcorn at the appointed time, but the former Cheshire Lines Committee Railway (CLC) runs one that departs from Central station at 5.05am. To travel by this service I need private transport so purchase a new 'Hercules' bicycle for the purpose. Before sun-up I make my way towards Garston CLC station via Smithdown Road, going steadily on the cobble-stoned surface, the fully charged head-lamp on my bike tracing the highly polished tram lines as far as Sefton Park station over-bridge. Here I turn right into Crawford Avenue which runs parallel to the LMS route to the south. Turning right into Penny Lane, then continuing along Dovedale Road, I again turn right into Rose Lane, then left just past Mossley Hill station. I cycle down Brodie Avenue, a tree-lined dual carriageway, followed by Long Lane, to arrive at the station opposite the Garston Cenotaph.

It is now 5am and the platforms are deserted, but I am attracted to the hiss and pale blue pilot light of a gas lamp near the steps, which I turn on, being bathed instantly in the incandescence given off by the mantle, as gas trapped within the glass bowl explodes. The signal box is closed, all signals showing 'proceed' aspects, and 10 minutes elapse before I observe, looking towards the Cressington curve, the dim headlight of a train flickering as the leading wheels of the locomotive strike the rail joints.

I arrive at Farnworth (for Widnes) station, my destination on the **'Premier Railway'** so-called in the conversation that takes place on the journey from Garston. I begin free-wheeling most of the way into Widnes, down Birchfield Road and Kingsway, before turning right into Victoria Road, which leads directly to Waterloo Road, where, on the left, is Widnes LMS station. Fifty yards further on is Waterloo level crossing; the controlling signal box alongside is in total darkness, the lights presumably having fused. Continuing into the West Bank area of Widnes I reach the bottom of a narrow pathway climbing an embankment up to the level of the Britannia Railway Bridge which spans, by means of two central piers, both the River Mersey and Manchester Ship Canal.

Sailing under the Runcorn railway bridge; the transporter is in the background.

Photo by Author.

Halfway up this path is a small wooden hut. Its occupant, employed by the railway, controls a metal turnstile released only when the toll has been paid: 1d for pedestrians, 1½d with a bicycle, but of course there is no charge for railwaymen, it being one of the perks of the job. Atop the embankment flagstones are laid for a length of 250yd, bordered by a five-foot-high sandstone wall on the right; this follows the curvature of the two lines running between Ditton Junction and Runcorn stations, as far as the bridge which has two small castellated towers, backed by two of a larger size, forming the entrance onto the girders. This pattern is reversed on the Runcorn side, giving uniformity to the vast structure. Looking over the four-foot-high cast iron lattice work fence on my left, I see the massive single-span transporter bridge parallel with the railway over the Runcorn Gap. Its platform is suspended on the end of steel hawsers, swaying gently in the breeze blowing up river, its squealing clearly advertising its lack of lubrication. The paved pathway gives way to wooden laths 5ft x3in across the bridge at intervals of 1in, the gaps being wide enough to permit a glimpse of the menacing tideway of the murky waters below.

A rumbling heralds an approaching train running onto the bridge from the Runcorn side, sending severe vibrations into the girders which resound with a thundering roar as it passes me. A flight of steps and wooden slope bring me to road level again, and a short cut over the two lock gates on the Bridgewater Canal leads to a gateway into Percival Lane, itself, in turn, leading to Folly Lane. I arrive inside the signal box at two minutes to six, relieving my mate who is at the ready, wearing his coat.

Here I am, the first time in charge of a signal box on my own and, I admit, a little apprehensive. It is still dark as I survey the surrounding countryside, which looks entirely different from that in daylight. The brilliant lights from the petrochemical plant just north of the signal box are the brightest visible, whilst in the far distance are the twinkling lights of south Liverpool. A little further left are the dim windows of the electricity works, and outside the Foreman's cabin the stationary diesel shunt engine is silhouetted against the yard lights, with the luminosity emitted from Castner Kellner works behind.

It soon becomes daylight. I have been on duty for two hours and still await my first train. Glancing over towards Widnes, behind Fison's fertilizer works, I observe two plumes of white smoke moving against an obscure background, obviously from a train negotiating the heavy climb up the Ditton Bank. The lower quadrant semaphore distant signal, sited on the small right hand castellated tower on the Widnes side of the bridge and controlled from Runcorn signal box, is in the 'Off' position as the train comes into view; it is hauled by an **LMS 0-8-0 'Super D'** locomotive, ably assisted by one of the same class in rear.

Target 92, the local tripper from West Deviation Yard, Widnes, runs twice every eight hours. Arriving at Runcorn, the train propels through the crossover road on the main line to the Down branch line adjacent to the station where the locomotive detaches and returns to Widnes.

Our shunt engine then proceeds on the Up line and couples onto the stabled wagons, propelling them down for shunting into their respective sidings. After all the wagons have been shunted it's time to settle down to my bacon and eggs, knowing I have successfully dealt with my first train. The three turns follow the same pattern in respect to traffic flow. Main line freight trains run to Alsager, Chaddesden and Longport, headed usually by **Class 4F 0-6-0** locomotives with shunting taking place intermittently, but on the whole it is an extremely boring job.

The absence of birds is noticeable in the area, undoubtedly owing to the scarcity of trees and bushes, but on occasions rabbits scurry about on the embankment a few hundred yards away. Compensating for this bleak outlook, a large ship on the canal brings a little colour into the drab scene with its escort of tugboats.

I am informed that railwaymen are entitled to free travel on the railways to enable them to get to work, so putting pen to paper I make an application for a pass from Liverpool Central to Farnworth station on the former Cheshire Lines Committee Railway. A few days later I receive a message that the pass is in the booking office at Central station awaiting collection. Arriving at the station the booking clerk informs me that there is a charge made for it, something of which I was unaware. Apparently, there is an outer limit of 10 miles, and the distance from Central station to Farnworth exceeds this, hence the charge. I tell him I haven't got any money on me at the moment but that I shall come and pick it up later in the week. Fancy having to pay to go to work! No way, considering the wage for a Class 5 signalman is only small, will I be paying for the pleasure. I don't bother going to Central to pick it up because I discover that, when in uniform, railwaymen are not challenged by the guards of trains or station staff to produce a pass.

Two gentlemen of foreign extraction, bedecked with turbans, are accepted for employment as 'Knobbers' (points men) in the yard. It amuses me to watch them walking - no, more of an amble - along the embankment, one behind the other, as is customary in their country of origin, after alighting at Runcorn station.

At this point I will explain the method of shunting at Folly Lane. This is done by gravitation, the foreman meeting the train at the Down line home signal, situated 200yd on the station side of the signal box. The sidings which are the destination of the wagons lie 200yd in the opposite direction. Jack, the foreman, well over 6ft tall and very strong and brawny, does have the tendency to be fiery; and woe betide anyone on the Runcorn bridge when he's about, speeding on his 50cc auto-cycle - how the frame stands his weight, beats me! - but a railwayman he truly is.

Uncoupling four rafts of wagons with his usual expertise and timing, he communicates to the 'Knobbers' by means of a system using hand signals, the road they should be placed on, but this time he does not bargain for the inherent habits of his aspirants: in single file they amble everywhere, so slowly that the wagons finish up in the wrong sidings. Taking off his cap, he slams it down in disgust and shouts obscenities, easily heard from here but not by the miscreants ½-mile away. No doubt they receive some good, old-fashioned Widnesian language as he re-marshals the wagons into their correct sidings. Finally I watch our intrepid friends walking - sorry, ambling - into the setting sun, sheep-like, never to be seen again!

By way of respite from the boredom, after being relieved at 10pm on Saturday late turn, the foreman Eric, George, the driver of the 350 (no mean player of the concertina), and I partake in liquid refreshment in the local public house. The hostelry stands beside the private level crossing controlled by Castner Kellner's own staff, where George entertains the customers with his squeeze-box. It is something I look forward to, and I quite often miss the last train home to Liverpool when faced with a daunting ride of nearly 14 miles, having had **one or two, or** .....?

The Widnes/Runcorn transporter bridge; mid-river, 1959. Photo by Author.

Walkway on Runcorn railway bridge; the transporter is on the left.

Photographer unknown.

Widnes and Runcorn bridges; Fiddlers Ferry Power Station is in the background.

Courtesy of Joe Gerrard. Pilot of Aeroplane: Author's son, Tony.

Having worked in Folly Lane signal box for six months it is time for a change. I am being transferred to Huyton Quarry Station signal box, on the Liverpool to Manchester railway, as a Class 4 Porter/Signalman.

CHAPTER FOUR

ROCKET'S RAILWAY

1951

HUYTON QUARRY STATION SIGNAL BOX

Huyton Quarry, a quaint village six miles from the centre of Liverpool, has been associated with the railways since the era of the famous 'Rocket' locomotive, and is situated at the bottom of the Whiston incline on the Liverpool to Manchester line. The stationmaster and I make our way to the signal box at the western end of the Up line platform.

Huyton Quarry Station signal box. Photo by J A Sommerfield, courtesy of Martin Bott.

The station, on the west side of Northview overbridge, is spotless, the waiting rooms freshly painted in red and cream, and rectangular plots, surrounded by whitewashed bricks, contain a variety of plants. At road level the booking office, again newly painted, has tubs of flowers outside, given by the travelling public and tended by the appreciative station staff.

Before I have a chance to weigh up the interior of the signal box, the stationmaster points to a wooden-handled brass bell which stands on a small shelf by the door. *'This bell should be rung on the approach of a stopping passenger train to enable my staff to get onto to the platform before it arrives; officially, that is, but, between you and me it will signify that you have brewed a pot of tea, and I have my cup over here ready.'* he says, producing it from behind the instrument shelf. *'Very good, Sir,'* I reply. *'No time like the present,'* says the signalman on duty, the familiar black kettle boiling away.

The LNWR Tumbler Frame is far too long for the amount of points and signals that it controls. Originally the quadrupled lines commencing in Liverpool terminated here, but during 1938 the lines were severed at the old Huyton Junction, about one mile to the west, stop blocks being erected east of the running lines which curve towards St Helens via Prescot.

These two redundant main lines now form the Delph Sidings, served through trailing points on the Up line quite close to the signal box.

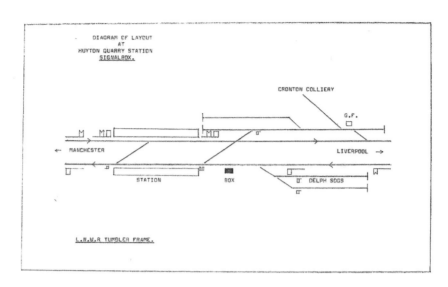

Huyton Quarry Station signal box.

Huyton Junction signal box. Photo by Terry Callaghan.

The original Huyton Junction signal box was closed after this remodelling, the work being transferred to the present signal box at Huyton station; consequently, the number of levers in use here at Huyton Quarry was reduced..

Huyton Quarry signal box controls the lines between Huyton station and the world-famous one at Rainhill. In addition to the sidings already mentioned, two on the Down line side are used by traffic to and from the Willis Branch leading, via a level crossing in Hall Lane, to Cronton Colliery just over a mile away.

One of the shunters in charge of these sidings received the British Empire Medal for his involvement when a munitions train, in Breck Road Sidings on the Bootle Branch line, was hit by a bomb during the 'May Blitz' of 1941. As a result of the same incident - one of the most memorable in the bombing of Liverpool, although not one person was killed - a goods guard at Edge Hill received the George Medal, and others, lesser awards for their bravery. These gallant men succeeded in uncoupling the unaffected wagons as others were exploding around them, and shunting them into adjacent sidings. The signalman on duty was actually blown off the signal box steps by the bomb blast; he now works in Edge Hill No 12 signal box.

Traffic from the colliery, worked principally by **LNWR 0-8-0 'Super D'** locomotives, travels to Edge Hill for marshalling, whilst the empty wagons are stabled in the sidings to await acceptance by the transport manager at Cronton. A ground frame released from the signal box gives access from the sidings onto the Down line.

The position of Porter/Signalman, as the name suggests, necessitates carrying out other duties quite apart from those of signalling. In this instance the signals are lit by oil lamps maintained by the signalman. So, in addition to learning the mechanical and electrical apparatus in the signal box, I have to learn about signal lamps. These are required to last for seven days on a full tank of paraffin, and if they go out within that period the most probable cause is bad maintenance. Wicks, glasses and all other component parts must be clean, and the flame not too high or low, for satisfactory operation. After completing my training in the signal box and mastering the art of wick-trimming I am passed out by the Signalmen's Inspector.

There are two turns of duty, the first being from 5.15am until noon, followed by noon to 7.15pm; from Monday to Saturday, with 20 minutes per day allowed for the signal lamps. At 5.15am on Monday I open the signal box (5-5-5 on the bells) only to be immediately offered a freight train from Huyton Junction to detach five wagons into the Delph Sidings. This train, known as the 'Tranships', runs every weekday morning so it is essential to arrive for duty on time, otherwise delay will be caused to the early morning passenger services to Wigan and Manchester. Having disposed of the train I attempt to get a fire going in the cold iron stove, the signal box cat sitting in front awaiting the first vestiges of heat, but it is quite some time before the kettle boils to allow me to brew up.

Passenger traffic along this line is constant. The expresses to and from Yorkshire are hauled mainly by Fowler **LMS 4-6-2 'Patriot'** or Stanier **LMS 4-6-0 'Jubilee'** class locomotives, and stopping trains usually have **Stanier 2-6-4 'Tanks'** up front. Freight trains are run in between, as margins allow.

Beyond the station bridge Whiston incline curves slightly to the right, disappearing under Pottery Lane bridge. A **'Jubilee'**-hauled express is approaching, coasting down the incline towards me; framed by the station bridge the scene looks like a postcard. In my quieter moments I often look from the box towards the Whiston incline and try to picture the scene 120 years ago with **'Rocket'** on its way to Manchester, struggling upwards through the peaceful countryside, or sedately cruising down towards me in the opposite direction, its passengers open to the elements; but every time my dreams are shattered by the **'Whoosh'** of a modern leviathan.

Looking at the signal box, it is evident that there was no paint left after giving the station a 'lick'; it has not seen a brush for many a year, and grime has rendered the front windows opaque. However, one day, I vow that I will attempt to clean them up.

Cleaning and lighting the signal lamps is not too bad on a nice day, but today, with wind and rain together, it is awful. Battling up the incline with a can of paraffin and a plentiful supply of Bryant & May's matches, the rain trickling down my neck, I curse as a gust of wind brings down a shower of water from the overhanging trees. Eventually I arrive beside the Down distant signal, and at its foot is a small pile of spent matches left from previous expeditions. I shall be adding to this before successfully lighting the sodden wick!

A lovely day dawns, so I decide to tackle the extremely dirty windows at the front of the signal box, having first borrowed a wooden ladder just long enough to reach them if wedged under the nearside rail. Armed with a razor blade I begin to scrape the glass. Every time a bell rings, down comes the ladder, until the opportunity arises to continue with the chore. Nearly time for the **11am Liverpool to Newcastle** express to pass Huyton Junction so, feeling proud of my efforts, I settle to watch the train approaching on the gentle curve, leaving an almost horizontal trail of smoke in its wake as it speeds to negotiate the Whiston incline. Suddenly fragments of wood fly through the air, the remains of the ladder which I have forgotten to remove!! Unfortunately, I am unable to finish the windows - and I would never discover who owned the ladder!

After brewing a pot of tea and ringing the bell I do not get the usual response. Five minutes later the stationmaster arrives, somewhat flustered.

'What's the matter, boss?' I enquire.

36

'Well, you'd better not ring the bell anymore.' He continued, *'I happened to be in a queue in the cake shop when you rang, and the assistant said to the people in front of me ...'* - he swallows to gain breath - *'Let me serve our stationmaster first, if I may. His tea is ready in the signal box.'* I burst out laughing at his obvious embarrassment.

Our little black cat is a permanent resident, taking leave of the signal box at will and often returning with the trophies of his excursions. The levers, bells and the trains passing by at speed do not seem to bother him too much. However, familiarity breeds contempt and it is a sad day indeed when, one morning, I find him dead beside the track. The porter and I bury him in the little flower garden which the station staff and I look after, close to the signal box.

Major engineering work takes place mostly at weekends, mainly to minimise inconvenience to the travelling public. Re-laying the tracks between here and Rainhill station requires the two signal boxes, normally closed at weekends, to be open. When the work is finished the signalman at Rainhill switches his signal box out of circuit but forgets to clear the signals for normal train running. As a result the next express passenger train is stranded in no-man's land. After 10 minutes the driver gains entry into the empty signal box and contacts Liverpool Control Office, who give him authority to take his train forwards under caution.

Before closing a signal box one rings the control for permission in case it may be required to stay open for traffic purposes. It is at this juncture that I am requested to go to Rainhill and clear the signals. By following the signal wires I find the signal box then switch it into circuit.

The Bourne wagon way, laid in 1824. Photo by Author.

Here I am on **'ROCKET'S RAILWAY'**, the scene of its triumph 120 years ago, in 1829, where the level track runs east to Lea Green signal box in the distance, on top of the Sutton incline. Only a few hundred yards from this signal box towards Manchester a railway was laid in 1824 in the form of a wagon way built by the Bourne brothers, and this required George Stephenson, in constructing the world's first railway bridge, to pass over a railway, albeit one made of wood.

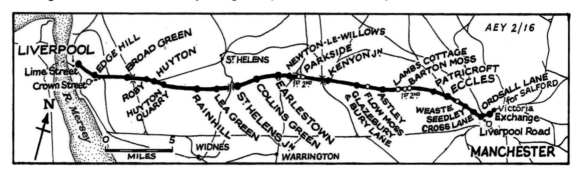

Rainhill Station signal box. Photographer unknown.

Skew Bridge, at the Liverpool end of Rainhill station, is the only structure on the Liverpool to Manchester railway to be emblazoned with George Stephenson's name. Further on towards Liverpool, on the left can be seen a square structure on top of an embankment. This is part of an engine house built to haul trains up the Whiston incline; however, it was never used as such because **'ROCKET'** was able to haul the trains up the gradient without assistance. I feel very proud to be here, considering my efforts a **'feather in my cap'**; but this, I am afraid is short-lived. My ego is cruelly deflated when I am summoned to appear on the carpet at Liverpool to receive a severe ticking-off for opening a signal box illegally.

'Lion' in Rainhill station. Photo by Author.

'Rocket' in Rainhill station. Photo by Author.

I have spent eight months in Huyton Quarry signal box and enjoyed every minute, but I am promoted to Signalman Class 4 at Farnworth & Bold, Widnes.

Incidentally, the bell still rings at brew-up time!

CHAPTER FIVE

STOP! PIN DOWN THE BRAKES

1951-52

FARNWORTH & BOLD STATION SIGNAL BOX

Travelling by way of the CLC railway to Farnworth (for Widnes) station, I am unaware of the exact location of my new post at Farnworth & Bold Station signal box, on the original St Helens & Runcorn Gap Railway, opened in 1833. The station porter directs me along Derby Road, where I come upon a large factory on the right with huge piles of asbestos pipes of various sizes outside, just prior to the T-junction at Lunts Heath Road. Here a small lane leads down to the station.

Farnworth & Bold Station signal box. Photo by J M Tolson, courtesy of Sankey Canal Restoration Society.

The signal box is actually situated on the Down Line platform which is overgrown with weeds. Opposite, the dilapidated station buildings are still occupied by the stationmaster even though passenger trains ceased to use this line several months ago. Looking left from the signal box the lines descend on a very severe gradient towards Widnes and are sandwiched between two large works: those of Messrs Turner's Asbestos Co and Peter Spence's chemical works, each with sidings connections from the Up line. To the right, two private coal sidings run behind the station buildings, and a lead from the Down line underneath Lunts Heath Road overbridge enters Mason's wood yard. In the distance, two gigantic slag heaps dominate the horizon, dwarfing the pit-head winding gear which spins almost continuously at Sutton Manor Colliery.

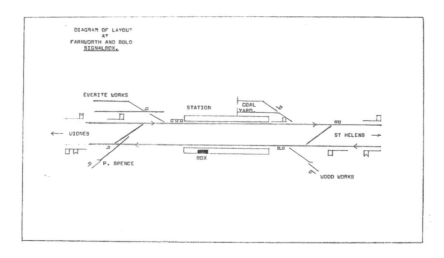

Farnworth & Bold Station signal box.

Approaching from the St Helens direction, and framed by the overbridge, is a fully loaded train from Clock Face Colliery hauled by a **Stanier LMS 4-6-0 'Black Five'** locomotive, the driver of which is preparing to heed the instructions on a signboard erected outside the signal box:

'STOP HERE TO PIN DOWN THE BRAKES'

The fireman and guard duly oblige and then come to the signal box to make a brew before proceeding on their journey to Garston Docks. I observe that the tea, sugar and 'conny-onny' are moulded into a round sticky ball, wrapped in a piece of greaseproof paper. This is dunked into a battered white enamel can of boiling water. I decline the offer of a drink, but I do mention the shortage of coal in the signal box bunker and that one or two lumps from the tender would suffice in return for my hospitality. With the shrill of binding brakes and a hiss of steam the train moves slowly forward on its downward journey, to pass over the CLC main line half a mile away, before disappearing on a right hand curve towards Appleton.

Controlling the lines from signal boxes at Appleton station and Clock Face Colliery Sidings, with a 50-lever LNWR Tappet Frame and upper quadrant semaphore signals, this signal box is by far the biggest on this stretch of railway. The interior is large in comparison to the length of the frame and the stove, for some unknown reason, is placed off-centre, much too close to the door. As a result I have difficulty keeping warm. The incessant rattling of the ill-fitting windows and blasts of arctic air through the gaps force me to stay close to the near-useless fire, wearing my coat.

Most trains on the route from Widnes to St Helens have to be assisted in rear by a bank engine. **Bank engines are located at points where passenger or freight trains have to travel over a line with a severe upward gradient.** This particular one is known as Farnworth Bank.

Its severity can be judged by records which state that a passenger who missed a train one morning at Runcorn Gap station was issued with a ticket and instructed to run up the line to catch it, which he duly did! The speed of trains has not increased a great deal on this stretch of line, and I imagine that a reasonably athletic person could emulate this feat today.

LNWR 0-3-0 'Super D' locomotives are invariably used to assist trains in rear from either Widnes No 2 signal box at Ann Street or Widnes No 1 signal box up to Lunts Heath Road bridge, where the gradient lessens appreciably. A local tripper, headed by one of these engines, is labouring up towards me from Widnes, being assisted. I am unaware that I am about to deal with my first emergency as a signalman.

After disposing of the engine in rear, the brake van is placed, via the crossover road, onto the Down main line; the train, consisting of wagons destined for Turner's works, is being propelled into their sidings, when I notice the brake van is beginning to move forward. I immediately send the bell signal for **'Train or Vehicles Running Away, along the Right Line'** (4-5-5) to Widnes No 1 signal box (Appleton station signal box being switched out of circuit).

This effectively protects the adjoining line. I leave the signal box and give chase to the runaway, and the guard - a 'para' colleague of mine in the Airborne - seeing me running and gesticulating, slides down the embankment on his posterior, continuing the chase that I abandon as a lost cause. By now the speed of the brake van has increased to nearly twice that of its pursuer, and I watch it hurtle out of sight to its inevitable destruction. Widnes No 1 signal box has no facing point connections to divert the van from the main line, so the signalman can only warn his counterpart at Widnes No 2 signal box, controlling level crossing gates, of the impending emergency. At No 2 signal box the points are set towards No 4 signal box and the runaway, travelling at speed, passes over the level crossing safely. Fortunately, shunting is not in progress on the single line leading to the Marsh Sidings where the finale is played out. Demolishing a stop block, not designed to withstand an impact of this nature, the brake van finishes up as a heap of scrap metal and firewood. Luckily, no one has been hurt, the only casualty being the guard's pride; but even he has some consolation, discovering that his corned beef 'sarnies' (sandwiches) are intact.

Food rationing still exists, and the free entitlement of tea, sugar and milk is issued once per month as usual. My family has access to these commodities, satisfying all our needs; but living in a small cottage, adjacent to the railway, is a retired couple, and I let them have my ration of sugar. Roger often pops into the signal box for a chat, the main topic always being his experiences at the Earlestown wagon works. I remind him not to forget the sugar that has just arrived today, which is exactly what he does! It is 9.30pm and I get relieved at 10, so I decide to deliver the bag before I go home. Entering the garden gate I am alarmed by a strange shuffling, and instinct makes me turn around. The fangs sink deep into my backside as I attempt to retrace my steps to the signal box, but the owner of these powerful jaws has the opposite idea. Roger comes out to investigate the commotion, not forgetting to collect the bag of sugar - which I have miraculously kept hold of - walloping his pet Alsatian until I am free. With blood running down my leg, I go to hospital for treatment and the regulation jab in my other cheek!

A small light glimmers in the stationmaster's office at 11.30 pm. Goodness knows what he finds to do at this time of night! Later he comes to the signal box for an out-of-hours visit.

Once every month all signal boxes must be visited out of the normal office hours by an inspector, or stationmaster, to check that the signalman is performing his duties correctly, always signing the train registers as proof.

On this occasion, he hands me a letter containing an allocation slip, informing me that I have been promoted to a Class 3 Signalman and am to be transferred to Woodside Siding signal box on the main Liverpool to London line next Monday. As a result I forgive his intrusion so late at night.

Stop signal with calling-on arm beneath.

Signalman Peter Worthington: self-portrait.

41

CHAPTER SIX

HARRY'S DOMAIN

1952-54

WOODSIDE SIDINGS SIGNAL BOX

Woodside Sidings signal box is on the main Liverpool to London line halfway between Speke Junction and Ditton Junction station. This line was opened in 1852 as a single line to Garston by the St Helens & Runcorn Gap Railway Company.

The signal box stands in a picturesque countryside setting and signals trains on the now four lines of way which are bridged by Old Hutte Lane, Halewood, 250yd to the west, and Higher Road, 60yd to the east. Behind the signal box stand two cottages occupied by railwaymen, and they are both well known throughout the area for their horticultural talents and have prize-winning chrysanthemums growing in colourful profusion in their gardens bordering the main road. Opposite is Liverpool's RSPCA home, and I can see several of the Edge Hill Gridiron horses cavorting in their idyllic surroundings having recently retired from active service. In the distance it is possible to see the ex-CLC railway with its motley collection of ex-LMS and LNER locomotives, running parallel to this line.

I am taken aback by the antiquated environment inside this signal box. An oil lamp, hanging in the centre, is supplemented by one fastened to the wall next to the desk, to provide the meagre form of illumination. Hand-generated telephones line the sidewall beneath the clock. Toilet facilities are non-existent - it's a case of an 'under the signal box job' - and water is supplied from a well 50yd away in the middle of a field by means of an old style village pump. However, the pleasant surroundings make up for these primitive conditions.

Traffic is particularly heavy on this stretch of line, and most of the 24 levers in the LNWR Tumbler Frame are in constant use. The signals controlled from this box comprise both upper and lower quadrant semaphores and colour lights. The Up line distant signals are of the lower quadrant type, requiring fog signalmen to be on duty when visibility is less than 200yd. The sidings opposite, used by local coal merchants and by farmers for the transport of potatoes, are connected to the Slow lines.

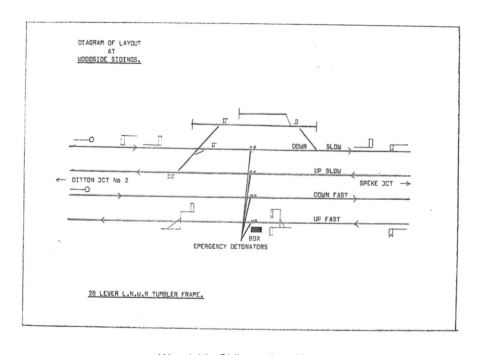

Woodside Sidings signal box.

Trains in transit from the Derbyshire, Yorkshire and Lancashire coalfields pass in continuous procession on the Down Slow line towards Garston Docks, being passed by the express freight traffic travelling on the Fast lines.

The **'Merseyside Express'**, **'Red Rose'**, **'Shamrock'** and **'Manxman'** are named passenger expresses that ply between Liverpool and the metropolis each weekday, hauled principally by **Stanier 4-6-2 'Coronation'** and **'Princess Royal'** locomotives. Some two miles away, just past Halebank station, are the water troughs, constantly filled in readiness for the thirsty engines to quench their thirst.

The **10.10am 'Merseyside Express'** left Liverpool on time and is approaching under clear signals, but it is apparent that something is amiss, judging by its speed. It comes to a stand at the Up Fast line home signal, and the driver informs me of a malfunction with the injectors on locomotive **No 46247 'City of Liverpool'**. The fireman has started emptying the firebox contents onto the small embankment alongside, setting it alight. Some passengers have alighted and are sitting on the grass verges viewing his labours, while others join in a conversation with the driver. It takes an hour for the assisting locomotive to arrive from Edge Hill Shed, passing on the Up Slow line, much to the derision of the waiting passengers, before travelling wrong line from Ditton No 2 signal box along the Up Fast line. In circumstances of this nature permission has to be received from the driver of a failed train to allow an assisting engine to travel in the wrong direction towards his train. This is achieved by issuing a **Wrong Line Order** form which is filled in by the driver and countersigned by the signalman. Also, a **Signalman-to-Signalman Wrong Line Order** form has to be issued to allow the assisting locomotive to travel between two signal boxes, as in this instance. After coupling up, the train departs, leaving a mound of smouldering ashes to mark the position of its unscheduled stop.

Oblivious to all this activity is a pair of starlings that have nested within the girders carrying the Up line home signals.

The fog has now become widespread, drifting from the surrounding fields. It is 1am, and the regulations for fog working are put into operation, during which it is necessary to obtain the assistance of fog signalmen. This is achieved by calling the 'knocker-up' who lives in one of the cottages behind the signal box. He goes to the various homes of those required for duty. A fog signalman's duties entail placing a detonator on the line while the distant signal is at the caution position; this signifies to the driver that the home signal is at danger. A freight train has just passed the signal box, complete with tail-lamp, clearing the rear section. I am immediately offered another train from Speke Junction signal box, receiving the 'Train Entering Section' straight away. Four minutes have elapsed, when, to my horror, this train passes the home signal at danger, travelling at over 60mph into the advance section which is still occupied by the previous train.

Speke Junction signal box. Courtesy of James MacKenzie.

Lever frame in Speke Junction signal box. Courtesy of J MacKenzie.

Sending the 'Train Running Away along the Right Line' signal to Ditton No 2 box, my concern is for the train crew and whether there will be a collision in this very dense fog. The signalman in Ditton No 2 signal box informs me that he has managed to cross the first train onto the Slow line, averting what could have been a very nasty accident, but the question remains;

'*How and why did it happen?*'

Apparently, the first of three trains travelling along the Up Fast line exploded a detonator, the central ring of which became embedded in the fog signalman's forearm. In accordance with the rules he replaces the detonator then makes his way to the signal box but, before arriving, the second train has passed, the driver having received a warning at the distant signal. As a result the driver of the third train is totally dependent on visual observations in what can only be described as a real 'pea-souper', and he obviously missed the signal indication. Subsequently, the injured fog signalman is sent to hospital for treatment and fog working is reintroduced.

During periods of foggy weather it is difficult to see trains passing on the four lines of way, so **'Tail Lamp Snatchers'** are employed, though not as the name suggests, to steal-them. Their duties entail watching each train passing and looking to see that it has a tail-lamp in rear, which enables the signalman to accept a following train.

Protection rules apply to all lines passing this signal box, and if any train is stopped by signals the fireman or guard must visit the signal box to be reassured that his train is protected by the signalman, either by placing reminders on the levers or on the commutator (switch) of the block instrument. At the same time he must sign the train register, which the signalman countersigns. Because of the density of traffic this occurs many times during a turn of duty, and one gets to meet a lot of train crews.

It is always sad to hear of the death of a colleague, especially when there are happy memories, and such is the case of Alfie Dunne, a goods guard at Garston; he often came to the signal box to sign the train register, **under Rule 55,** and brew up a can of tea. I recall just one of his many attributes: the perfect mimicry of birds and animals. A cockerel crowing in the middle of the night could only be him, out here in the wilds!

Time passes.

The night is cold, and mist blankets the surrounding fields. Eerie patterns are cast about me by the flickering oil lamps. Suddenly the uncanny silence is shattered by the crow of a cock! It is 2am, and a shiver goes down my spine. Someone is coming up the signal box steps. I peer over the desk into the semi-darkness near the door, and ever so slowly a figure, whose facial features are covered by a scarf, approaches, writes in the register and leaves.

'There is no signature in the book!'

This spiritual visitation disturbs my previous tranquil mind. Five awful minutes later I am again subjected to the presence, but this time I am handed a piece of paper, on which is written.

'As you are aware our friend and colleague Alfie Dunne passed away recently, and anyone wishing to contribute towards a floral tribute, please append below.'

A list of names follows, each donating 2s 6d. *'I have found out who my true friends are, and you don't come into that category,'* he says, waving the list under my nose.

Quick as a flash, in reply, and still in a state of shock, I respond, *'I am sorry to hear he has died, but the list was not sent to the signal box, and if it is any consolation, I promise to put five shillings in the collection when he does go,'* adding, *'Make it next Friday, because I've got a big week in!'*

We both burst out laughing simultaneously, as I realise that I have fallen for a ruse, and *'Alfie Done It!'*

My signalman colleague, Harry, on the other turn of duty, has devised an ingenious idea in the form of a periscope which gives a perfect wide-angled view on the other side of the road bridge, 60yd east of the signal box. Visible now are Widnes trains negotiating Ditton Bank and the spray thrown up by the locomotives on the Halebank water troughs. He has also begun to grow his own tobacco, and bunches of the drying leaves are hanging from the roof beams in colourful array, being tinged by the paraffin fumes which, I am informed by him, improve the smoke.

Now, who could argue against the old stager? In his domain he excels, making a contraption that shuts the door, if left open by an unthinking visitor, and turning the fire-bars around in the stove to conserve fuel. A nuisance, but a likeable man.

Harry, a man of small stature in his late 50s, paints landscapes as a hobby, and some of his work is very good; but behind the innocent smile hides the truth. He only uses the pictorial work to cover up his real passion, and that is painting and sculpting the nude female form, getting such a lot of satisfaction out of showing it to me. As far as relieving me is concerned, it is possible to set the clock by him. At five minutes to the hour a cyclist approaches along Halebank Road at a steady 3mph. It's always Harry, **'bang on the nail'** - but, with a head-on wind, his timing is very unreliable!

Signalmen accept that things can go wrong while they are on duty, and more so in a very busy signal box such as this. The **3.30pm from Liverpool to Birkenhead** passenger train has just arrived at its destination, and station staff find a travelling case on the luggage rack in one of the coaches, but no indication of whose it is. British Transport Police consider that the line should be searched, suspecting that someone has fallen out of the train. The entire route the train took is examined on foot, but nothing is found so normal train running is resumed and, like most occurrences of this nature, it is quickly forgotten.

A new name is added to the missing persons file when the police succeed in identifying the ownership of the case; that is until two days later when one of our platelayers walking his length discovers the gruesome remains at the bottom of a small embankment, only 300yd from this signal box.

A few days after this incident, on a bitter winter's night a freight train *en route* from Edge Hill to Crewe passes the signal box, on the Up Fast line, without a brake van in rear. On the adjacent track the **8.30pm Birkenhead to Liverpool** passenger train has just passed, heading towards Speke Junction. An empty wagon train destined for Rowsley is in section on the Up Slow. I carry out the emergency regulations applicable to this situation and await developments. Five minutes go by, and it is obvious that something is amiss. A telephone message from Ditton No 2 signal box confirms my worst fears: **the Crewe train has broken into two portions.** Several more minutes pass before the guard of the Birkenhead train arrives in the signal box and informs me that his train has crashed into some wagons and that all four lines are blocked. The collision has taken place only one mile from the signal box, on the Liverpool side of Old Hutte Lane overbridge but, owing to the darkness, it is not possible to see anything from my position. Travelling home on the Birkenhead train, a signalman becomes aware of the approaching Rowsley train and somehow manages to attract the driver's attention, enabling him to bring his train to a stop only yards from the obstruction. The prompt action by both of these men almost certainly averted a more serious accident. It is subsequently established that a vehicle on the Crewe train had become derailed at Speke Junction and travelled in this condition until it hit the structure of a farm track underbridge, which caused the train to break in half, fouling the Down Fast line in the process. Miraculously, no-one is seriously hurt, but the lines remain blocked for several days. Severe damage is caused to the bridge, which has to be supported with huge baulks of timber and necessitates cautioning trains at 10 mph over this section of line.

I am living in the Old Swan district of Liverpool at this time, but unfortunately get a puncture on my bicycle in Gateacre village on my way to work and am forced to finish the journey using a Corporation bus. Rather than walking to the terminus at Old Hutte Lane for the return journey when finishing my turn of duty, I decide to ask the driver for a lift on the **'Merseyside Express'**, in transit from London to Liverpool, which had to be stopped outside the signal box so he could be notified of the situation, and be cautioned. Climbing aboard none other than **46247 'City of Liverpool'**, we begin our ascent of the slight gradient towards Speke Junction, the engine oscillating from side to side as it comes to grips hauling 12 coaches towards the bridge where speed must be reduced. It is the very first time I have been aboard such a powerful locomotive and enjoy the experience all the way to Lime Street station.

Today at 8.19am telephone calls are being received relating to an horrific train crash that has occurred at Harrow & Wealdstone, just north of London. I am on a 12-hours turn of duty and, all day, up-to-date information is being relayed. Two of the locomotives **46202 'Princess Anne' 4-6-2 ex Turbo,** and **45637 'Windward Islands'**, a 4-6-0 'Jubilee', regularly ran between Liverpool and the south along this line, **'Princess Anne'** on express passenger trains and **'Windward Islands'** on freight. I look back to the times that I observed them on so many occasions, whether on Edge Hill Shed or in full steam, going flat out past this signal box

Returning to a more wholesome subject, electric trains have been running between Manchester and Crewe for a while but plans are afoot to extend them to Liverpool. The beginning of this large project takes me back to my army days when orders were issued to paint anything that did not move! Men armed with brushes begin painting everything white: stop blocks, manhole covers and the like. This operation, using aerial photography, highlighted the obstructions that could impede the erection of stanchions to take the overhead line equipment.

Re-laying, bridge alterations and rationalisation take place simultaneously, and the first work to be carried out is the re-laying of the Up Slow line opposite my signal box. The permanent way between Ditton and Speke Junctions is maintained to a very high standard by three gangs of men, and all have figured in the prizes in competitions for the best kept lengths.

White stones are meticulously placed along the edge of the ballast for miles; in fact, it is possible to cycle beside the track to Ditton Junction, with Halebank station the only site where one must dismount. Levelling the track to the optimum is achieved with the use of sighting boards and jacks, the Ganger, Albert, placing three or four cans of chippings under the sleepers with a special shovel. This has been the practice from the early days, but notices have been issued detailing instructions that must be observed when the **'MATISA'** tamping machine is on a running line. This machine was developed to replace the sighting boards and jacks.

Approaching on the Up Slow line is 'MATISA', looking for all the world like a contraption from a science fiction film. It stops outside the signal box, and the operator spends half an hour setting it up ready for work. With a few whirrs, clangs and hisses the big moment has arrived; new technology introduced into railway engineering.

'Absolutely fantastic!' exclaims an observer, as four steel arms thrust deep into the ballast! Eight hours later the machine is still locked in the same position, caressing the same sleeper!

'Er, let's send for Albert,' someone says, sarcastically. *'I'll second that,'* concurs another.

Testing of locomotives, coaches and wagons often takes place on this stretch of line, and lately two engines coupled have been running up and down the Slow lines between Speke and Ditton, hauling empty wagon trains every day.

Now they have graduated and are travelling on the Fast lines, pulling empty coaching stock with the same monotonous regularity. I notice the approach of Train No 54, the **10.10am Liverpool to London** and its sign advertising the **'Merseyside Express'** in vermillion on the front, brightening up the drab-coloured **1,600hp 16 cylinder Co-Co English Electric diesel locomotives Nos. 10,000 and 10,001.**

Eventually, diesel locomotives will replace steam, but it will take many years.

Signal boxes can be strangely eerie at times but, then again, one experiences some lighter moments. As I sit, deftly balancing on the hind legs of the chair, the full moon takes on an extra brilliance through the top left-hand window of the door opposite me as the flames of the oil lamp slowly dim, owing to fuel starvation. The subjects under discussion on the telephone are horror films: **'Frankenstein'** and **'Dracula'** have been dealt with, followed by **'The Mummy'**. Synonymous with this type of movie is the **'Werewolf'**.

Broken clouds drift across the heavenly orb, creating sinister shadows on the two lower panes of glass in the door. It is at this precise moment that the animal monster enters into the conversation. Staring into the gloom I try to convince myself the shadowy form is not moving, but - the frightening thing - it is! I feel my heart begin to pump a little faster, when there before me two eyes appear, looking in my direction.

Then the face! I completely lose my balance and drop the telephone, as the chair crashes through the window with me on it. A block bell rings as I struggle to regain my feet, being careful not to injure myself on the shattered glass. **Eyes!** belonging to the most hideous looking cross-bred Alsatian dog I have ever seen, are fixed on me. I shudder to think of the consequences had the door been open; and it had walked into the signal box I would probably have been a victim of heart failure! Shooing it away, using words justifiably subject to expurgation, helps to release the tension brought on by this frightful experience.

On the lighter side, Halebank station is illuminated by paraffin lamps, the oil for which is stored in a cabin only 200yd from here. Stanley, the porter, in his early sixties, has requested a lift back to the station with the full cans of fuel. I inform him that an engine and brake van is approaching on the Up Slow line and that I will stop it for him. Minutes later, the **10.15am Liverpool to Birmingham** express, travelling at speed on the Up Fast line, passes the signal box with its brakes hard on and sparks flying from the wheels, stopping opposite the oil cabin. I watch in amazement as Stanley struggles over the lines with his cans, for a lift. In a cloud of steam the express departs, leaving behind a dejected soul. On arrival at Crewe the driver reports being flagged down at Woodside Sidings signal box. It was our **Stanley!**

One of the platelayers in our gang has a smallholding, and one day he brings me a chicken, still with its feathers on. I explain that I have never plucked one before, so he sets about showing me. After half an hour the operation is complete but, as I wrestle with the levers, flurries of air spread the feathers into a uniform carpet covering the whole floor. The head and giblets are on a piece of newspaper ready for discarding when, of all people, in walks the Block Inspector! Looking around the signal box, and sensing my embarrassment, he warns me:

'It's against the rules having a bird in the signal box, me lad!' with a smirk on his face.

Each week a list of signalmen's vacancies is sent to every signal box. At the moment a 48-hour week is worked by most, but it is being reduced, making it necessary to create a new grade of Rest Day Relief Signalman. I apply for 25 vacancies, getting writer's cramp in the process of filling in the application forms. In these circumstances, order of preference is requested. Most of the older hands go for these new positions because they do not include night turns of duty. As a result I finish up with a 'plum' job' as a General Purpose Relief Signalman Class 1 based in Widnes: at the age of 21, the youngest ever, at this time. The Block Inspector is a little reluctant to transfer me to this position, owing to my lack of experience, so it is some time before the move materialises.

Edge Hill steam crane passing Speke Junction.

Photo from Richard Mercer collection.

Speke/Garston Shed seen from train on Down Fast line at Allerton Junction.

Photo by Les Fifoot.

CHAPTER SEVEN

A RELIEF SIGNALMAN AT WIDNES

1954-57

Relief Signalmen are required to have knowledge of several signal boxes to enable them to be used for holidays, sickness and emergency duties. In the Widnes area the number of signal boxes to be covered in my new position is 16, but to gain the increase in pay for this job, I must be passed competent for Ditton Junction No 2 and Runcorn station signal boxes.

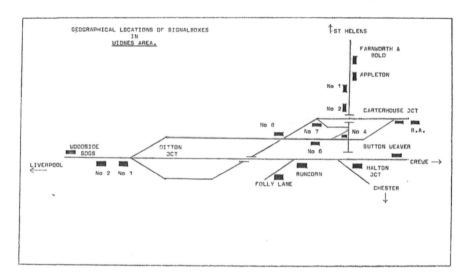

Locations of signal boxes in the Widnes area.

Six weeks of intensive training culminate in my receiving a rate of pay amounting to £5-6s-0d per week, plus travelling time from my home station (Widnes) and shift allowance. After the above-mentioned signal boxes, I 'train' the remainder, although I am called upon in the meantime to take duty in those of which I already have knowledge, as the need arises. I will deal with each signal box, though not necessarily in the order they were trained.

DITTON No 2 SIGNAL BOX

Ditton Junction No 2 signal box is sited between the Down Slow and Up Loop lines, 200yd on the Liverpool side of Ditton (for Hough Green) station. Behind the signal box, running parallel to the Up Loop line a yard, consisting of eight sidings plus the Down Loop, stretches in an easterly direction to the station overbridge. In addition to the foregoing and the main lines, there are junctions from the Up Fast to Up Slow and Down Slow to Down Fast lines, all controlled by a 75-lever LNWR Tumbler Frame. All signals are of the upper quadrant semaphore type, except the two Up Distant signals, which are electrically colour-lit. Near the station a crossing from the Down Fast line leads to Runcorn Bay and No 1 siding, north of the platforms, and on the south side is a lead from the Down Slow into St Helens Bay line, thus completing the layout.

Opposite the signal box a large yard is stacked high with pit props, and beyond that lies the vast Ditton Sleeper Depot, with its pickling plant used to inject creosote into the newly arrived timber, already cut to size, transported by the trainload direct from Garston Docks. The main lines rise slowly from sea level, westwards, up a sweeping curve to the advanced starting signals, just prior to the commencement of Halebank water troughs, with Woolton Church visible in the distance in its prominent position on the outskirts of Liverpool. Behind the signal box the main road through Halebank village, half a mile away, traverses the railway via an overbridge, with an extremely large booking hall built on top, obscuring a decent view in that direction.

Ditton Junction Yard is perpetually filled with wagons as it is the transfer point for traffic from the south destined for Widnes, and vice versa.

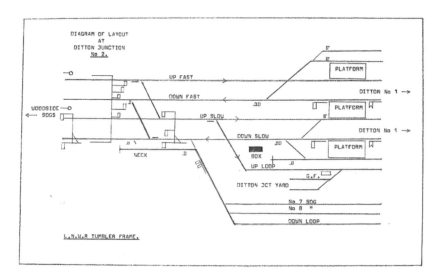

Ditton Junction No 2 signal box.

Target 92, tripping between Widnes and Runcorn every four hours, runs round its train here, and is signalled under the Permissive Block Regulations, using Single Stroke Block Instruments, to Ditton No 1 signal box.

Permissive Block Working permits more than one train in a block section at the same time. With the exception of an Officer's Special (railway big-wigs), a propelling movement must not be allowed to enter an occupied section, unless for attaching or detaching purposes.

There are three types of lines:

1. **Goods Lines.**

2. **Passenger Lines,** and

3. **Lines used by passenger and freight, with Permissive Working for freight trains only.**

   (During fog or falling snow, Permissive Working must be suspended.)

Halebank water troughs, over ¼-mile long, are continuously filled with water treated through a softening plant, the residue of which is pumped into a shallow depression between the railway and Halebank village, giving it the appearance of a snow-covered field all year round. During winter the troughs freeze over, and platelayers are on permanent standby to break the forming ice. In long periods of adverse weather their task becomes a losing battle, and piles of ice-blocks line the edge of the tracks to a considerable depth, obstructing the cycle path and taking weeks to thaw. The Advanced Starting signals are also affected in these conditions because spray from passing locomotives ices up the wires, causing them to become inoperative. This malfunction is detected within the signal box using electrical repeaters of the signal arms.

This signal box is renowned as a heavy one to work. The amount of traffic dealt with, and the strength needed to pull the worn-out and hard levers, confirm its reputation; however, being young the physical exertion does not bother me, and I quite enjoy the challenge of a busy signal box. Over the lever frame is a large illuminated diagram which has a detailed plan showing all points, signals and relevant information to assist the signalman in his duties. Track Circuits give a visual indication on the diagram of the exact geographical location of trains within the area of control. As the train proceeds, electrical impulses are transmitted to the signal box, activating relays that lock all points until that section is clear. Prior to these diagrams being installed in signal boxes, the signalman never knew the position of a train unless he could actually see it.

Not all signal boxes have this useful equipment, but two earlier types are more widespread. The first of these are **Home Signal Berth Track Circuits,** which are 200yd long and, when activated by a train, an annunciator sounds in the signal box for 10 seconds in conjunction with a small indicator changing from **'Line Clear'** to **'Line Occupied'** position. This effectively locks the Block Instrument needle to **'Train on Line'** and cannot be released unless the train is allowed to proceed, thereby coming under the protection of the Home signal. The second is used specifically at Goods Lines Home signals and is, operated by the fireman of a train. Aptly titled the **'Fireman's Plunger'**, like the Home Signal Track Circuit, it activates an annunciator, but the indicator shows **'Train Arrived'**.

The widely-known named expresses that run between Liverpool and cities in the south overshadow two trains that serve this area well. These also are named. I refer to **'The Ditton Dodger'** and **'The Ditton Warrior'.** The 'Dodger' runs between Ditton Junction and Timperley, via Warrington, along the Low Level line, with the local passenger service plus a small amount of freight work. 'The 'Warrior' is a real slogger, tripping between Garston and the Ditton Yards, loaded with timber, coal, molasses, sleepers or other goods, hauled by **Webbs 0-6-2 'Coal Tanks'** or **'Super D'** locomotives, and clearing out Messrs Evans' and Montague Meyer's timber yards, along with the Sleeper Depot and Prop Yard. This train is aptly titled, struggling with up to 70 wagons on its upward journey to Garston, very rarely needing assistance but often having a few stops to blow up!

A shunting neck in Ditton Junction Yard runs parallel to the Down Slow line for ¼-mile. A Crewe to Edge Hill freight train with a **Stanier 4-6-0 'Black Five'** up front has finished shunting but the driver, unfortunately, misreads the signals on the large gantry nearby. Opening the regulator his train gathers speed, not on the Down Slow line, as he thinks, but along the Neck! With a resounding crash the stop block is demolished and the engine finishes up on its side in a farmer's field, covered over with the remains of smashed wagons. The fireman bales out seconds before impact, and the driver survives without serious injury.

On the Up Fast line at Ditton No 2. Courtesy of Mick Langton.

On the Up Slow line at Ditton No 2. Courtesy of Mick Langton.

Two miles away to the east of Ditton Junction is:

WIDNES No 8 SIGNAL BOX

(WEST DEVIATION JUNCTION)

This signal box is on the former St Helens to Runcorn Gap Railway extension line to Garston Docks. It is built between, on the one side, a bridge carrying the CLC Railway (opened in 1878) from Moor Lane signal box to the West Bank Hutchinson Estate and, on the other, a road bridge leading from Ditton Road to the same industrial area. Opposite the signal box a large water tank for supplying locomotives tilts perilously to the right, giving the impression that it is about to crash down onto the three lines in front of the signal box, whilst in the rear an embankment rises to the CLC Railway. This combination requires artificial lighting to be used at all times within the signal box.

The Up and Down Fast lines (opened in 1865) run parallel to the main line on Ditton Bank on its northern side, while the Up and Down Slow lines (one of which was opened in 1852 as a single line to Garston) join the Fast lines close to the signal box, after first passing under the main line half a mile away.

Widnes No 8 signal box (West Deviation Junction). Photo by A W Hobart, courtesy of Ernie Brack collection

Traffic passing over these Fast lines is minimal, the chief reason being the reluctance of the signalmen in Ditton Junction No 1 signal box, to use them to run freight trains. As a result they have received the infamous title of the **'Sacred Lines'**! Running contiguous with, and parallel to, the sacred lines are Clare's Sidings - who Clare is I have never been able to establish - used specifically for timber destined for Messrs Evans' works at Ditton Junction.

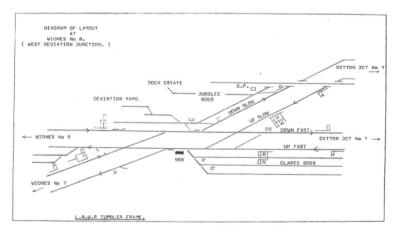

Widnes No 8 signal box (West Deviation Junction).

A ground frame released from this signal box controls the entrance to Jubilee Sidings, on the Down Slow line near the main line overbridge, with one of the sidings continuing under the fourth arch of the massive Ditton Viaduct into the Dock Estate. A trailing lead from the Down Slow line serves West Deviation Yard via a shunting neck that terminates at the said Jubilee Sidings ground frame. Looking east, the Up and Down lines rise sharply to Widnes No 7 signal box, and a pair of worked catch points (which are installed to derail runaway vehicles that could otherwise foul the junction points) protect the junction to Widnes No 6 level crossing signal box, to the left, half a mile away. Almost all of the signals, operated from a 50-lever LNWR Tumbler Frame, are of the upper quadrant semaphore type. Unique to this signal box is No 8 lever, minus its catch handle. It is attached by wire to a gong half a mile away, close to Jubilee Sidings ground frame, and requires a heavy pull when used. Pulled twice, it is an indication to the driver that the ground signal (Dummy) is in the 'Off' position and that he can now propel his train into Deviation Yard. Using this lever is particularly hazardous, because an unusual method is adopted to clean the floor. Paraffin is poured onto the dark beige linoleum, and with over-shoes made from sacking by the resident signalman, one shuffles from lever to lever, thereby polishing the floor, giving a mirror-like finish. I, like others before me, have finished up with a bruised posterior using this novel procedure.

A trainload of timber has just arrived from Garston to be shunted into Clare's Sidings, and the guard detaches his brake van behind the Up Slow home signal, as is the usual practice. Drawing the train forwards up the bank towards No 7 signal box (3-3-2 on the bell - **Shunt into forward section)** the driver misjudges the length of his train and does not fully clear the aforementioned catch points. As a result the couplings stretch, and the two rear wagons become derailed and fall on their sides, strewing timber all over the place. Following trains are diverted along the Goods lines to No 6 signal box until the breakdown train clears the track, which takes several hours.

Traffic into and out of Deviation Yard is particularly heavy, with most trains calling to attach or detach wagons. Trippers running between St Helens, Warrington, Dock Junction and Ditton Junction are frequent and, as mentioned earlier, Target 92 commences its many journeys to Folly Lane from here.

It is not often that the signalmen in Widnes have the opportunity to witness the passing of a new class of locomotive, but today one is being released from the works and is scheduled to visit Deviation Yard. I refer to the **English Electric Co-Co 'DELTIC' 3,300hp** with **two 18 cylinder Napier Deltic Engines.** Pale blue in colour with yellow chevrons decorating the front, it glistens in the bright sunlight against the dull landscape of Widnes. This powerful engine is now backing into the yard, when **'BUMP!'** It's a **'CRANE'** job! The rails have spread and **'Deltic'** has the ignominious distinction of being derailed on its maiden journey.

Passing West Deviation Junction signal box. Photo by Les Fifoot.

I have been working for a week in this signal box and have yet to signal a train. The temperature is in the 80s, so I take advantage by sitting on top of the CLC embankment, sunbathing, waiting for the bells to ring; but I know this is not to be, because ASLEF, the drivers' union, has called strike action for extra remuneration. After three weeks this action is called off, the drivers receiving one shilling per week (at today's price, 50p) but the hard-working firemen received nothing!

'Deltic' at Widnes. Photo from Richard Mercer collection.

Leaving this signal box, to walk through Deviation Sidings, we arrive at:

WIDNES No 6 SIGNAL BOX

(WATERLOO ROAD LEVEL CROSSING)

This signal box, as previously mentioned, controls a level crossing in Waterloo Road, Widnes, signalling trains on the Goods lines between Widnes No 8 and Widnes No 4 (Dock Junction) signal boxes, with Single Stroke Permissive Block instruments, using an LMS Standard Frame. In 1852 a new station was built here, replacing the original Runcorn Gap station, retaining the same name until 1864 when it became Widnes, but there are no physical remains at the location today. Railway traffic is light across this very busy main road which leads from Widnes town centre to the transporter bridge, and it is always difficult to open the gates for trains, especially during the peak hours.

Widnes No 6 signal box (Waterloo Crossing). Photo by Eddie Bellass.

A 4ft-diameter wheel is turned to operate the gates, and mechanical stops in the roadway protrude upwards to prevent the gates from passing this pre-selected point. Unfortunately, these stops have a tendency to stick from time to time causing traffic to build up at the crossing and it is, with embarrassment, that one must leave the signal box to give them a hefty whack with a hammer - one of those usually used by firemen on locomotives to break coal - to free the unseen obstruction.

'WHAT A RAILWAY!'

Physically, it is a very easy signal box to work and one of the three in the Widnes area to employ signalwomen, but today the number of women operating signal boxes throughout Britain is on the decline. **(Incidentally, my previous assumption regarding the fused lights was quite wrong?) (Was I?)**

Time exposure at Waterloo Crossing. Photographer unknown.

Walking along Waterloo Road in the direction of the town centre, Widnes LMS (named Widnes South from 1959) station is on the right-hand side, and at the end of the Down line platform is:

WIDNES No 7 SIGNAL BOX

This signal box stands atop an embankment on the Warrington side of Widnes LMS station (built in 1870, replacing that at Waterloo Road). The Up and Down lines (opened in 1869) from Widnes No 8 continue on to Carterhouse Junction signal box, just over a mile away.

The junction here diverts trains on a downward right-hand curve to Widnes No 2 (Ann Street) signal box, passing first Widnes Locomotive Shed on the left.

Widnes No 7 signal box. Photo by Graham Earle

All signals are of the upper quadrant semaphore type, worked from an LNWR Tumbler Frame, and Absolute Block Regulations apply on all lines. This is the second signal box to be built on this site, for in 1892 the LNWR erected this one of 20 levers for the outrageous price, in present-day terms, of only £265!

There is no shortage of visitors to this signal box; it serves as the relieving point for train crews in transit from the Yorkshire and Derbyshire coalfields via the Low Level line, also those from Wigan and beyond leaving the St Helens Branch line. In addition the booking office, now closed to the public, is used solely for paying wages to railway staff working in the area.

Widnes South (ex-LMS) station, looking east. Photo by H C Casserley

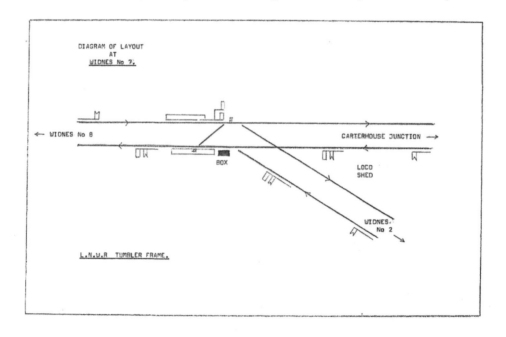

Widnes No 7 signal box.

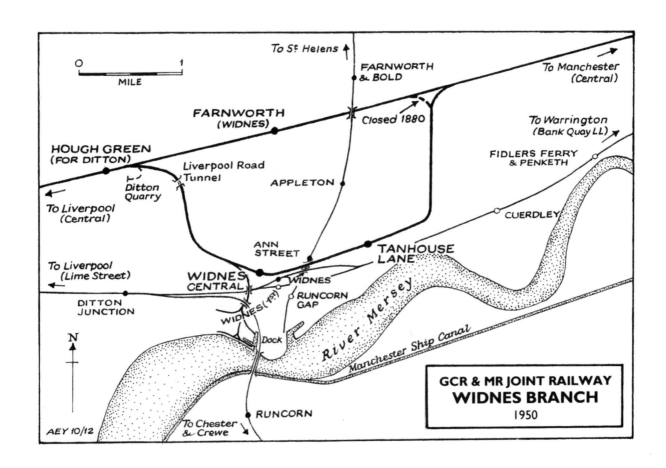

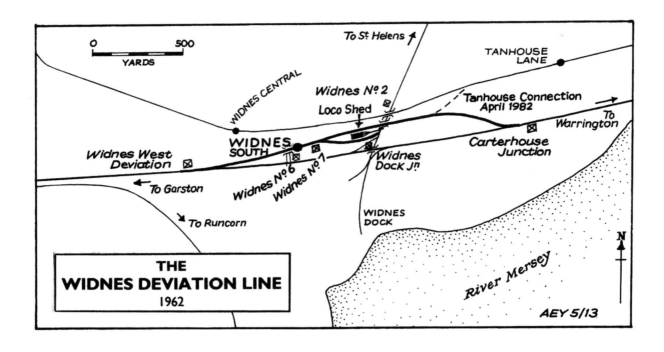

Widnes area maps by Alan Young

Retracing my steps to Waterloo Road Level Crossing signal box, it is only a short distance to:

WIDNES No 4 SIGNAL BOX

(DOCK JUNCTION)

Earlier, I mentioned Widnes No 7 signal box being renewed in 1892. In 1894 this signal box was also rebuilt with an LNWR Tumbler Frame costing £934! Surrounded by railway lines and factories, Widnes No 4 signal box has a bleak outlook, and the work is equally uninteresting because it controls shunting into the Marsh Sidings, which fan out towards the River Mersey in the distance, plus trippers between the various yards in the area.

Widnes No 4 signal box (Dock Junction). Photo by M Humphries, courtesy of 8D Association

The Goods lines between No 6 and Carterhouse Junction signal boxes, are crossed at right angles by the St Helens Branch, itself terminating at the single line which crosses over a bridge spanning the St Helens Canal, just prior to the Marsh Sidings. This bridge marks the site of the original Runcorn Gap station, opened in 1833, which stood here until the year 1852 when it was rebuilt at Waterloo Road. Two junctions, one 200yd towards Widnes No 6 signal box, close to the site of the second Runcorn Gap station connect the Goods lines, via the Curve, to the next junction on the St Helens Branch line, towards Widnes No 2 signal box. Both these junctions are controlled from this signal box.

Permissive Block Working applies on all lines, but there is a need to be extra careful when operating the lever frame because the sequential locking is minimal and many of the points have free levers. In overall charge of the various yards in the Widnes area (including Folly Lane at Runcorn) is a Chief Inspector, stationed here at Dock Junction. At most times he can be seen outside the signal box on the walkway covering the points rodding, directing traffic movements into Messrs Albright and Wilson's, Muspratt's and Lugsdale Sidings, and onto the Marsh.

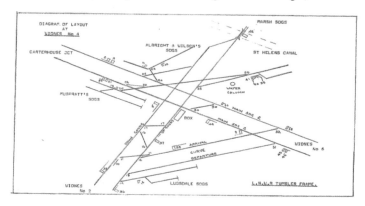

Widnes No 4 (Dock Junction) signal box.

Dock Junction looking west.

Photographer unknown.

The site of the original Runcorn Gap station.

Courtesy of the Railway & Canal Historical Society.

A temporary cessation of activity brings the shunting staff a welcome rest in the early hours, so for a change of scenery, and of course, a cup of tea, I join them in their cabin nearby. One of the lads is relating his war experiences to an attentive audience.

'Just before the battle of El Alamein our platoon was resting, when orders came from headquarters that certain tasks had to be carried out to keep us fit.' The captain came to me and said, **'Corporal, take five men to chop some trees down.'** handing me the required number of axes.

There is a stunned silence for several minutes until a bleary-eyed shunter quips, **'Hey, Thatch, there's no trees in the desert.'**

The old soldier hesitates, looking at the knowledgeable gentleman. *'I know,'* he says, looking a little embarrassed:

'WE CHOPPED EM' ALL DOWN!'

Hearty laughter is directed at the now-awakened recipient of the leg-pull. A bell rings in the signal box, so I leave, with the strains of continued exultation from within this den of jocularity fading behind me.

By far the busiest signal box in the Widnes area is only a few hundred yards in the St Helens direction from here. I refer to:

WIDNES No 2 SIGNAL BOX

(ANN STREET LEVEL CROSSING)

This box signals trains between Widnes No 1 and Widnes No 4, and also, via a deviating line, up a sharp curving gradient to the right which in turn merges with the Low Level Line at No 7 signal box. In addition it controls the connections to Widnes Shed. It is sited adjacent to the Up line on the northern side of three consecutive overbridges, the first of these being a pedestrian footbridge for use when the level crossing gates to the left of the signal box are set against road traffic. Next is the bridge that carries the former CLC Railway between Hough Green and Widnes East junctions, and lastly, the one carrying the Low Level line from Widnes No 7 to Carterhouse Junction.

Ann Street, leading from Widnes town centre, is not a main thoroughfare although a lot of traffic passes along it to Messrs Albright and Wilson's factory nearby. The usual procedure adopted during the peak hours is to give preference to road traffic, and this is accomplished by allowing trains to approach, under the control of signals, before actually opening the gates.

Widnes No 2 signal box (Ann Street Crossing). Photo by R W Mercer.

Seldom are the gates across the road open for more than two minutes, but an irate cyclist has just entered the signal box, complaining that he has been sent home for arriving late for work, and blames me because I opened the gates to run a light engine; a move that takes less than a minute. I advise him to leave home two minutes earlier in future, or carry his bicycle over the footbridge provided, thereby obviating the cause of complaint - not forgetting to tell him I have a railway to run.

The majority of freight trains require assistance from here to travel up the Farnworth Bank. The procedure is to stop clear of the level crossing gates and await the **'Super D'** bank engine, already stabled on the Through Siding. With a series of whistles the two identical locomotives begin to move forwards, pumping volumes of grey, dirty smoke skywards, with sparks flying as the wheels struggle to gain adhesion. Eventually the train gets away, the sanders proving their worth.

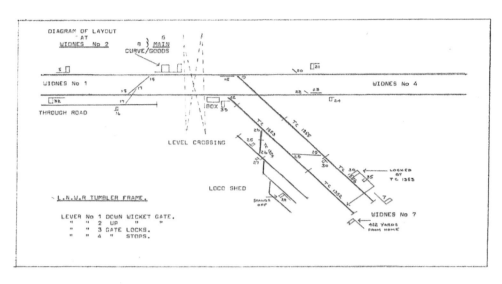

Widnes No 2 signal box (Ann Street Crossing).

Drivers bringing locomotives back to the shed must stop outside the signal box and request a time to book the engine 'home'. A quick glance at the clock, plus seven minutes, will usually satisfy most of them, and in some instances the crew will manage to elude cleaning the firebox out. The number of the engine and time are recorded on a special sheet, and this is sent every 24 hours to the shed offices for scrutiny. Occasionally locomotives from other depots visit the shed to fill up with coal and water in readiness for their return working home. There is never any shortage of coal for the signal box stove because many drivers push off a few-lumps of 'best Yorkshire' as they pass!

Widnes Locomotive Shed.

Locomotives in front of picture stabled in West Deviation Yard.

Lines between them, left-to-right, from No 7 to No 2 signal boxes.

Photo by Eddie Bellass.

Most train movements taking place require the gates to be opened, and the 4ft-diameter wheel needs a lot of strength to operate. Four levers (painted brown) in the LNWR Tumbler Frame are connected with the gates. Levers Nos 1 and 2 work the Down and Up wicket gates (for pedestrians only), No 3 the Gate Locks and No 4 the Gate Stops. These four levers are worked twice for every train, and adding the points and signals plus the turning of the wheel makes this the 'slogging box' of Widnes; not forgetting that the signalman has responsibility for cleaning and lighting the oil lamps atop the gates.

If a track circuit becomes occupied owing to an electrical fault, any points within it are locked. To enable a signalman to release the points in these circumstances there is, fastened to the instrument shelf, a small box 6in x 3in x 2in with a glass cover, very similar to a fire alarm. When this glass is broken with either a poker or another implement, a button is exposed which is pressed to free the electrical locking. I am on duty at Widnes No 1 signal box, and get a **flat 'un** on the bell.

A flat 'un is achieved by holding the block hammer when ringing. This in effect stuns the normal resonance, and is an indication that the signalman sending it requires immediate attention on the telephone. This practice, frowned upon by the Block Inspectors, is always used when they are not on the war-path! Anyway, Phil, the signalman on duty - who hails from the country of Wales - rings to tell me he has a track circuit failure on the shed and cannot release a locomotive. I ask, *'Have you broken the glass on the instrument shelf?'*

'No, man, I have not,' comes the reply.

'Well, get the poker and give it a whack, but hold the shovel under it - otherwise the glass will fly all over the signal box - then press the button,' I suggest.

'Okay, boyo,' comes an instant reply. I hear the sound of tinkling glass falling onto metal. I think to myself, *'that seems a lot!'* and he returns to the phone.

'There's no button here, boyo,' he informs me.

'No button?' I reply.

'No, there's no button, only needles, and I still can't get the engine off the shed.'

'What have you smashed?' I enquire.

'The glass, boyo.'

'Which glass?'

'The glass on the instrument shelf, like you told me, boyo.'

I think, *'The needles.'* *'I'll turn my needle to "Train on line", just a sec.'* *'Is that it, bach?'* I say.

'Yes, that's it, boyo.' *'Well, Taffy, I reckon you've broken the wrong glass!'*

I attempt to explain about the small box, etc. Another tinkle of glass (not so much this time) but the engine still remains on the shed. He has another go. Still no joy.

I am unable to establish whether he manages to release the engine, before wrecking the signal box completely!

WIDNES No 1 SIGNAL BOX (VINEYARD)

This seems a completely inappropriate name for a signal box situated in derelict surroundings, without a trace of greenery to be seen, but I have recently been informed that there were once extensive vineyards located to the east of the line here.

Widnes No 1 signal box (Vineyard). Photo by Graham Earle, courtesy of 8D Association.

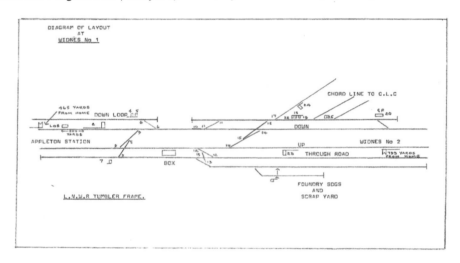

Widnes No 1 signal box (Vineyard).

Absolute Block Regulations apply in this signal box, sited between Widnes No 2 and Appleton Station signal boxes, adjacent to Lugsdale Road overbridge on the Up line side. The upper quadrant semaphore signals are connected to an LNWR Tumbler Frame.

Lever frame in Widnes No 1 signal box. Photo by Graham Earle, courtesy of 8D Association.

Sidings on the southern side of the signal box, under the control of a shunter, serve the nearby iron foundry (where during the war Bailey bridge components were manufactured) and scrap yard. One line runs parallel to the Up line (the Through Road) from Widnes No 2, which is used occasionally to run the Vineyard tripper to Dock Junction, depending on the traffic situation. On the Down side a Loop line, commencing at Appleton station, terminates here. Prior to the withdrawal of the passenger train service on this route, freight trains were regulated from the latter signal box, for the next recessing point is at West Deviation Junction, a few miles away. Today this line is used solely to stable traffic for Messrs Southern's timber works at Appleton.

Ditton Road, two miles long, commencing at Ditton Junction station and running straight to Victoria Road in Widnes, is lined on the right hand side with numerous chemical works. This has given an apt title to the road, the **'Stinky Mile'**. Cycling along this stretch, in thick, yellow chemical fog, I inhale fumes that take my breath away, yet it appears to have a clearing effect on the lungs. I reach the sanctuary of this signal box at 5.45 am to take up duty. Smoke from fires lit by a group of gypsies, camped on waste ground opposite, mixes with the already dense atmosphere and seeps under the frame into the signal box.

Shortly after, I hear the distant continuous popping from a locomotive approaching down Farnworth Bank with a train that has not been accepted by the advance signal box, No 2. I telephone Phil informing him of my suspicion that the train is running away and, if this proves to be correct, I shall send him the appropriate bell signal. Minutes later the heavily laden train looms from the curtain of fog, after passing the home signal at danger, and is travelling at 50mph or more into the section. Sending the 'Train Running Away Right Line' signal, I expect it to be acknowledged by repetition; but no, I receive nothing.

The telephone rings.

'What is that, boyo?' he enquires.

'4-5-5, train running away,' I reply.

'You must not let him come man, I cannot deal with it!'

'Open them gates, smartish!' I shout, slamming the phone down in disgust.

I head for the door to listen for the demolition job that is about to take place. I hear only the usual muffled traffic noises and those from the forge, but none that would indicate a collision with the gates. The upward gradient to Widnes No 7 signal box is steep enough for the driver to regain control of his train, but he was not aware that **'Boyo'** only just managed to avert what could have been a severe accident; it was very close indeed.

Hough Green Junction signal box controls a loop line deviating from the main CLC railway, passing signal boxes at Moor Lane, Widnes Central station and Tanhouse Lane, before re-joining the main line at Widnes East Junction. Passenger train services along this line are light, and it is the Railway Executive's intention to withdraw them altogether, but the United Sulphuric Acid Co has built a new factory at Tanhouse Lane, requiring bulk train loads of Anhydrite from quarries at Long Meg, on the Settle & Carlisle line, for processing. This traffic, at present, is routed via Halewood on the CLC railway. To bring the plan to fruition, consideration was given to the future supply of traffic to USAC Ltd, and it was decided to construct a new link line from this signal box to the factory. It has now been completed; traffic is routed via St Helens and the Loop line from Hough Green to Widnes East Junction is finally closed.

I had the honour to be the first signalman to divert trains onto the newly opened line!

It is only five minutes walking towards Farnworth Bank before one arrives at:

APPLETON STATION SIGNAL BOX
(THE SECOND-HAND SHOP?)

This small signal box, situated on the Down line side on the platform of the now defunct station, controls the entrance to the Down Loop line, commencing at the other end of the platform. It is used now solely to stable timber trains destined for Messrs Southern's large yard; their own engine transferring the wagons into their premises as they require. All the signals are of the upper quadrant semaphore type, worked from an LNWR Tumbler Frame.

Appleton Station signal box: note both lower and upper quadrant signals.

Photo by J M Tolson, from Richard Mercer collection.

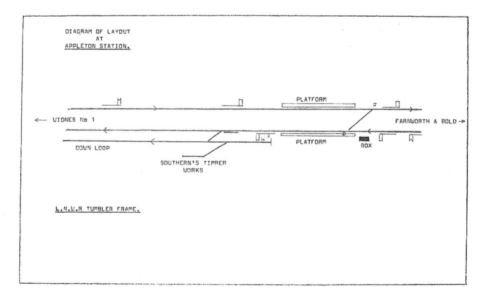

Appleton Station signal box.

Second-Hand Shop! How does this box receive this *nom de plume*? Well, during the austerity years in the war, and shortly after, railwaymen like many others would attempt to find ways of getting extra money to supplement their meagre wages and make ends meet. George, the resident signalman in this box (nearing retirement age) is a good exponent of such practices. He has his fingers in many pies, from illicit contraband to second-hand goods, and is quick off the mark in notifying his prospective customers of bargains they can obtain from his connections. I don't hesitate, jump on the bandwagon and manage to get some bargains in the process. Not forgetting the famous wartime slogan:

'WALLS HAVE EARS'.

I work in this signal box on only a few occasions, and nothing of note takes place operationally. By road, just over a mile to the east is:

CARTERHOUSE JUNCTION SIGNAL BOX

Carterhouse Junction signal box. Courtesy of H.G.

This signal box controls a junction. In one direction it deals with the Up and Down Goods lines to Widnes No 4 signal box, opened in 1854, and signals trains under the Permissive Block Regulations. The other route on an upward gradient, the Up and Down main lines to Widnes No 7, are worked under the Absolute Block Regulations. Outside the signal box is a level crossing, used only by a local farmer to drive his cows over a small bridge spanning the St Helens Canal to the field on the other side, which borders the River Mersey a few hundred yards away. The canal running behind the signal box follows the same course as the railway as far as the eye can see in each direction.

Lever frame in Carterhouse Junction signal box. Courtesy of H.G.

Towards Widnes a small sidings in the 'V' of the junction, manned by a shunter, stables tank trains destined for Messrs Albright and Wilson's factory. On occasions I am requested to report to this signal box to await the tripper destined for Pilkington Sullivan's chemical works. Getting aboard, the train is allowed into the advance section up to the next signal box:

BRITISH ALKALI SIGNAL BOX

The box is half a mile east of Carterhouse Junction, and shares the same exposed position near the banks of the River Mersey on the other side of the St Helens Canal, with the Manchester Ship Canal and Cheshire countryside beyond. I open this signal box which has a small LNWR Tumbler Frame, two block instruments, one circuit switch, and a stove, and these make up its entire contents; comfort is unattainable. Even the windows are somewhat different from the norm in that they do not require cleaning. **There is no glass in them**, making the stove a useless asset, as the prevailing wind from the river whistles through, chilling me to the bone.

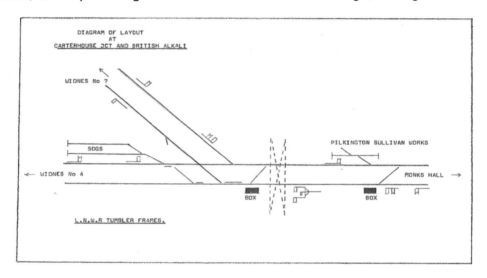

Carterhouse Junction and British Alkali signal boxes.

The LNWR company concentrated on building new signal boxes in the Widnes area in the 1890s, and this one was erected in 1896, costing a mere £206; but plans have been made to dispense with it and replace it with a ground frame controlled from Carterhouse Junction signal box. This signal box is opened only as required, the next box along the line being at Fiddlers Ferry Power Station. I have the honour of being the last signalman to work British Alkali signal box before its final closure.

Tamping machine at Fiddlers Ferry Power Station signal box. Courtesy of Ray Burgess.

This completes the signal boxes I work in Lancashire, so over we go to the Cheshire side of the River Mersey:

RUNCORN STATION SIGNAL BOX

Trains leaving the girders of Britannia Bridge enter a rising curve, passing through Runcorn station, where 200yd ahead on the Down line side is the brick-built signal box at the northern end of a deep cutting. Looking out of the windows of the signal box, beyond the station only a portion of the bridge is visible as buildings obstruct the field of view. On the left, and running behind the station down platform, is the single line that branches into two from the Up and Down lines to Folly Lane. Little can be seen to the south, owing to the cutting mentioned above. Opposite the signal box are a large goods warehouse and sidings. The LMS Standard Frame has 45 levers and, above it, a large illuminated diagram.

Runcorn Station signal box. Courtesy of Joe Gerrard.

All signals are of the upper quadrant semaphore type, the exception being the Up line distant on the northern side of the bridge, which is a lower quadrant semaphore. Between this signal box and Ditton Junction No 1 there was at one time a signal box called Ditton Bank, which stood almost opposite West Deviation Junction on the Low Level line, but it closed in the early 1930s. However, in its place Intermediate Block Signals were erected.

Intermediate Block Sections are Track Circuited throughout, and they allow for a train to leave the signal box in rear, before the previous train passes the advance signal box, provided that the line is clear to the Intermediate Block Home signal, and the overlap track circuit, (usually 200yd) in advance of this signal is not occupied.

A telephone is provided at the IB Home signal for train crew use. It must be in working order at all times. If for any reason it fails, Absolute Block Working must be instituted until the fault is rectified.

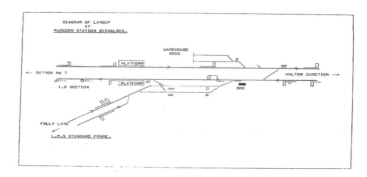

Runcorn Station signal box.

Most passenger trains stop at Runcorn, but the station platforms cannot accommodate the longer ones, owing to their insufficient length, so these must draw up to allow the rear vehicles to be dealt with. As the number of people using this station is considerable, excessive delay to traffic is unavoidable because of this operational difficulty.

Leaving Runcorn Bridge. Courtesy of Mick Langton.

Author in Runcorn Station signal box. Courtesy of Joe Gerrard.

Freight traffic is only moderate, compared to the passenger trains, but it requires more handling time, especially those trains approaching from the Ditton Junction direction destined for Folly Lane, which have to propel through the main line crossover road situated in the cutting. If they are assisted in rear, the banking engine stops opposite the signal box to await disposal of the train, and a margin, before returning to Ditton Junction for further work. Target 91, the Folly Lane trip engine, is propelling two vehicles into the Warehouse Sidings and has just become derailed on the runaway catch points operated from the signal box. It does not take long, with a little pull from the **350hp diesel,** to re-rail it, but there is a malfunction of the point mechanism which calls for examination by the signal lineman. A couple of whacks with a hammer and a drop of oil soon rectify the problem!

There are three shunters stationed at Runcorn, working on different turns of duty. They are responsible for shunting the Warehouse Sidings, detaching and attaching wagons on trains *en route* from the Crewe or Chester directions to Liverpool and vice versa, and also stabling trains on the Folly Lane Branch. One of these shunters domiciles himself in the signal box, always sitting on the locker underneath the clock, complaining all day about the amount of work he does. At times, I must agree, it does get hectic, but on the whole he tends to exaggerate. Even so, I wind him up by saying, *'I wouldn't put up with it, if I were you.'*

His reaction is to ring the Yard Master at Widnes. Usually the conversation at this end is:

'Could I have a word with the Yard Master please?'

'Is that you, Mr. Hughes? I am fed up with this job. Send my cards over on Target 92.'

Despite his grumbles and incessant complaints he is really a damn good worker, but I think he likes everyone to think he is badly done-by.

Another day dawns, and he is his usual loquacious self. Having just shunted two wagons into the Down Sidings, off the Crewe to Edge Hill train, watched by a host of passengers waiting for the train behind it, he returns to the signal box and slumps onto the locker, muttering:

'That lot there don't know what work is. Give them a bloody shunting pole, and they wouldn't know what to do with it!'

On and on he goes.

'Joe, guess what, we've got a visitor,' I say, as I spot the Yard Master approaching through the private coal yard behind the signal box.

'Good morning, Signalman. Good morning, Joseph.'

'Goo .. goo .. good morning, Mr Hughes,' replies Joe, sheepishly.

Joe then begins to advise him of the traffic situation, adding, *'I've done this, Mr Hughes, and I've done that.'*

I think, and know, he's talking a load of waffle.

'That's very good, Joseph. By the way, the reason I have come to Runcorn is to deliver this letter to you,' he says to Joe, giving me a wink as he hands it to him.

Joe sits down and nervously opens it. Out comes documentation. *'They're fully stamped up,'* quips the boss, as Joe eyes his cards.

'Bu … bu … but hey, Mr Hughes, I didn't mean it!'

'Now, now, Joe, you rang me before, didn't you?' Joe by now is in a terrible state, and I don't help the matter by confirming the telephone message, and saying;

'A good boss always takes notice of his men.'

'I've been on the railway for nearly 30 years and never before been treated like this.' whispers Joe, his eyes filling up with tears.

Patting him on the shoulder, the boss says, *'Oh, all right, Joe. Let me have them back.'*

As he is walking back towards the station, Joe mumbles*, 'Give that fella a bloody shunting pole, and he wouldn't know what to do with it!'*

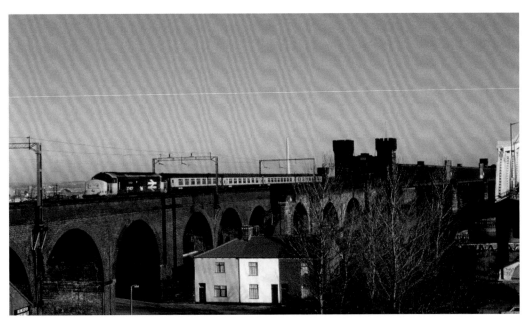

Leaving Runcorn Bridge. Courtesy of Mick Langton.

A freight train coming from Liverpool, hauled by a **4-6-0 'Jubilee'**, creates a wonderful picture as it emerges from the girders of Runcorn Bridge. It is enveloped in smoke and steam, gaining but little respite on the small length of level track there, before again labouring up the severe gradient that ends two miles away at Sutton Weaver signal box, passing first the junction at:

HALTON JUNCTION SIGNAL BOX

This signal box is situated just over one mile south of Runcorn, controlling a junction with the main line in front of the signal box, and behind, the Chester Branch, signalling trains to Sutton Weaver and Frodsham Junction respectively. Similar to Woodside Sidings signal box, it is illuminated entirely by paraffin lamps and has no toilet, which is no problem to a good boy scout! However, it does boast a modern water supply, complete with taps.

Halton Junction signal box. Train from Chester branch. Courtesy of Ray Burgess.

The Signalmen's Inspector has just passed me competent to work the signal box, after one week's training, and he requests me to take up duty on the afternoon turn on Saturday. Cycling from my home in Halewood I reach the start of the 'Stinky Mile', assisted by the prevailing wind, when I am suddenly passed; travelling at speed on his 'Cyclemaster', by another Relief Signalman who is stationed at Widnes, probably going to Waterloo Crossing signal box. Knowing him, he always seems to get the cushy jobs! From Runcorn it is an upward climb to Halton Junction, with at least ¼-mile being along a muddy farmer's track running parallel to the railway.

Diagram in Halton Junction signal box. Courtesy of H.G.

I arrive on duty, but the early turn signalman is reluctant to leave me in charge because I have come to relieve him at the unofficial time of 1pm, which is normal practice for a Saturday in the majority of signal boxes. However, he goes home at 1.10pm, only to return at 1.59pm on the pretence of forgetting something in his locker. Such is his confidence in me?

We are in the throes of winter and it has started getting dark early, so I lift the oil lamp from its holder, suspended at head height in front of the instrument shelf. Examining it closely, I think, 'I've not seen one of these before'. The lamp has a steel tube with a mantle on top, and fastened to the oil container is a pump handle. Out with the Captain Webb's to light the mantle, but I am drenched by the paraffin spurting all over the place, which I am powerless to stop. A bell rings, and in the unfamiliar surroundings I fumble, bumping into the levers. **'Blast it'**, I mumble to myself. Lighting the hand-lamp, that gives as much illumination as a dynamo on a bicycle when travelling up Gateacre Brow (a very steep climb in Liverpool) which is all I have, I persevere with it and, after two hours, still no success. In the end I give it up as a bad job! I work until 9pm with just the hand-lamp, booking trains, operating the levers, the Block Instruments and everything else! I get through the shift all right, but it turns out to be a long eight hours. To add insult to injury my relief asks me if I enjoy working in the dark. I could answer him, but choose not to.

I did wonder why that bottle of methylated spirits was on the shelf in the corner!

'Some scout, eh!'

HST on Up line at Rainbow Bridge, Halton Junction. Courtesy of Ray Burgess.

All the signals worked from this box, with a 25-lever LNWR Tumbler Frame, are of the upper quadrant semaphore type, except the Up line distant which is colour lit. On the Down line there is an Outer Home signal for acceptance purposes, which I recall relates to the very first question put to me at the beginning of my training period at Pighue Lane Junction signal box.

The theory of railway regulations is far more difficult than the practical application, and this is a good example:

Regulation 5 of the Absolute Block Regulations, (Warning Arrangements) bell code 3-5-5 deals with the acceptance of trains where the mandatory distance of 1¼-mile clearance is not possible.

However, only in exceptional circumstances can this regulation apply to passenger trains, but the signalman in this signal box is authorised to warn such a train in accordance with this regulation from Frodsham Junction, the clearance being less than 100yd. (There may be other signal boxes in the Liverpool area where this is authorised, but I do not know of any myself.)

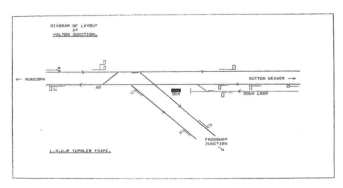

Halton Junction signal box.

Clearance points of at least ¼-mile, as previously mentioned, are mandatory in basic signalling principles, covered by the Absolute Block Regulations, but where the junction home is less than this distance the signalman is not authorised to accept a train if he has already accepted one from another signal box that would foul the clearance point:

The signalman in Box 'C' (see diagram on next page) accepting a train under regulation 4 from signal box 'A' debars him from accepting a train under the same regulation from Box 'B', or cross one in transit from signal box 'D' to 'B', unless the train from 'A' has come to a stand at the home signal, or has passed the clearance point. This signal box, however, is equipped with an Outer Home Signal for acceptance purposes, which is more than ¼-mile from the Inner Home Signal. Therefore the signalman can accept a train from Sutton Weaver signal box, another from Frodsham Junction and still cross one in transit from Runcorn to the latter at the same time, but prior to operating the Outermost Home Signal for a train, the line must be clear as far as the clearing point, and all points within that section of line set to their correct position for the approaching train. (In foggy weather or falling snow, different regulations must be adhered to.)

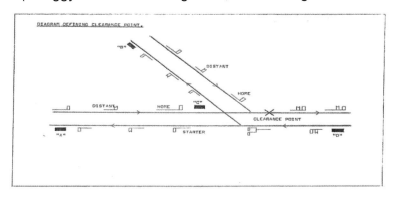

Illustration of 'Acceptance Clearance Point'.

Stopping train from Crewe at Halton Junction. Courtesy of Roy Gough.

Leaving this signal box, in a southerly direction by way of the beautiful Cheshire countryside, we arrive at:

SUTTON WEAVER SIGNAL BOX

The Liverpool Administration Area and signal boxes covered by the Signalmen's Inspectors is vast, stretching from Lime Street station to Gerrards Bridge Junction at St Helens, Lea Green, Canada and Alexandra Docks, all Widnes and St Helens, and on the Cheshire side of the River Mersey, as far as this signal box. Sutton Weaver box overlooks a quaint hamlet a few hundred yards away, signalling trains between Halton Junction signal box and that at Birdswood, (colloquially 'Dicky Bush'), this being administered from Crewe.

Sutton Weaver signal box, standing adjacent to the Up line, controls facing points on the Down line side into the Loop line terminating at Halton Junction, and has an LNWR Tumbler Frame with upper quadrant semaphore signals. Freight traffic climbing the 1 in 101 gradient from Weaver Junction is almost invariably regulated into the loop line, firstly to give preference to passenger trains, and secondly to enable drivers to take on water for their locomotives at the column near the exit at Halton Junction.

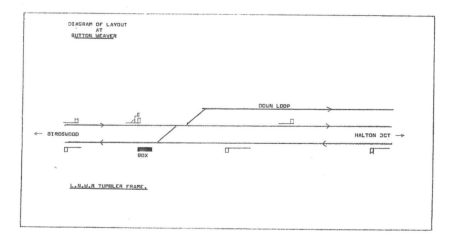

Sutton Weaver signal box.

This completes the list of signal boxes covered by a Class 1 Relief Signalman stationed at Widnes, and for three years, I have been requested to work in each of them at management's discretion. The usual procedure is to leave each relief man in a signal box for three weeks before moving on to another. This keeps him in touch with traffic variations and locking of the lever frames, etc., which are all different.

A signalman must be prepared to work on his own, but it is always possible to pick up a telephone if he gets bored. Omnibus telephone circuits allow more than two people to be on the line at once, and many interesting conversations take place during a shift. A typical night turn, for example, will be for six signalmen to pick up their telephones at 10.15pm. Each one will give a general outline of the day's events, as far as he is concerned. Television sets are outside the scope of railwaymen at this time, because of their exorbitant cost, but Liverpool boasts many cinemas and theatres, so films and shows are discussed in some depth.

Rules and regulations follow, and the knowledge attained is of a very high standard, especially considering that most of us attend evening classes at Liverpool on advanced signalling. Hypothetical situations and emergencies, that at some time could arise, are put to the group, who must solve the problems correctly, using the numerous rules and regulations appertaining to the safe running of trains; but care is needed because trick questions are thrown in. Much time is spent discussing signalling principles and the Signalmen's Inspectors appreciate our interest knowing that, at any time, one of us is likely to fire a difficult question at them. Later, when everyone is mentally exhausted, the subject is changed to the oldest in the world, bringing a period of relaxation prior to the end of the shift.

I mentioned earlier the driver at Runcorn playing the concertina. It is not unusual to hear the strains of a saxophone wafting from the confines of a brake van in the Widnes area, because one of the guards is an expert musician, but numbers of men in these grades are far more limited than signalmen. Most signalmen follow some sort of hobby to while away the time, in what can be a lonely profession. Within the wide spectrum of subjects one would find:

BOOK READING (including rules and regulations), **SHOE REPAIRING, PHOTOGRAPHY, PAINTING** (both portraiture and landscape), **HAIRCUTTING, FURNITURE** and **WINE MAKING,** and finally, **SEXOLOGY (much of this, wishful thinking)** with many practising prestidigitators - **Relief Signalmen being the best exponents, especially when it comes to rostering work!**

At times, especially in the smaller signal boxes, it helps to follow an interest, mainly to break the monotony, whilst taking care not to contravene the 'rules and regs'. For instance, the use of television sets and radio receivers is totally prohibited and a disciplinary offence. Television sets in signal boxes: what a laugh! There has not been one invented that I know of powered by paraffin or gas, and anyway a signalman's wages would only buy a 'cat's whiskers', and the only whiskers permitted in a signal box belong to the **Moggie!**

In addition, all signal boxes must be kept private and no unauthorised person allowed in them. However in one signal box it is customary for the shunter to go and cook his breakfast, until one morning he is busy cooking his bacon, sausage and eggs on the signal box stove, when approaching, easily distinguished by his regulation bowler hat, is none other than the Signalmen's Inspector.

‘Don't let him catch you in here,’ says the signalman, as the shunter makes a hasty exit.

‘I'll keep it cooking for you, and make an excuse to get rid of him.’ ‘Okay!’ the shunter acknowledges, with thumbs up.

‘Good morning, Signalman,’ says the inspector, breathing in deeply to sample the appetizing aroma. *‘I see you're cooking breakfast. Don't let me stop you.’* removing his coat and blocker.

‘Er, it's all right, sir. I'll wait 'til you go,’ edging him towards the door.

A block instrument rings, the inspector answers it.

‘Come on, sit down,’ he says. The obedient signalman duly obliges and only when the meal is completed does the inspector take his leave.

Enter the shunter!

I end this chapter with a particularly amusing story, but one which could have caused an accident. By good fortune it did not, but it did make me smile.

Widnes is renowned for its vile, acrid chemical-bound fog, and I am on duty at West Deviation Junction signal box. It is very early in the morning, and all sound is deadened by a blanket of dense fog, coloured yellow by sulphurous emissions from the several chemical works nearby. Visibility is nil, and no trains have been signalled on any line, when the eerie silence is shattered by a metallic thud from underneath the signal box*, followed, almost immediately, by binding brakes and hiss from a locomotive's safety valve.

[* If points are set for the wrong direction and a train passes over such, they are termed as being 'Run Through'. This effectively damages the points, and it is necessary to call out the Signal and Telegraph Engineer to repair them.] Which did occur in this instance.

Referring to the Train Regulations, a signalman must make sure the points are set for the safety of an approaching train, especially in foggy weather; but in the following incident, I was unaware of a train's approach.

The red glow emitted from the firebox pierces the murky atmosphere, and a mysterious voice calls, '**Hey, Bobby,**' (derived from the slang word for the peelers)

'**Where are we?**' '**West Deviation Junction, brother,**' I shout.

'**Where the blinkin' heck is that?**' comes the reply, echoing through the gloom. '**I am going to Crewe.**'

'**Well, you won't get to Crewe, this way, mate,**' I shout. The driver and fireman climb into the signal box (for the first time ever) to discover they are completely disoriented because of being wrongly routed at Ditton Junction No 1 signal box.

It is time to move on; my time as a Relief Signalman at Widnes ends.

Frodsham Junction signal box. Photographer unknown. Courtesy of 8D Association.

CHAPTER EIGHT

TWO MEN IN A BOX

1957-62

DITTON JUNCTION No 1 SIGNAL BOX

This new signal box was built two years ago on the Down Slow line side 50yd east of Ditton Junction station overbridge. It replaced the very old and dilapidated LNWR type formerly situated directly opposite, adjacent to the tidal waters of Ditton Brook. Consisting of a 100-lever LMS Standard Frame, this signal box is by far the busiest in the area and warrants two signalmen being on duty to deal with the heavy flow of traffic.

Ditton Junction No 1 signal box. Courtesy of David I Ingham.

Promotion to this level usually takes many years of service in lower grade signal boxes, and very few signalmen under the age of 45 ever work here. Consequently, it is hard for the resident signalmen to accept a youngster with much less experience than they have, when I turn up at the tender age of 26. The supercilious attitude adopted towards me by most of them is, I feel, totally unnecessary; however, I can see their point of view.

The junction at Ditton No 1 signal box in 1959. Photo by Author.

Three weeks of training culminate in a gruelling test by the Signalmen's Inspector, before he passes me as competent to work the signal box on my own.

The track layout controlled from this signal box is thus: from the Down Loop line in Ditton Junction Yard a siding, running east, passes in front of the signal box, leading to the large Hutchinson Estate (mentioned earlier) at Widnes, with a hand points connection 100yd away serving Messrs Montage Meyer's timber works to the south-east. The Down and Up Slow lines between West Deviation Junction and Ditton Junction No 2 signal boxes come next, followed by the Down and Up Fast lines between the same points. 200yd from the signal box the Down and Up Main lines, via the Ditton Bank to Runcorn, run between these Fast and Slow lines, merging at the complex junction controlled from here. Messrs Evans' massive timber works in Ditton Road are serviced by a connection from the Down Fast line at the bottom of the said bank. The Sleeper Depot and Pit Prop Yards are connected to the Up Fast line via trailing points, close to the station. Ditton Yard has already been described in the previous chapter, also the St Helens and Runcorn Bay lines which are still used by the few remaining local passenger trains to Birkenhead and Warrington.

Referring to the layout diagram and photograph it will be noticed that the two crossover junctions run in the same direction, with No 2 signal box controlling the opposite routes.

These two junctions are known locally as the 'Top' and 'Middle' crossings.

It was on the middle crossing that the infamous Ditton Junction disaster took place in 1912. The driver of a Chester to Liverpool express train, hauled by a **2-4-0 'Precedent' Class locomotive,** ironically named **'COOK',** misread the signals on Ditton Bank and became derailed at speed on the points set for the Down Slow line. After colliding with the buttress of the station bridge a fire started, fuelled by the gas lighting cylinders in the carriages, and many unfortunate people were killed. Evidence of this catastrophe can still be seen underneath the bridge, the charred woodwork serving as a poignant reminder.

Ditton Junction. X marks the spot of the 1912 disaster.

Courtesy of Widnes Library.

Ditton Junction disaster 1912: note the name of the locomotive.

Courtesy of Widnes Library.

The signals worked from this box are a motley collection of lower and upper quadrant semaphores and colour lights. Seventy-foot-high posts carry the Up Fast and Slow lines home signals, which are duplicated at locomotive height. In windy conditions these posts sway considerably, which may be ideal for training trapeze artistes but, for sure, a lamp man's nightmare.

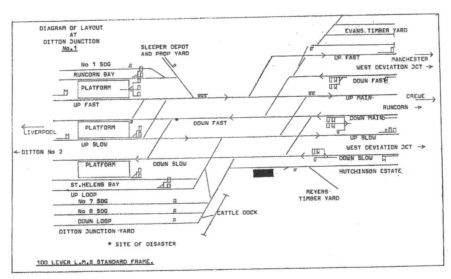

Ditton Junction No 1 signal box.

The two signalmen here are delegated certain duties within the signal box. The first is responsible for all telephone messages, train recording, regulating traffic through the junction and operating levers Nos 1-39. The other operates only levers Nos 40-100 which keep him busy for most of a turn. Each day the roles are reversed. Ditton Junction Telegraph Office is situated within the signal box and has a 40-line switchboard, plus numerous telegraph instruments worked by needles using the Morse Code system. Between 8am and 4pm these are operated by a clerk, but after these hours the signalmen are responsible for connecting through calls. However, we are not trained to use the telegraph instruments, so they are ignored.

Opened in 1869, Ditton Bank rises steeply to Runcorn Bridge, and just prior to the 59-arch viaduct (constructed with 17,000,000 bricks) is one of the world's first Intermediate Block Sections. The signals appertaining to this portion of line are of the electric searchlight type, so normal signalling conditions apply in all kinds of weather, the exception being a telephone failure, as mentioned previously. The long, steep gradient of 1 in 114 warrants a bank engine, **(usually a 'Super D')** to provide assistance to any trains requiring help, which can be a frequent occurrence during a 24-hour period.

Ditton Bank c1910. Courtesy of Widnes Library.

Signalman Dougie Doughty in Ditton No 1 signal box. Photo by Author.

I am working with one of the old codgers, who unfortunately still bears a grudge against my intrusion into his domain, to the extent that I get the **'White Line treatment'***. He is sitting on his chair, avoiding any attempts I make to have a casual conversation with him. It is during one of these solemn moments of silence that he bursts out with two *'HALLELUJAHS!'* I nearly jump out of my skin, but seize the opportunity to compliment him on his dulcet tones. This, I fear, proves to be an error of judgment on my part, because from then on I am subjected to continuous hymn singing. *'Onward Christian Soldiers'* - **BANG, BANG, BANG** go the levers as he strides up and down the signal box like a turkey cock. I try to regulate the traffic while he practises for next Sunday. He goes on to tell me of his long association with the church choir, also the history of his railway career, which I find interesting. As a result, his attitude changes considerably, and now we work in harmony - if you will pardon the pun.

*THE WHITE LINE

In a two-man signal box, each has a prescribed number of levers to operate, and where they join, an imaginary demarcation line is drawn.

In normal circumstances the White Line is ignored, but if an altercation occurs for any reason between them, it is a case of, *'you stay your side of the line, and I'll stay mine.'* Hence the **'White Line Treatment'**. In fact, in some signal boxes this line is actually painted across the floor, but here it is seen only on the 6in-wide foot-board in front of the frame.

In excess of 250 trains pass this signal box during an 8-hour turn of duty, the Up and Down Slow lines being used mainly by freight traffic to and from Garston or Edge Hill. Passenger trains must be given preference over those carrying freight which, from the fastest Class 4 down to the slowest Class 9, are allowed a specific margin of time to run in front of Class 1 expresses. This margin depends entirely on the distance to the next recessing point. At Ditton Junction No 1, a Class 9 running to Weaver Junction Loop line requires 21 minutes; yet, a train of the same class for Folly Lane needs 29 minutes, this allowing for the train to be propelled from the Up Main line into the Down Sidings at Runcorn. These laid-down margins are adequate in normal circumstances, but intuition plays a great part in their practical application.

Signalmen get to know drivers that usually get a good head of steam on their locomotives and will arrive at the recessing point well within the time allotted. (This is more pronounced on 'pay day', when train crews prepare for a quick dash home!) Target 92, for instance, with Widnes drivers aboard, when travelling to Runcorn will easily clear the main line in 18 minutes instead of the 29 but, by giving 18 minutes, the signalman takes the risk of stopping the following express whose running is monitored by the Control Office staff at Liverpool. More often than not the gamble pays off, but now and again miscalculations take place, owing to diverse circumstances not apparent beforehand, such as bad wheel adhesion or duff coal on the engine. In this event a report must be sent to management and is followed by a verbal censure. Still, it makes a change to see the **'Merseyside Express'** with a **'Lizzie'** up front, pushing Target 92, hauled by a **'Super D'** and laden with 25 wagons of coal, over the viaduct and bridge!

It is cold, and flurries of snow change to a heavy downfall as I cycle along Halebank Road at 9.30pm heading for work. When I enter the signal box I resemble a snowman, but the efficient central heating soon relieves me of my newly acquired covering. Jammed points at Speke Junction cause traffic to build up, and a Crofton Colliery to Garston coal train has just arrived at the home signal on the Down Slow line from West Deviation Junction. Our platelayers, called out for snow duties, are themselves fighting a losing battle against the persistent white flakes as the points here become inoperative. Only the Up and Down Fast lines remain open, and Liverpool Control 'block back' on further freight traffic approaching from other areas. The position remains the same throughout the night, and by morning the Crofton train is well and truly embedded in a huge snowdrift.

With difficulty I arrive home, after negotiating the many blocked roads, and even though the snowfall abates during the day, I leave earlier than usual for the night turn, allowing for the inclement conditions, and when I get there the situation is almost the same as when I left 16 hours before, with the Crofton to Garston still buried! Conditions improve somewhat during the night, and 30 hours after its arrival at Ditton Junction, the signalman in Speke Junction signal box is in a position to accept traffic. It takes a further two days to clear the backlog that has accumulated in various yards and sidings.

Two signalmen in their early twenties have replaced the old codgers who have recently retired. This young blood injects a new vitality and brings changes to practices that have remained unaltered for years. For instance, the 'Sacred Lines' mentioned in the previous chapter are now used regularly by coal trains, to the obvious delight of their crews, but bringing frowns from the remaining old stagers! Many of these trains continue down the Fast line to Speke Junction, rarely seen when I was a signalman in Woodside Sidings signal box. In all, the transition makes for a more interesting signal box to work in, speeding up the disposal of traffic in the process, which is the essence of good signalling.

Working in a double-manned signal box is entirely different from one that is single-manned. After years of seemingly solitary confinement, one must accept other signalmen's ideas and mannerisms, and understand their likes and dislikes. Occasionally though, one meets a signalman who is 'game for a laugh', and I wish to refer to a relief signalman from Edge Hill, a past master in the art of practical jokes.

Electrification work is well advanced between Weaver Junction and Liverpool, and my next door neighbour, Ted, aged 62, is domiciled in the signal box to assist in hand signalling duties as they arise; I note also that he has pinched the best seat in the signal box.

On the Up line, Ditton Bank. Courtesy of Mick Langton.

Old Ted is a perfect subject for Jack. Over the last couple of weeks, Jack has surreptitiously asked him questions relating to his working life.

'Now, Ted, the other week you told me that from leaving school at 13 years of age, you worked on a River Mersey tugboat for 15 years,' says Jack.

'That's quite correct, Jack,' replies Ted, awakened from his nap.

'Then you spent 25 years in the Merchant Navy as a stoker, followed by a further 15 years as a stevedore at Garston Docks.'

'How long have you worked on the railways?'

'25 years come next year, Jack.'

'Hmmm,' murmurs Jack, making a quick mental calculation.

'That makes you 93. Isn't it about time you retired?'

Ted responds with a sheepish grin!

Ted assists in the marshalling of two empty wagons, one on the Up, the other on the Down Fast line underneath Ditton Road bridge, for demolition is about to begin of the booking office which straddles these two lines. Resounding crashes from the masonry falling into the wagons causes alarm to the unsuspecting residents in a small row of terraced houses nearby. This is not surprising considering the work is being carried out at 2am, and simultaneously engineers are erecting a Bailey bridge above the seven tracks so that the road bridge can be strengthened prior to electrification. Relaying the tracks and stanchion-erecting is in progress adjacent to No 2 signal box. The noise generated by all of this activity is unbelievable, and I doubt whether anyone can sleep through it all.

The bridgework has now been completed, and new buttresses are built alongside the embankments. Traffic during these engineering operations is switched from the Fast lines to the Slow, and vice versa, as the necessity arises. This causes a certain amount of delay, but it is minimal. In addition to the work already mentioned, Multiple Aspect Colour Light signals are being erected and will replace the existing semaphores in the near future. Week in, week out, the work continues. The walls of the buttresses have now set, and mobile cement mixers are at the moment pumping their loads into the cavity between the bricks and soil, but the weight of the cement is too great for the high, flimsy wall, causing it to collapse with a mighty crash onto the tracks at the entrance to Ditton Yard!

Target 92 has opened up to get enough speed before the start of the bank. It comes ploughing through the conglomeration, sending bricks and debris in every direction but staying on the rails. Little damage is done, but the whole process of rebuilding must be carried out again.

Not so lucky is an incident that occurs a few days later. Again Target 92 is involved, hauled by a **'Super D'** locomotive. Owing to a serious malfunction of the signalling apparatus, the driver receives a 'proceed' aspect over a portion of line that has been taken up in readiness for relaying. At speed the train plunges into the ballast resulting in the engine falling on its side, coal from the tender completely burying the driver and fireman, who are both taken to hospital for checking. Fortunately, they are not seriously hurt and return to work in a couple of days.

An even more incredible incident occurs a few weeks later. Before engineering work can commence on the line, the Permanent Way Supervisor must first obtain permission from the signalman who, using reminder appliances placed on the levers, protects the affected portion of line. Only then can material trains be allowed to enter into this section, and then on the authority of this supervisor. When, after the work is completed, the supervisor informs the signalman, the latter handing a 'restoration ticket' to the driver of the first train to pass over this line instructing him to travel with caution. Re-laying operations are taking place between Allerton Junction and Mossley Hill stations on the Down Fast line throughout the weekend. On the Sunday evening it is dark before the Permanent Way Supervisor completes his work and informs the signalman that normal train running can be resumed. The driver, in accordance with the regulations, is handed the restoration ticket and allowed to proceed into the advance section, unaware that the **'Trap is set'**. Extricating himself and the fireman from underneath the pile of coal that has spilled onto them from the locomotive tender, he finds the engine on its side and the two following wagons smashed to pieces, decorating it. After protecting the adjoining lines, they return to investigate the cause of the accident and find to their dismay:-

A RAIL IS MISSING ON THE DOWN FAST LINE!

I am never to establish the origin of the nickname 'The Old Dog' given to Stan, Ditton Junction's top class relief signalman, and in my opinion a more apt title would be **'Bloody Wars'** Stanley, for any outrageous story related to him always receives the same response, using these two words. I notice a certain agitation and frustration as he looks under papers, in the desk, and all over the signal box, until I say:

'What's the matter, Stan?'

'I can't find my glasses or pipe. Can you see them anywhere?' he replies.

At this juncture I would explain that he does not see too well without his glasses - which at the moment are perched on his forehead. As to the pipe, well that is in his mouth!

Forgetful he may be, but a genial character liked and respected by all his fellow signalmen. On one occasion he offers me this advice.

'If, as you go home, you see a body in the middle of the road, don't stop; forget it, and carry on.'

'How strange,' I think.

'Why's that, Stan?'

'Well, a few years ago, I am on my way home off the night turn when I come across a body in the middle of the road. Like a good citizen I notified the police and kept watch, from a safe distance, of course, until they arrived. I am astounded when I am arrested as a suspected hit-and-run driver.'

'Blimey, Stan, it must have been a terrible shock for you,' I say.

'Yes, it was, Tony,' his voice wavering.

'As you know, I only ride an auto-cycle!'

'BLOODY WARS,' I utter.

In addition to the electrification scheme and Multiple Aspect Signalling, signal boxes are being modernised with the introduction of Train Describer Equipment, ultimately to replace the Absolute Block Working with Track Circuit Block. The instrument shelf has been totally removed from the signal box to enable the roof to be strengthened for the new equipment. The block instruments are transferred onto a table beside the desk - much to old Ted's disgust, because he sits there - with the associated wires pinned to the walls and ceiling. Upwards of 30 men are engaged within the signal box carrying out various tasks, mainly of an electrical nature, and management has issued a directive instructing us to order out of the signal box any person not working. Of course, our first attempt to carry them out received the 'two finger exercise', but, we really knew it could not be enforced. In fact, the only time we have a little respite from the incessant noise is when three or four card schools open up in the few vacant spaces, and even then we are stepping over legs and ducking under temporary wires festooned all around. Mind you, they do have the decency to invite us to join them, but we decline the offer!

Three weeks of continuous activity, night and day, terminate, when the Signal and Telegraph 'high-ups' pass the equipment as working satisfactorily. Delays to traffic during this extremely busy period were minimal and management appreciated the extra burden placed on signalmen in every signal box, but was not forthcoming with any extra remuneration to which we were undoubtedly entitled!

The big weekend arrives for the transition from Absolute Block to Track Circuit Block working. There is a vast difference between the two methods of signalling. Basically, in Absolute Block working, permission must be obtained from the signal box in advance before a train is allowed to proceed. Track Circuit Block, on the other hand is defined thus:

Track Circuit Block signalling permits a signal to exhibit a proceed aspect when all track circuits in the line ahead are clear up to, and including, the overlap beyond the next stop signal, and all necessary points within that distance are set in the correct position for the safe passage of a train. Therefore, under this system, a signalman is permitted to allow trains into the forward section without permission, the governing factor being clear track circuits, which are indicated on illuminated diagrams in each signal box.

In Absolute Block it is essential for each signalman to observe a tail lamp on every train, which indicates the train is complete, but in Track Circuit Block this is not obligatory. Signing the train register in accordance with Rule 55 no longer applies, because each stop signal has a telephone nearby, in direct contact with the controlling signal box. The definition of Rule 55 is thus:

Rule 55 is applicable on all running lines not equipped with track circuits, except those signalled in accordance with the Permissive Block Regulations.

The object of the rule is for the train crew to remind the signalman of the presence of their train and see that he has protected it, either by means of a collar placed over the signal lever, if inside the home signal, or a cover on the block commutator, if outside. In addition, the fireman or guard, as the case may be, must sign the train register and have his entry countersigned by the signalman. Only when the train has proceeded on its journey must the signalman remove the reminders.

The District Operating Superintendent enters the signal box.

'Good Evening, Tony, Good Evening, Doug,' he says.

'What an amazing memory he has,' I think to myself, considering the number of railwaymen under his charge!

On the stroke of midnight, technicians, armed with pliers, commence to cut the exposed wires at random, but one of them inadvertently severs the lighting cable serving the signal box, plunging it into darkness. Oil-filled hand and 'Tilley' lamps are hastily lit to provide temporary illumination, but the signal box becomes full of acrid fumes and smoke. However, the essential work must continue, to keep up the schedule. All traffic over the lines is suspended for the weekend while this major operation is taking place, employing hundreds of men. A new signal box at Ditton Junction No 2 is being commissioned, and at the same time my old haunt, 'Harry's Domain' is being closed. Old Harry, who has worked there for 26 years, requests the honour of closing it. It is, indeed, a sad day for him, but a post at Widnes No 7 has been earmarked for him for the few months up to his retirement. Sutton Weaver, Birdswood and Mossley Hill Station signal boxes are also being closed this weekend (6th March 1961) but all the resident signalmen have new positions to go to, carrying their memories of their former places of work with them.

In connection with the electrification the decking on Runcorn Bridge requires renewing, and a unique engineering operation is planned.

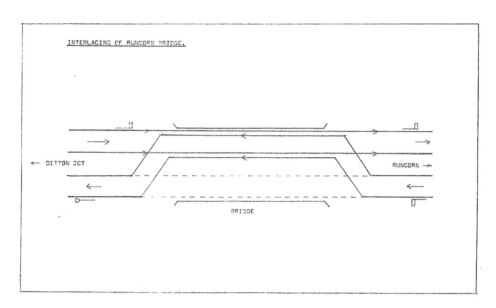

Interlacing Runcorn Railway Bridge.

The lines are to be interlaced on the bridge itself, to avoid the likelihood of serious delay to traffic if Single Line Working were put into operation. Absolute Block signalling remains in force between Runcorn Station signal box and here, with track circuits controlling all movements over the bridge, without the use of points.

When the Up line is completed the track will be transposed to allow similar treatment to the Down line: see the picture on the next page.

Interlacing Runcorn Bridge. Courtesy of 8D Association.

Progressing simultaneously with this work, although unconnected with the railway, is the new road bridge linking Widnes and Runcorn which will eventually replace the aged transporter. To construct this massive structure, work started from opposite shores, the girders soaring out over the Manchester Ship Canal and River Mersey. Many hawsers, anchored in concrete, take the strain of the tremendous weight, increasing as each piece is added, like a jigsaw puzzle. Let us hope they get it right!

Building the new Widnes to Runcorn Road Bridge, 1960.

Transporter in the background.

Courtesy of Ron Couchman.

Runcorn road and rail bridges. Photographer unknown.

Jack, the relief signalman is back, and Ted is still here, reclining on the most comfortable chair, pretending to be asleep. I have just placed my breakfast of two boiled eggs on the stove and am busily getting on with the work of train regulating, when Jack enquires,

'What have you got for breakfast, Tone?' (Surely he knows?)

'Two boiled eggs,' I say, pointing to the pan.

'Where do you get them from?' Jack, enquires.

'From the shop in Hunts Cross, owned by the father of Rita Tushingham.'

'In that case they will have the little lion on them.'

(The Egg Marketing Board directed that all their eggs should be stamped with this emblem.)

The inquisition continues. *'Does the lion come off in boiling water?'* he asks.

'No, they're indelible,' I say. (Being an authority on such matters?)

Old Ted, still relaxing and with his eyes closed, not taking any part in this ridiculous conversation, stirs when Jack requests him to have a look at one of the eggs.

'Hmm, I thought so,' he mumbles, repeating it louder, to get the interest of Ted.

'*Now Ted, did you hear Tony tell me where he got his eggs from, and that they had a little lion on them, which doesn't come off in boiling water?*'

'*Yes, Jack, I certainly did.*' (I knew he wasn't asleep!)

'*Can you see any lion on this egg, Ted?*' asks Jack, handing it to him.

'*No, Jack, I can't.*'

'*No, and you won't. Just have a close look at this egg and tell me.*'

'*Does it look very much like one laid by one of your chickens?*'

'*You know, Jack, you're right. It certainly looks like an egg laid by one of my chickens.*'

'**Heaven's above!**' I think.

'*He never got those eggs from a shop,*' Jack insinuates, continuing,

'*He pinched them from your hen coop!*' Ted's face drops, because Jack has convinced him that I am a thief.

To the day he died, old Ted thought I was guilty, but Jack knew the truth, having switched his new laid ones for mine, perpetrating a perfect ruse at my expense. The swine!

My mate and I have found a perfect stooge also, and we use our cat to instigate our dastardly intentions. The cat happens to be a stray that was adopted by the signalmen, who named it after the 'pea-souper' smogs that frequently blanket this area. Now Smoggs sleeps in a box, advertising on it a famous brand of beans. All the local policemen visit the signal box on night duty for a chat and a cup of tea, but primarily to find out whether we have seen anything suspicious that may warrant investigation. One of these policemen, just out of training, tries to impress us by quoting this law and that law; in fact, he becomes quite a bore. Late one night, the local Co-operative store is broken into and some merchandise is stolen. Brian, our subject, happens to be on duty. Smoggs is turfed out of his box which we up-end, and in block capitals write on it '**CO-OP**'. Enter Brian for his usual tipple, and normal conversation. After a while we ask him if he is interested in buying some tins of beans, but all he seems bothered about is where we obtained them, so we drop it, moving onto something else. Not to be outdone, before he goes he once more broaches the question of the beans and, so as not to disappoint him, we point to Smoggs box. He takes his leave, only to return an hour or so later with his sergeant to examine the evidence, finding only Smoggs curled up inside! No doubt he received a severe ticking off, for time-wasting. Later, we attempt to sell him a sewing machine, and he alerts the whole Widnes police force about the unscrupulous signalmen in Ditton Junction No 1 signal box.

It is ironic that the frequent break-ins around here followed a set pattern, and a police officer was subsequently apprehended and charged with the offences - but not our Brian!

In addition to the major re-signalling scheme just completed between Speke Junction and Weaver Junction signal boxes, is the implementation of a new panel-operated power signal box at Edge Hill, replacing those existing at Edge Hill No 2, No 3, No 12, Wavertree Junction, Waterloo Tunnel Mouth and the previously mentioned Mossley Hill.

Panel-operated signal boxes are a new concept in railway signalling, but I shall deal with this subject in a later chapter.

Multiple Aspect Colour Light Signals allow a greater braking distance for trains travelling at high speed, with each one being positioned at least 1,000yd from the next. In a series of four consecutive signals, a driver will receive first a single **GREEN** aspect, followed by **DOUBLE YELLOW** at the second, which signifies to him that the next will be displaying **SINGLE YELLOW**, and to commence braking in readiness to stop at the next signal in advance, which is showing **RED**. Therefore, 2,000yd is the minimum distance allowed for a train to stop. Undoubtedly, MAS increases line availability and certainly speeds up the disposal of traffic. An excellent example for comparison can be seen on the Up Fast line between Speke Junction and Ditton Junction No 1 signal boxes, a distance of 4 miles. Prior to the installation of MAS only four stop signals existed between these two points, but now there are seven.

Coinciding with the MAS scheme an Automatic Warning System (AWS) is being introduced. Drivers in the past have always had to rely on visual observations of the position of signal arms. With the normal running speed of trains being increased to 100mph there was a need to introduce a system to **assist** the driver, using electronics. **I emphasise the word 'assist' to point out that the AWS does not in any way excuse the driver from observing the signals.**

The basic principles of the system are thus. A magnet is secured between the railway tracks, approximately 200yd in rear of the signal to which it applies. An engine passing over this magnet completes an electrical circuit, indicated on the instrument panel in the driver's cab, accompanied by an audible alarm, i.e. **a bell, if the signal is exhibiting a GREEN aspect, or a HORN, when showing DOUBLE, SINGLE YELLOW or RED.** If the horn sounds, the driver must acknowledge it by depressing a button. Failure to do so activates the train's braking system after 10 seconds. The introduction of this safety feature and the intensified beam of colour light signals allow the abolition of fog signalmen, which quite possibly brings much relief to people residing within earshot of the exploding detonators.

Monday morning arrives, to the 'burps' emitted by the new Train Describing equipment. A four-digit description appears in the receiver when it is transmitted from the next signal box, the accompanying burp attracting one's attention. Each train has a different number, such as 1A07, 5F61 etc. The first digit defines the class of train 1-9, a locomotive being 0. A letter follows, signifying the destination, *i.e*:

A = LONDON, F = LIVERPOOL, H = MANCHESTER, and **P = PRESTON,** for trains running within the London Midland Region.

Inter-Regional trains are lettered thus: **E = EASTERN, M = MIDLAND,**
O = SOUTHERN, S = SCOTTISH, and V = WESTERN.

The final two numbers refer to the train number. The **'Merseyside Express'** was train **No 54,** so the new description will now be **1A54.**

In this signal box there now exist four different types of signalling:

Track Circuit Block, Absolute Block, Permissive Block and Single Stroke Instrument Block, each with its own regulations. It is doubtful whether this number could be equalled in any other signal box in this country, or, in fact the world.

Today the Runcorn Gap will be bridged **(we hope)** when the two sections of the new road bridge are lowered towards each other. With binoculars trained in that direction it is possible to see the space diminishing, ever so slowly. A workman has completed the physical connection, placing one foot on the Runcorn side, the other on the Widnes side, high up on top of the girders. A miscalculation of 2in is soon rectified, with the two sections marrying perfectly, everyone breathing a sigh of relief because the engineers had got it right! However, further up river a rescue operation is taking place.

Ditton Brook runs underneath the railway, at an oblique angle, from north-west to south-east, and is tidal (as mentioned earlier) up to Halewood, three miles away. It meanders through a channel 10yd across and is, at high tide, 10ft deep. Purely by chance I see a youth falling into the swollen water, now on the ebb. Leaving the signal box I manage to attract the attention of the Signal Lineman and his mate, working nearby. We form a human chain, with me in the middle, then wade into the dirty, chemical-bound liquid and succeed in grabbing the lad's coat as he appears from under the railway arch. The swift current increases suddenly and we have great difficulty in regaining a firm foothold on dry land because of it. Fortunately, the chain remains unbroken; otherwise we and the lad could have been carried away through the barren and uninhabited area down to the River Mersey, to an uncertain end. Luckily, the lad survives his ordeal; even more so, the fact that I spotted him! Returning to the signal box, dripping wet, my mate, the Edge Hill hairdresser Charlie, himself now a relief signalman, utters some facetious remark about my taking a swim whilst on duty, to which I reply, **'B***** ***!'**

The electrification work is well advanced, with most of the wiring completed. New words are entering into railway terminology, such as Catenary, Contact Wire, Return Conductors, Pantographs, Droppers, Neutral Sections - and many more. Operating instructions are issued to all signalmen and personnel involved prior to the switch-on to enable them to be fully acquainted with the new methods. In addition, the signalmen have received instructions on first aid in connection with electric shock, hoping they never have to use it.

The first electrically-hauled train at Ditton Junction: note station buildings to the left under construction.
Photo by Author.

Pre-planned isolation procedures place a great deal of responsibility onto the signalman. Each electrified line is divided into sections and sub-sections, which are numbered to correspond with the diagram in the signal box. Before the electrical current to any particular section is switched off, the Electrical Control Room Operator must obtain permission from the signalman via Traffic Control. This allows the signalman to regulate trains that he may have approaching the signal box, and to confirm that any electrically-hauled trains have passed clear of the section to be isolated. Only then can such permission be given. Traffic Control contacts the signalman requesting an isolation. The signalman fills in an 'AS' form by dictation, and when the full procedure has been completed, the power can be switched off.

On the Down line, Ditton Bank. Courtesy of Mick Langton.

Further responsibility is now placed upon the signalman because he must ensure that no electrically-hauled train enters the isolated section. He is authorised to stop trains in order to ascertain their traction for this purpose. Provided that there is no physical blockage of the line, diesel-hauled trains may be allowed into the section. When the power is subsequently switched on, the Electrical Control Room Operator contacts the signalman again, via Traffic Control, after which normal working can be resumed. In its pale blue livery, the first electric locomotive approaches Ditton from the Crewe direction under the canopy of steelwork stretching as far as the eye can see!

Many minor accidents involving personnel occurred during this period, and the signal box first aid boxes were used regularly. There were two serious incidents. The first concerned a tamping machine operator who had alighted at Halebank station and was struck down by the following passenger train whilst walking on the sleeper ends, on his way to Woodside Sidings signal box. In the second, at a location not far from Woodside Sidings, an Overhead Line Equipment Inspector received a 25,000 volt electric shock when he inadvertently touched the live contact wire. Both men were lucky to survive.

At the site of the old Woodside Sidings signal box large earth-moving equipment is at present levelling the land and steelwork is being erected to accommodate a giant motor car plant, owned by the Ford Motor Company. The smallholding owned by the platelayer **(who gave me the chicken to pluck)** has been demolished because it occupied part of the site. At the same time, new railway sidings are being installed to service the finished factory, taking in the original sidings that have been unused for some time. Controlling the traffic to and from the new yard will be the signalman in Ditton Junction No 2 signal box, with a small direct wired panel positioned on the instrument shelf. Also taking place, but not connected with the above work, is a major road-widening scheme, and the two railway cottages at Woodside are being demolished.

The new direct wired panel to work Ford's Sidings in Ditton No 2 signal box.

Black switches operate points; red switches operate signals.

Courtesy of Ray Burgess.

A colleague from the Signal and Telegraph Department comes to the signal box, enquiring about the next train to Runcorn. We tell him the one now entering the Up Fast platform. With thanks he dashes over to catch it. The next day he re-visits us, and on entering says,

'Hey, you's two! What was you playing at yesterday? I finished up in LONDON!'

We burst out laughing; winking at each other, but our friend was not amused one bit.

'Let's go through it. You came to the signal box, asking for the next train to Runcorn,' but, adding, *'You didn't ask if it stopped there!'*

Modernisation has cost many millions of pounds, so management must find ways to recoup some of their investment, and they look no further than this signal box. They make me redundant, along with two of my colleagues.

Leaving Ditton Bank. Photo by John Wilson, courtesy of 8D Association.

Passing Ditton Junction No 1 signal box. Courtesy of D I Ingham.

By the way; the District Operating Superintendent didn't have such a good memory, as I thought. I am told, before coming to the signal box, he had enquired who was on duty!

I see a high embankment, on top of which is a brick-built signal box, isolated, backed by a vast expanse of sky, with its name proudly embossed in concrete on its eastern façade; the name nearly as long as the signal box.

'I've been here before!'

CHAPTER NINE

ON THE WEST COAST MAIN LINE

1962-69

WIGAN No 2 SIGNAL BOX

A hybrid is the best description of the interior of this signal box. It has an LMS REC 65-lever Standard Frame, with catch handles similar to those used by the LNWR, underneath a 12ft-long NX panel. I realise at once, not only have I to learn the workings of the signal box, but also the language. The signal box will be relatively easy; the language I am not so sure, because words are used here which are not found in any English dictionary, some even defying translation.

Wigan No 2 signal box. Courtesy of Peter Cooper.

This signal box is one of three at Wigan built in 1941 and all were modified from the original design owing to the intervention of World War 2, to LMS Air Raid Precaution standards. These required walls 14in thick, topped by 6in concrete roofs, which give them a robust appearance. The frame, built at the Railway Signalling Co, Fazakerley, Liverpool, has a mechanical locking-box running behind the levers along its entire length, but levers Nos 21-25 and 41-45 and their slides have been omitted, leaving spaces up to the locking-box fascia. This enables the signalman to operate the panel without stretching over the frame. The front of the enamelled 12ft by 4ft NX panel, made by Messrs Seimens, is dark green in colour, and in contrast, the track circuited lines are depicted by strips of white plastic, cut to length to correspond with the physical layout outside. Two small red lights, one at each end of the strip, give a visual indication when the relevant track circuit is occupied. Sidings and lines without track circuits, are signified by dark brown strips, and have no visual indications.

Author arriving for duty, 1962. Courtesy of P Worthington.

In 1834 the North Union Railway Company merged with the Wigan Branch Railway Company, whose lines from Parkside terminated at Chapel Lane, but it was 1838 before they were actually connected by rail, via the new iron bridge passing over Wallgate, one of the main thoroughfares of Wigan. North Western station, having 10 platforms, was erected adjacent to this bridge, on its southern side.

Wigan, now famous for its Pier, Pies, Rugby League team and Uncle Joe's Mint Balls, was once a Roman settlement, bearing the name Coccium. This settlement was situated on a knoll in the centre of the River Douglas valley, an ideal site from which to observe intending attackers. The high embankment upon which Wigan No 2 signal box stands is level with the church on the highest point of the knoll; Wallgate station, on the former Lancashire & Yorkshire Railway, is placed between the two. Behind the signal box the view of the valley, several miles across, and backed by the three large slag heaps at Garswood Hall Colliery, known locally as the 'Three Sisters', is very picturesque.

The Up and Down Main lines, from the northern direction, run into a complex junction prior to entering North Western station and continue to the junction controlled by Wigan No 1 signal box at the southern end. Looking towards the station, a pair of facing points from the Up Main line lead to No1 platform, next, the Up and Down Main lines run through No 4 and No 5 platforms respectively, followed by Bay platform No 9. Platforms Nos 8 and 10 complete the station layout at this end. Nos. 2, 3, 6 and 7 platforms are controlled solely by Wigan No 1 signal box.

Absolute Block Regulations apply between Rylands Sidings signal box, the next one north, and here, but Permissive Passenger Station Working applies to No 1 signal box, with bi-directional working authorised on all through lines in the station.

Passing Wigan No 2 signal box. Courtesy of Ron Couchman.

This signal box is quite the most comfortable I have worked in, having central heating fed by a gigantic coke boiler which requires constant attention, a modern toilet and electric cooking facilities. There is even room for a bed, if ever management were to make them statutory equipment in signal boxes, although it would hardly be used here owing to the density of traffic! All main line running signals are of the Electric Colour Light type, controlled by three position switches, incorporated into the NX panel. The function of these switches depends under which regulation the train is to be accepted. Under Regulation 4, with Line Clear, a large green light confirms acceptance, the switch being turned to the left position to obtain a proceed aspect in the signal. (These block lights replace the usual needle.) In the case of a platform being occupied (a red block light shows) the switch is turned to the right position, giving a subsidiary aspect at the signal. If for any reason the switch is accidentally turned in the wrong direction, the signal will not clear. The ground signals, on the other hand, are mechanically worked from the lever frame and illuminated by floodlights, all controlled with one master switch on the instrument shelf, rather than being paraffin-lit, as is usual in this type of signal.

The **'Royal Scot"** and **'Mid-day Scot'** are just two of the many named expresses on this route, most of them being hauled by **'Princess Royal'** and **'Coronation'** class locomotives. Firemen aboard often take advantage of the stop at Wigan to fill up the tender with water from the columns suitably situated at the platform ends. The amount taken depends on the speed of the train over the Moore troughs, south of Warrington, and the likely needs of the locomotive before reaching the next ones at Hest Bank, north of Lancaster. In the depths of winter each column has a continuously burning brazier alongside, bringing warmth to the overall dismal scene, but occasionally even these are not powerful enough to stem the freezing process, and icicles build up in grotesque patterns.

Panel in Wigan No 2 signal box. Courtesy of Adrian Vaughan.

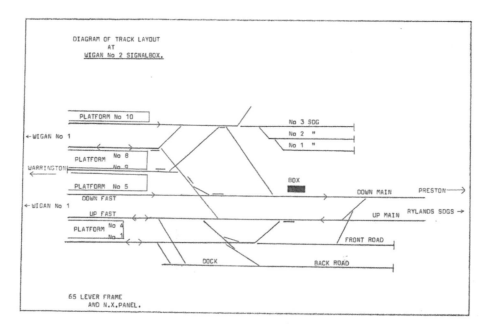

Wigan No 2 signal box.

Locomotives hauling 14 coaches out of platform No 5 have difficulty on the slight upward gradient, propelling red-hot cinders like rockets high into the sky, as the wheels send sparks flying in their efforts to gain a grip on the slippery rail; meanwhile the signal box foundations shake in unison with the oscillating traction, as it nears the start of the 1 in 104 gradient which stretches for six miles up to Bank Top, near Coppull, before gaining respite on the long easy run into Preston.

Entering Wigan North Western station. Courtesy of Wigan World.

Freight traffic runs through Wigan frequently, despite having the Whelley Branch avoiding line east of the town, running from Bamfurlong Junction in the south to Standish Junction on the north side, but these trains consist mainly of vehicles with oil-filled axle boxes which travel at a faster speed. Coal trains from the many collieries around Wigan are generally diverted onto the avoiding line, these wagons having grease-filled axle boxes and being correspondingly slower.

Absolute Block Regulation 20 deals with trains which become divided (bell signal 5-5).

Basically, if a train is on a gradient falling in the direction of travel, the signalman replaces the signals to danger only after the first portion has passed, then does all in his power to stop the second portion by diverting it onto a clear line or siding, etc. (if possible).

It is 3am on a Sunday; Rylands Sidings signal box is switched out of circuit, and the section extends from Boars Head Junction. I receive the 'Train Divided' signal for a freight train, and George, the signalman at Boars Head Junction box, informs me that the two portions are some considerable distance apart. I go to the window and hear a tremendous crash, intimating there has been a collision, probably in the region of Mesnes Park. This is confirmed ten minutes later in a message reporting that three large tanks and the brake van have become derailed but that the Down line is clear, which enables the introduction of Single Line Working. In the event of there being only one running line available for traffic, owing either to an obstruction similar to that above, or for planned engineering work taking place, Single Line Working is instituted.

This method of working allows for trains to pass through the affected section on the unobstructed line.

The acceptance of trains is governed by the situation in any given locality and can vary quite considerably but, basically, permission must be obtained by a person acting as a Pilotman before any train is allowed to foul this line. The Pilotman must wear a distinctive red arm-band with 'Pilotman' printed in white upon it; if one of these is unavailable, a red flag will suffice to signify his authority to all personnel. He must personally see each train enter onto the single line, so that in the event of a train having arrived at the opposite end, he must travel through the section to that point.

In theory, Single Line Working rules are extremely complicated but, practically, they are easier to understand.

I send my report of the incident to the office stating that Regulation 20 was carried out during this emergency, but some bright spark gets a moment of inspiration and decides to send me a letter, asking the following question:-

'Could you please let me know whether you replaced the signals to danger in front of the divided train?'

Thinking to myself that this person has definite management potential, I reply thus:

'I wish to inform you that I did in fact replace the signals to danger against the first portion of the divided train, and you may consider that I have contravened Regulation 20 clause 6, but in accordance with clause 10, I ascertained that the first portion had come to a stand in the rear section.'

There was no further communication!

At times North Western station gets packed with passengers, but today there appear to be more than normal. I am informed that a special locomotive is expected, so delving through the reams of notices; I come to the one relating to it. The northern approach of the long sweeping curve from Rylands Sidings signal box to North Western station is obstructed from view by a building two miles away and it is here that I focus my attention, awaiting the first sighting of this famous locomotive. Coloured like a summer's day sky, sending wisps of pure white smoke into the atmosphere; it sedately approaches the signal box, creating a wonderful picture (with bearded driver) reminding me of days gone by. Built in 1886 by Neilson and Company for the **Caledonian Railway, 4-2-2 'Single' No 123** became, **No 14010,** on the Grouping in 1923, giving good service until eventually being withdrawn. Fortunately, it was saved for posterity from the breakers' torches, reverting to its original number and Caledonian livery, and so it enters Wigan, to the delight of the many enthusiasts waiting to see it. In addition to **Caledonian '123',** many other 'foreign' locomotives have visited Wigan recently, probably the most famous being **Gresley's 4-6-2 No 4468 A4 'MALLARD',** world record holder for steam traction, with a maximum speed of 126mph achieved on the East Coast Main Line between Grantham and Peterborough way back in 1938. Standing at the signal on No 8 platform, dwarfing a **'Super D'** on the next line, its dark blue livery contrasts with the dull cream brickwork of the station buildings. The renowned **4472 'Flying Scotsman', 'Sir Nigel Gresley'** and **'Bittern'** have put in an appearance on No 8 platform, leaving the main line open for the incomparable, ubiquitous **'Princess Royal'** and **'Princess Coronation'** classes in their maroon livery!

I am led to believe that, when installed, all levers in the frame were painted white in this signal box for the purpose of deceiving the enemy if ever they were successful in invading Britain, and ended up in Wigan! A novel idea, but highly improbable! However, they now have their correct distinguishing colours.

To assist the signalman, duplicated block bell hammers have been incorporated on the panel, opposite the spaces in the lever frame, making it possible to accept trains from whichever position he happens to be in. Eight telephones line the wall: three for the signalman, the others for the box lad. Express trains departing from Preston are wired to this signal box by telephone, this information then being relayed to several other points. This process is repeated when the trains pass Euxton Junction signal box, five miles south of Preston. Similarly, on the Down line side messages from Crewe and Warrington are received and relayed. Considering that well over 250 trains are dealt with during a turn of duty, hundreds of calls are received and sent, and liaison with local signal boxes and the inspectors at North Western station account for many more.

'Ayrshire Yeomanry' at Wigan. Photo by Author.

Scottish express passenger trains dominate the workings at Wigan on the night turn of duty, for no sooner have the northbound ones been dealt with, than the southbound begin to arrive.

Of particular interest are the working arrangements for the **12.30am from Liverpool Lime Street to Glasgow.** This train arrives on platform No 10 simultaneously with the **1.0am from Manchester,** at the southern end of platform No 8, the latter engine being detached and sent back to Manchester for further work.

The North Western station shunt engine propels the Manchester portion through the scissors crossing between the two platforms (No 8 and No 10) onto the Liverpool train. On arrival at Preston, coaches off the **1.50am from Liverpool Exchange station** are then coupled to it, completing the formation. Platform No 10, after the departure of this train, is used to marshal parcels traffic from Manchester, Bolton and Liverpool, for loading and unloading prior to travelling north.

Vehicles left on any running line in the station are protected by a 'Vehicles on Line' switch (VOL) operated by the inspector in charge of that particular platform. Operation of this switch gives a track circuit occupation indication in the signal box and locks the block light to 'Train on Line' position.

Three sidings behind the signal box are used to stable the passenger coaches which work locally between Wigan, Preston, Chorley and Blackburn, whilst opposite, on the Up line side, two sidings are utilised for Manchester and Warrington direction stock.

It is 7.50am and a locomotive has become derailed opposite the signal box while backing up onto its stock to work the **8.5am Wigan to Warrington.** By chance, a ramp for re-railing vehicles is close to hand and with the assistance of 'Doc', the station inspector, in less than five minutes the locomotive is back on the rails, and the **train leaves on time!**

Enjoying my pipe, I notice more smoke than usual floating in the signal box air, and the smell of tobacco turns to one of burning rubber! Soon the operating floor is engulfed by a black cloud of acrid smoke - which has definitely nothing to do with my pipe. Two track circuits become occupied, replacing the signals to danger in front of an approaching express train. Time, just, to call the fire brigade before my mate and I evacuate the building. Sparks from a passing train have ignited tinder within a cable trunking which, travelling via the ducts into the relay room, sets fire to it. Flames 10ft long shoot out as firemen smash the door down, and in minutes the fire is extinguished. Little damage is done and the signal box becomes fully operational again within an hour, after the electrical apparatus has been checked by the Signal and Telegraph staff.

My box lad, Horace, is a great exponent of the 'Wigin' lingo, and he attempts to teach me a few phrases, which I find baffling because each sentence is compacted into a one polysyllabic word; but I try to teach him the true Queen's English which, as any well informed person knows, is spoken only in Liverpool!

Allow me to give some examples of **'Wigin' lingo,** and the way we Scousers (myself adopted) say it!

'Owzeenoo?'	**'How are you now?'**
'Thakonifthawants.'	**'You can if you would like.'**
'Izeeonthneetturn?'	**'Is he on the night turn?'**
'Thaluksowderbartteeth.'	**'You look older without your teeth.'**
'Atowdimbureewuntlissen.'	**'I told him but he wouldn't listen.'**
'Daasgointgerit.'	**'You go and get it.'**
Thanoosnowtabartit.	**'You know nothing about it.'**
'Weevgorracar.'	**'We have got a car.'**
'Tha'dberrargeronthbuz.'	**'You had better get on the bus.'**

This really is worse than learning the 'rules and regs'. I wish he would **learn to talk proper!** Descriptive words are vastly different also, and considering the short distance between Liverpool and Wigan, this is surprising. Two public houses in Wigan are called **'Buck i' th' Vine'** and **'Bird i' th' Hand',** the **i' th'** translated from **'in the'.**

Behind the signal box stands a long row of terraced houses, and a cat is doing a balancing act on the apex of the roof.

'Hey, Horace, come and see this moggie.' I say.

'Icontseenomoggie, burracanseeacat!' he replies.

He goes on to inform me a **'Moggie'** is a **mouse**!

I give up!

Still, I have many a smile in my attempts to master the vocabulary in this locality, but it will remain an enigma forever!

Having a signal box lad has many advantages, including fish-and-chip suppers. One night I am teasing Walter the signalman at Standish Junction signal box, as I enjoy my piping hot food.

'I'd give my right arm for some,' he says. The nearest 'chippy' is three miles away from him; he's on his own, so he has no chance. However, I write on a piece of paper:

'Horace, go and get some fish and chips, and run up to Standish.' (On his motor-bike, of course.)

A little later, Wal says to me over the telephone:

Ring Boars Head and Coppull Hall, tell them to put the one's up (work to rule) *there's someone approaching.'*

'Why, it is Horace, and he's got fish and chips. Isn't that great.'

Half an hour later, Horace rings to say he is on the way back. Two hours later he has still not arrived, and I begin to get worried, knowing only too well that box lads should not be employed as fish-and-chip distributors. Eventually, about 3am, he walks in, calmly telling me:

'I ran out of petrol between Standish and Boars Head, and had to walk the rest of the way.'

'Do you realise that I have done all your work while you've been away?'

'Get cracking!' I order him, as I mount the locker and get into my favourite reposing position. **(By the way, I never received that right arm!)** We must not forget through all this frivolity that we run a railway, and a new diesel locomotive is being tested on the main line.

Approaching from the north, with all signals 'Off', it hurtles around the curve in its distinctive chocolate brown and cream livery, silent, until thundering past with a deafening roar. In that split second I spy the name **'KESTREL'** on the side plate. This powerful **Hawker Siddeley 4,000hp Co-Co** locomotive passes regularly for several weeks and then becomes conspicuous by its absence. Later I hear of its departure to Russia, possibly on the Trans-Siberian run from Moscow to Vladivostok.

A very small leak has appeared in the lead water pipe leading to the sink, sending a spray just a few inches along the floor. The ever helpful 'Doc' is on duty at the station, and he arrives armed with a fireman's hammer! Giving the pipe a hefty whack, we have a new river flowing the full length of the signal box! Doc decides to summon a plumber to finish the job!

In addition, the electric kettle has been out of action for several weeks owing to a wiring fault, and during this period a paraffin stove, placed on the concrete window shelf, has been used to boil water in a new aluminium kettle. However, the electrical supply has been reconnected and there is no further use for the steaming kettle, still on the stove. Grasping hold of the handle without thinking it may be hot, causes me to drop it and knock the stove off the shelf, which explodes into a massive fireball setting the signal box on fire. The flames spread rapidly along the linoleum, stopping us from retrieving our coats hanging on the door, and we can only watch helplessly as they disappear in the inferno. In minutes the brigade arrives to extinguish the blaze. Fortunately, none of the signalling equipment is affected, and normal working is soon resumed. There is no doubt, had this signal box been built of timber, it would most certainly have suffered the same fate as Wavertree Junction signal box a few years ago. Management were sceptical of how it started, and I get the feeling that they presume they have an arsonist on their pay-roll, especially after the previous incident!

Hand-lamps are an integral part of a signalman's equipment, and great care must be exercised in their use. They are capable of showing Red, Green, Yellow and White, the coloured glasses being mounted on an internal plate which fits into the main casing. This circular plate revolves around the oil container and wick holder, and to change from one colour to the next entails turning the inner plate with a swivel like action, using the carrying handle.

A rear-end collision occurs on my turn of duty between a Scotland-bound express passenger train and a failed Liverpool Road (Manchester) to Carlisle freight, between Rylands Sidings and Boars Head Junction signal boxes during thick fog at 9pm. The locomotive hauling the express becomes derailed and several passengers are injured, together with the guard of the freight train. At the subsequent enquiry it is established that the driver of the express train had, in fact, run past the home signal at danger, but he insists that he received a green hand signal at

Rylands Sidings signal box. This is denied emphatically by the signalman but, when asked to explain his actions that night, he admitted changing the hand-lamp indications outside the window of the signal box, turning it through Green to Red. It was at this split second that the driver observed the Green light, continuing into the occupied section. This was a pure and simple accident.

Even though the railways have been nationalised, rivalry still exists between signalmen who worked in signal boxes originally belonging to different pre-grouping railway companies - never mind pre-nationalisation. Promotion is limited to the areas covered by these pre-grouping companies, and in the case of the London Midland & Scottish Railway, the seniority of signalmen is common knowledge making it possible to know who would fill a particular vacancy. Many signalmen worked in one location for years, waiting for a signalman to retire, or pass on, **(to fill a dead man's shoes)** but now a decision has been made to amalgamate all the signal boxes into one large group. This causes great consternation among the senior signalmen on the former LMS and bitterness sets in, when a signalman from the former Lancashire & Yorkshire Railway fills a vacancy in Wigan No 1 signal box; an affront which takes years to be forgotten!

Learning of a new classification formula for signal boxes, and that those on the Liverpool to Crewe main line have been designated 'Power Signal Boxes', on behalf of the signalmen in this signal box and Wallgate, I apply to be placed in the same category. (Our colleagues in the top signal box, No 1, are not interested in being included in this application.) Our request is declined by management. However, I persist for 18 months, and to our benefit the decision is reversed. We all receive over £400 in back pay, which is quite considerable given that our rate of pay is only £24 per week. The signalmen in Wigan No 1 receive nothing, so their representative protests, but it is a further 18 months before they are re-classified and receive their entitlement.

A locomotive is detached from a train in the station and is destined to run light to Crewe. The normal procedure is to use the main line crossover road, but express passenger trains are being given preference so I decide to utilise platform No 8. The subsidiary signal is off towards No 2 siding behind the signal box, but, for some unknown reason the driver has misread it, and his engine completely demolishes the stop block in a reverberating crash, finishing up halfway down the embankment, overlooking Wallgate Junction. The driver and fireman are not seriously hurt.

Young Horace turns out to be a good signal box lad, and the time has arrived for him to have a signal box of his own. He successfully passes his rules and regulations examinations; and Reggie at Pighue Lane Junction signal box immediately comes to mind, for now I have found that personal satisfaction in giving the benefit of my experience to others, as he did. I mention to him a quotation from a publication issued by the London, Midland & Scottish Railway Company, 'On Time'. The extract is from the January 1936 issue:

'ON TIME'

'10,000 Sentinels of Safety. Smoothing the Way for "ON TIME" Running. LMS Signalmen and their Work.'

'In this expressive phase may we sum up the first duty of those 10,000 and more signalmen, who, in 4,000 odd signal boxes throughout the system, skilfully and patiently transmit to their colleagues of footplate, guard's van, and shunting-pole the vital orders:

"Stop", "Go Slow", or "Right Away". But although we must think always of this great army of signalmen as standing primarily for safe working and all that is implied in the regulations designed with this object, theirs is a wider responsibility by far.

For upon judgement of the signalmen, upon his skilful management of block instrument, telephone and lever frame, depends to an increasing extent the smooth and punctual working of the huge traffic passing over the LMS metals.

The part played by the signalmen figures prominently for good or ill in the punctual working of our traffic.

102

It is in full appreciation indeed, in recognition of the splendid work which LMS signalmen are doing to maintain the company's record, both for Safety and for Punctuality, that the Chief Operating Manager has decided to include, in this and future issues of "ON TIME" a series of news items and articles of special interest to signalmen.'

This generosity, after iterating such kind words, merits far more. A wage rise would be more appropriate!

So Horace is joining this affluent breed of railwaymen, and no doubt he will succeed in emulating the signalmen of the past, so sincerely acknowledged and illustrated above. Signal box lads can graduate into signalmen, provided they show an interest in their work. I have been lucky in having two who are already successful signalmen on the Whelley line.

When I was a lad, my mate allowed me to operate the levers and block instruments, and after several months I could work the job on my own, although he kept a wary eye on me, of course. The normal duties of a box lad are quite boring, so pushing and pulling levers adds a little responsibility, and is so rewarding as well as helping towards the transition to manhood. A signal box lad's importance must never be belittled, for at the enquiry into the Winwick Junction (near Warrington) collision in 1934, the signal box lad was severely censured for the part he played.

My new box lad, Cyril, is very keen and has had a little experience working on the 'switchback' railway at Wallgate. He soon settles down to learning the rules and regulations, and the operation of the signal box, in fact, becomes quite proficient.

If I am not careful will he be pinching my job?

He is responsible for all train reporting, and the present method of using the telephones is being superseded by the introduction of tele-printer machines in most main line signal boxes. Now, whilst I welcome anything that brings about efficient working, I must say that these machines are a blasted nuisance, 'rat-tat-tatting' away like Bren guns, adding further disruption to our already noisy environment!

Back to the trains.

I hear the muffled sound of a collision involving a train, very early in the morning. The Manchester to Southport newspaper train, travelling along the L&Y route, is diverted every weekday into No 1 platform at North Western station to unload the papers for the Wigan area. To regain its proper route onto the 'Lanky' (as it is more affectionately known) the train is propelled behind the signal on the Up East Loop line at Wigan No 1 signal box, but today the signalman omits to pull one set of points over, resulting in the train being wrongly routed onto the shunting neck where it becomes derailed, the vans finishing up in a jumbled heap outside the signal box!

The introduction of diesel traction and subsequent withdrawal of steam locomotives - a crying shame - brought about the abolition of turntables. Some of the larger types were turned by using steam from the attached locomotives, but the smaller ones, similar to the one at the bottom of the embankment on the 'Lanky', were operated manually using a handle.

Contractors are engaged in dismantling this one, and just as a little diversion. I say to Cyril:

'Let's have a little fun with the men doing the work!'

I have an egg surplus to my requirements, so taking careful aim I lob it, grenade-fashion, in their direction. The aim is so perfect that it lands only inches from one of the men, whose immediate reaction is to look up into the sky where, by chance, a seagull far from its usual habitat is flying overhead. From the gesticulations on his part I am convinced that he thinks the bird laid the egg **in flight!**

A sad day arrives with the last steam passenger train running from Liverpool to Manchester over the original route. Hundreds of people, including myself, flock to Parkside to witness the train, stopping in deference to **Mr William Huskisson, MP for Liverpool, who died on that fateful**

opening day. This solemn occasion draws to a close when the continuous sound of the locomotive's whistle slowly diminishes as the train draws away from the countryside setting, little changed since the railway opened. **(See the picture on the Back Cover.)**

So many diverse events occur when working in signal boxes, and it is impossible to remember them all; but one incident that I shall never forget takes place in this signal box. It will be necessary, first, to set the scene.

The home signal on the Up Main line is situated north of Wallgate Junction overbridge ½-mile from North Western station. On numerous occasions this signal has been passed at danger owing to drivers being deceived by its sighting in relation to the sweeping curve approaching it. Because of this history, one becomes prepared for it happening again. The curve leading to Platform 1 (occupied at this time with a parcels train) is restricted to a 15mph speed limit. Platform 4 is also occupied, with the **'Royal Mail Train' - the one which was involved in the 'Great Train Robbery' of 1963 -** the last three coaches of which are protruding from the station, but clear of the facing points leading to No 9 Bay and No 8 Platform lines. In No 9 platform, coaches are stabled for the early morning train to the Royal Ordnance Factory at Chorley, and an express passenger train, with a Wigan stop, has just arrived at the signal on No 8 platform. The fireman of a freight train is busy filling up the tender of his locomotive with water on No 5 platform, and shunting is taking place from platform No 10.

In other words, the station is totally '**stitched up**'.

Darkness surrounds the luminosity of Great Universal Stores premises in north Wigan as I await the glimmering headlights of an express passenger train coming into view; but I have a premonition that something is wrong. Quite suddenly the night is illuminated by a line of Catherine wheels, travelling forward at high speed: a sure sign that the train is running out of control.

The points are set towards the mail train in platform No 4, and a collision is inevitable, that is, unless the runaway train can be diverted. Of the alternatives open to me, it is folly to think about platform No 1, because certain derailment would occur on the sharp curve. In seconds the road is set towards platform No 8, as track circuit indications confirm the signal is being passed at danger. A **'Royal'** train is due to run through Wigan on its way to Scotland in a very short time, and this necessitates a visit to the signal box by the Signalmen's Inspector, who is now watching the drama unfold, ashen-faced and silent, as the locomotive lurches and squeals in opposition to the permanent way. With wheels red hot the train comes to a stand no more than 2ft from the one standing at platform No 8, both locomotives hissing, as if in defiance of each other, ready for a trial of strength.

The now tranquil scene is broken by the intermittent clicking of cooling steel, and an intoxicated passenger hanging out of the window shouting:

'Hey, mon, where's are we?' then bursting out into song, giving us his rendition, in his best operatic voice:

'I belong to Glas-geee.'

A lone figure approaches and enters the signal box, dressed in civvies. He says:

'I am a Train Crew Inspector, and I was driving the train.'

'Didn't make a very good job of it, did you, pal?' I reply.

My superior and he get involved in a conversation as I carry out the duties I am here for, until one of them asks, *'What are we going to do now? Are you going to report it?'*

I say, *'Now look here, I am only "piggy in the middle" of you two, and all I want is to shift this blasted train from outside of my signal box,'* continuing:

'For one thing, that bloke singing out of tune is annoying me; and two, I want to be left alone, in peace, and I hate wasting ink on reports!'

104

Making a hasty exit, the inspector returns to his train, which leaves Wigan from the same platform as the mail five minutes later,

'ON TIME!'

The Royal train passes through safely, its occupants unaware of the emergency that had taken place earlier.

I enjoyed working as a Relief Signalman at Widnes, and a vacancy has arisen in this area, so I apply for it.

An amusing story to finish this chapter.

Wigan is well known the world over for its **Pier, Pies, Rugby League team and Uncle Joe's Mint Balls.** Uncle Joe's Mint Balls are made in the 'Santus' factory opposite Wigan No 2 signal box, the factory being built at an angle to the West Coast Main Line, and passengers *en route* to Scotland get a good view of it before they reach it. One day I observe two men in white overalls putting up ladders in readiness to re-paint the now deteriorated sign. It is a beautiful day, with the sun cracking the flags, and I soon come to the conclusion this pair have a humorous side.

The first word they paint is **'BALLS'**. This actually takes much of the day, with the regulation tea breaks in between. The next day **'GLOW'** is finished (missing out the 'A'). **Not bad for two days' work!** The following day they climb a little higher and paint **'JOE'S'**.

All of a sudden the heavens open, and this very important work is suspended for at least a week, leaving the sign for the travelling public on the passing trains to see. I expect there must have been a few smiles and titters aboard!

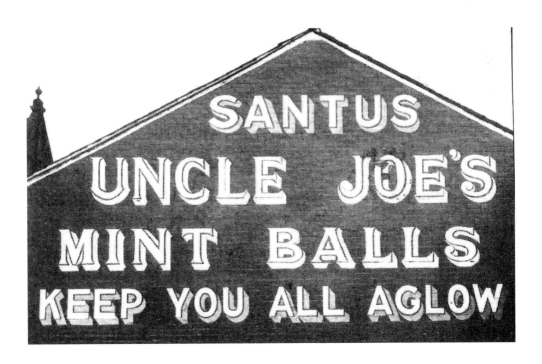

Uncle Joe's sign.

Time exposure at Wigan North Western station.

'A Signalman's Hard Day's Night at Wigan No 2.' Photo by Author.

CHAPTER TEN

A RELIEF SIGNALMAN AT WIGAN

1969-72

The area covered by a Wigan Relief Signalman is large, taking into account the recent amalgamation of the former L&Y signal boxes with those on the former LNWR. **Employees working on the latter always considered themselves 'LMS' – even though, technically, the L&Y was just as much part of the LMS – and by 1969 they were both part of BR London Midland Region.**

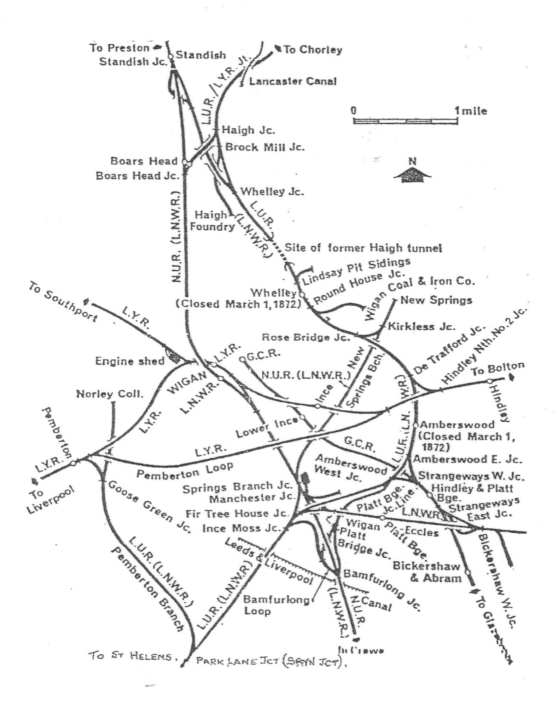

Railways in the Wigan area.

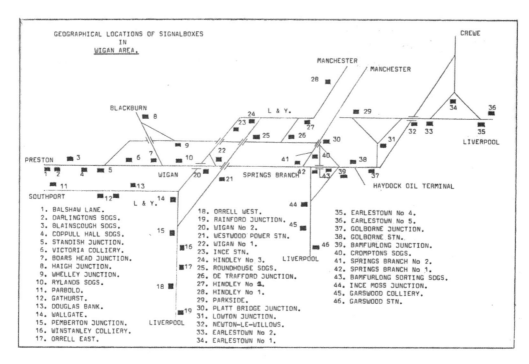

Locations of signal boxes in the Wigan area.

Before I can qualify for the rate of pay going with the position, it is stipulated that I must train Wigan No 1 and Standish Junction signal boxes, after which, and in full agreement with the management, I train others in any order that I wish.

I will take you to each one but, as in the case at Widnes, not in the sequence found in this chapter.

First we will visit:

WIGAN No 1 SIGNAL BOX

Signalmen Gerry Lomax (left) and Frank Ormshaw. Photo by Author.

Entering Wigan No 1 signal box, up the twisting concrete steps, I am faced by two lever frames of different lengths, back-to-back. The longer of these, having 85 levers, controls all movements on the former LMS (LNWR), passing in front of the signal box, whilst the frame in rear, with 40 levers, overlooks and controls the former L&Y Railway. All main line running signals are incorporated into the instrument panel fascia, 84 on the LMS side and 22 on the L&Y, together making a signal box with in excess of 280 levers, taking into account the fact that most of the switches are multifunctional.

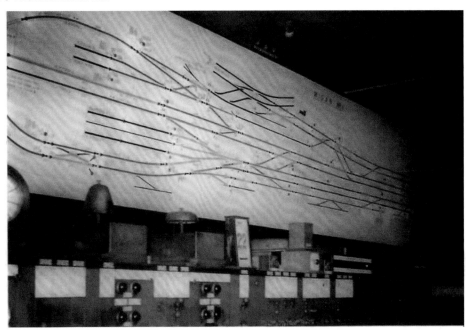

Illuminated diagram in Wigan No 1 signal box.

Courtesy of Adrian Vaughan.

'The Orange and Lemons' signal box, is not, as the name suggests, surrounded by groves of fruit trees in the middle of sunny Lancashire, nor does it even boast the tang of sweet smelling blossom. In fact, Wigan Gas Works, a stone's throw away, fills the air with a noxious stench: so unlike the aroma emanating from Uncle Joe's Mint Balls Factory, opposite Wigan No 2.

So how did the nickname arise?

Recalling a nursery rhyme, the residents on my turn of duty in this signal box for the last seven years bear the names PEEL, SEED and CLEMENTS! But make no mistake: it is not child's play working in one of the largest and busiest signal boxes in North-West England.

On the Up Sidings at Wigan No 2. Courtesy of Peter Worthington.

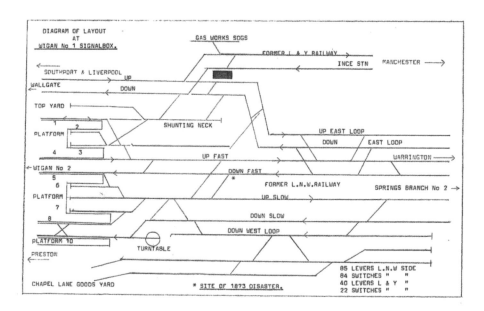

Wigan No 1 signal box.

The three signalmen here have the following duties to perform:

The first controls all traffic on the LMS Fast lines and the Up and Down East Loop lines to Springs Branch No 2 signal box on its southern side. In the opposite direction he controls Platforms Nos 1-5, the Top Shunting Yard, situated adjacent to platform No 1 and the Down Wallgate line, also the connections between the two former railway companies - these connections being interlocked in both lever frames.

The second signalman controls the slow lines from Springs Branch, the down West Loop, platforms Nos. 6-10, and traffic into and out of Chapel Lane Goods Depot. The third solely controls movements on the L&Y side, which includes the connections to Wigan Gas Works.

On this site, during the construction of the Gas Works, remains were found of Roman burials.

The geographical location of the signal box is in the 'V' created by the L&Y lines and the Up and Down East Loops, a few hundred yards south of North Western station, high above the River Douglas wending its way to the sea. A similar building to Wigan No 2 signal box, the façade is emblazoned with a large sign in moulded concrete, 'WIGAN No 1'. The frame was built at the Railway Signalling Company in Fazakerley, Liverpool.

Passing the site of Wigan No 1 signal box. Courtesy of Mick Langton.

110

Absolute Block Regulations apply on the main passenger lines, except those described in the last chapter, whilst Permissive Block operates on the Goods lines.

In 1873, a serious accident occurred here involving an express passenger train at the facing points on the Down Fast line (see diagram on previous page) and, unfortunately, a number of people were killed. The cause was never really established, but at the official enquiry recommendations were made that all facing points should be provided with locks to prevent them moving under trains. Facing Point Bars and Locks (FPLs) were thus devised and introduced into the railway system: an afterthought on the part of the railway hierarchy!

Something they are very clever at. **One is always wiser after the event!**

The old Wigan No 1 signal box, demolished in 1940.

The 'Blackpool Belle' in Wigan. Courtesy of Wigan World.

Aftermath of the train derailment at Wigan, 1873.

Both pictures courtesy of Wigan World.

I train for three weeks on the LMS Fast line side, then transfer a few yards to learn the slow line equipment and traffic movements. During this period the railway comes to a standstill owing to heavy snow blocking the points. A diesel passenger train from Liverpool has been standing for well over half an hour when the guard informs us that a lady in advanced stage of pregnancy has been taken ill. After making a can of 'Good Railway Tea' I plough through 18in of virgin snow on my St Bernard mission to give sustenance to the patient. Our train eventually begins to move, arriving at the station where an ambulance is waiting. Later in the day we hear of the safe delivery of a girl. This happy event is followed by an appreciative letter from the Stationmaster, but why not to me? It was delivered to the senior signalman on duty. I did think it was a bit of an affront, but I could see the delight in his eyes as he read the glowing appreciative words.

Because of this, I made no comment!

To facilitate regulation of trains between this signal box and Springs Branch No 2, and also to reduce the need for telephone messages, a 'Train Destination Describer' has been installed. Behind the glass inserted into a brass frame, a plate bears six segments, on each a separate destination. When the pin is slotted into the relevant hole the needle moves, ratchet-like, to that point, which is repeated on a similar instrument in Springs Branch No 2 signal box.

Chapel Lane, the terminating point of the former Wigan Branch Railway, runs under the tracks at a point equidistant between North Western station and this signal box. It is here that one appreciates the geological problems that confronted the early engineers, and also the reason why it took so long to bring about the connection with the North Union Railway. The line from Springs Branch runs through a cutting of no great depth to North Western station and on to Wallgate, the main thoroughfare in Wigan, the latter being at a much lower level, which made matters difficult for the builders.

Commencing on the northern side of Wallgate a long, high embankment stretches for nearly two miles to Beech Hill and Boars Head cutting. The iron bridge over Wallgate successfully completed the uniting of the two railways.

To return to Chapel Lane.

Prior to the advent of railways, road traffic consisted of horse-drawn vehicles, and the need for wider roads was not evident so the railway companies built over the existing features as they were. On the introduction of mechanised transport these thoroughfares became inadequate, as is the case in point, and the lane under the railway is much narrower than its widened approaches.

Electrification of the railways provided the opportunity to rectify such anomalies, with many bridges being renewed. This particular one has many sets of metals passing over it, so its replacement can rate as one of the largest bridge operations on the West Coast Main Line modernisation programme. To a layman, the widening of Chapel Lane is fraught with difficulties. However, this operation is carried out with little delay to railway traffic movements by adopting a method that can only be described as simplicity itself, using modern technology unheard of a few years ago. Snow has turned to ice in the freezing weather and covers the permanent way in a large white sheet. Arc lights, erected near the bridge, illuminate the area with a remarkable brilliance, dimming those on the station platforms beyond.

Trains are being diverted away from the lines that are blocked, and engineers, sporting yellow safety helmets, begin to drill deep into the ballast, disturbing the tranquillity for people living nearby and for us in our signal box. Every night for weeks on end the work progresses from one side of the bridge to the other, a few lines at a time. A silicone substance is pumped under great pressure into the boreholes, permeating the ground from the southernmost buttress to a point where the new one will be built. This silicone sets and allows workmen to excavate a deep channel, wide enough to build the new buttress without fear of collapse. After several months the buttress is finished and girders for the new bridge are positioned, followed by re-laying of the track, as traffic schedules permit.

Finally, Chapel Lane is spanned, leaving a massive heap of unwanted soil which is soon removed.

Rationalisation is proceeding in conjunction with bridge alterations and electrification, the Slow lines having already been severed at Springs Branch No 2 signal box and slewed into the Down Fast line. Platforms Nos 6, 7 and 10, plus the Middle road, are dispensed with. No 8 platform, on the other hand, remains, as does Chapel Lane Goods Yard on the slow line side. The track layout at the newly built North Western station on the Fast line side remains basically unaltered, but the junction itself is substantially changed. No 1 platform is reserved for the birds on Friday nights in the summer. Pigeon fanciers from all over the North-West congregate in a waiting room placed at their disposal, while hundreds of baskets containing their feathered friends are loaded into 15-or-more vans destined for Craven Arms - and even more exotic places, one being Nantes.

On Saturdays and Sundays in the autumn there is an almost continuous procession of express trains heading for Blackpool, their passengers *en route* to view the famous illuminations. It is difficult to regulate the traffic, owing to the bottleneck junction at Wigan No 2, and partake in liquid refreshment, because of the number of trains. As if this were not enough, one is mindful that they have to come back!

I mentioned earlier some of the accidents that occurred during the modernisation of the Liverpool to Crewe section. The current major operation on the West Coast Main Line is no exception, and many incidents, some serious, others not so, occurred. In one incident the Fast line signalman has turned the signal switches for a Liverpool-bound Diesel Multiple Unit (DMU) from No 2 platform at North Western station to travel along the bi-directional line to join the Up Main towards Springs Branch. Approaching on the Down Main (formerly the Down Fast line) is another DMU, destined for the vacated platform. For some inexplicable reason the same signalman operates the switches for the new facing crossover road.

In normal circumstances this would be electrically locked to prevent the points operating, but, owing to a malfunction of a Track Circuit, the lever is free, and this error places the two passenger trains on collision course.

At the point of impact, opposite the large electricity works, the trains are travelling slowly, and by good fortune no-one is seriously hurt. However, the trains are badly damaged and taken out of service. The signalman involved was completely exonerated from blame.

Before I leave this signal box, I should like to relate a particularly funny story.

Even though signalling must be taken seriously, it does no harm to have a laugh; that is, when one has time!

Horse-racing pages of the daily newspapers cover the train register as Jack, the signalman working on the 'Lanky' side, studies form, using a secret formula known only unto himself. His success is phenomenal, averaging five winners per day, most at extremely good prices; but he refuses to divulge his selections beforehand, perhaps because of superstition.

'*How many winners did you get yesterday, Jack?*' enquires old Harry, who always works the signal box wearing his 'wellies' (Wellington Boots) and peering over the pince-nez balancing on the end of his nose.

'*Five, Harry,*' he replies, going through an impressive list.

'*It would have been six, but, old Lord Thingymebob fell at the last, when well in the lead,*' he adds.

'*Very good,*' says Harry and, trying it on, continues:

'*And what have we got today?*'

'*Haven't picked 'em yet,*' mumbles Jack, placing noughts and crosses on his selections in red pencil, here, there and everywhere.

Early the following morning, Jack informs us that he had a bad day, managing only four winners.

Harry picks up his paper and reads:

'ALL MEETINGS ABANDONED YESTERDAY DUE TO FOG'

He makes no comment, as he gleefully waves the page, unseen by Jack! Jack overcomes this minor setback, and still manages to keep up to form, and make it pay!

'Duchess of Sutherland' at Wigan. Courtesy of Lawrence Thorpe.

Going flat out. Courtesy of Mick Langton.

'Wigan North Western'
Courtesy of John Harrison, railway artist.

115

Passenger train on Down L&Y Railway passing No 3 box. Photo by Author.

I will now systematically examine all of the signal boxes in which I worked under the Wigan administration, starting at the northern extremity of the area at:

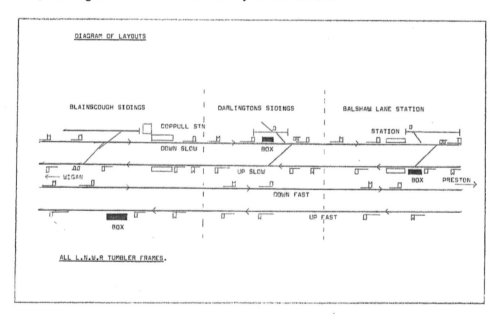

Balshaw Lane, Darlington's Sidings and Blainscough boxes.

BALSHAW LANE STATION SIGNAL BOX

Balshaw Lane & Euxton station is served only by trains travelling over the slow lines, and this small signal box stands at the northern end of the Up platform, controlling, with an LNWR Tumbler Frame and upper quadrant semaphore signals, traffic into a small goods yard opposite, and signalling trains between Euxton Junction and Darlington's Sidings signal boxes on the quadrupled lines.

Euxton Junction signal box comes under the Preston administration.

A steeply rising gradient commences outside the signal box, the line following a southerly route towards Wigan as far as Bank Top at Coppull, 2½ miles away. Running beneath the railway, a short distance away up this incline, is a narrow farm track bearing the infamous title 'German Lane'. German Lane bridge is to be renewed under the modernisation scheme, but first may I digress a little?

Re-laying of the Fast lines is well in hand and I change from bashing levers to wielding a shovel, not permanently, but as a temporary platelayer, at weekends when I am not required to work in a signal box. The Permanent Way Inspector seems impressed with the efforts of his motley crew of Drivers, Firemen, Porters, Signalmen and Shunters; so much so that he suggests that we all transfer to his department but I, myself, decline the offer! Anyway the work is far too strenuous for me having being reared as a hot-house plant!

Let us get back to the bridge. The new girders for it are sited beside the track in readiness. It is a **'Crane'** job. Edge Hill locomotive shed steam crane, normally used to re-rail engines and vehicles, is requisitioned for the work. On arrival at the bridge, preparatory operations are conducted then the hawsers placed in position:

'Take the strain,' shouts a bowler-hatted gaffer. Slowly, the wires tighten as the lift begins.

'Whoa!' A slight adjustment is necessary.

'Okay! Lift!'

Slowly, ever so slowly, the bridge becomes airborne, the hawk-eyed chief signalling with his hand, higher, higher.

'Whoa!'

The girders swing and bits of ballast are dislodged, falling into the gaping void. The crane then begins to move, on the falling gradient.

Surely, Mack Sennett is not filming this? Nearer and nearer …. and our friend the farmer gets something he didn't bargain for: a British Railways' crane on his land!

And yes, it is yet another 'CRANE JOB'!

Miraculously, no-one is hurt. Proceeding from German Lane towards Wigan, we arrive at:

DARLINGTON'S SIDINGS SIGNAL BOX

About one mile north of Coppull stands Darlington's Sidings signal box, adjacent to the Down Slow line, at the southern end of a small cutting. It signals trains between Balshaw Lane and Blainscough Sidings signal boxes and has upper quadrant semaphore signals worked from an LNWR Tumbler Frame. An open-cast coal mine behind the signal box is life-expired, and the sidings are no longer used so, as a result, the signal box is normally switched out of circuit, being open as required.

Royal trains often use the West Coast Main Line during the course of a year, and regulations stipulate that all signal boxes must be open so the signalman can observe their passing. On one occasion only am I requested to work in this signal box, and that is to signal the 'Royal Train' through. The acceptance of trains in these circumstances is slightly different from the norm, inasmuch as the train must be accepted by the signal box in advance before being accepted from the one in rear.

Dominating the countryside in Coppull is the giant Ring Mill, built during the Industrial Revolution for the manufacture of cotton materials, but today the weft-threading shuttles no longer fly between the warp, a casualty of economics and progress. Part of the building is now being used by small factory units, but for how long?

Coppull station, like Balshaw Lane, is served only by the slow lines. It stands above the main Wigan to Chorley road running through the village, opposite the Railway Hotel situated adjacent to the Up Fast line. Further on, in the far distance, can be seen Winter Hill on the outskirts of Bolton, its giant television masts prominent on the summit, pointing skywards.

Leaving the station and continuing towards Wigan, on the Up Fast line side, there is a small row of terraced houses owned by the railway, where I once lived.

Just past these stands:

BLAINSCOUGH SIDINGS SIGNAL BOX

This signal box, I believe, derived its name from a long-closed colliery west of the railway, the only sign left being a small embankment through which the connecting railway line ran. Unlike the Darlington's Sidings, these here are still used, albeit only occasionally, to serve the small goods yard and warehouse backing onto the station.

The LNWR Tumbler Frame controls upper quadrant semaphore signals on all four lines. Trains heading south are nearing the top of the long upward gradient, and pass only feet from the signal box structure causing severe vibrations as the wheels hit the badly positioned rail joints outside, the oil-lamps flickering in perfect unison.

Blainscough Sidings signal box. Courtesy of Cyril Peers.

Animals often gain access to the railway through broken fences, and on one occasion here an express passenger train arrived, the engine covered in blood. Examination of the line confirmed that six cows had been killed and several injured, but this incident was nothing compared to that experienced by Walter (now a relief signalman) after gaining promotion from Standish Junction signal box. He booked on duty here one sunny summer's day. Normally, very few people venture close to this signal box as it is a little off the beaten track, but on this particular day a middle-aged man, perched on the fence opposite, was indulging in the fascinating pastime of collecting engine numbers. The signals were off for a freight train, which was approaching on the Down Slow line, going at a steady pace on the downward gradient. Suddenly, the train spotter jumped off the fence and walked into the path of the train, with the result that one might expect!

Another incident that occurred here, though not so gruesome, concerns a young booking clerk at the station who was very interested in railway locomotives. The local tripper had just shunted the warehouse, and the driver was partaking in a cup of tea. Up comes our budding railwayman and asks the driver if he can have a go on his engine.

'Take it away!' he says obligingly.

Opening the regulator, the engine careers down the sidings and finishes up on top of the **Stop Block!**

Still on the route to Wigan, but further away from civilisation, we arrive at:

COPPULL HALL SIDINGS SIGNAL BOX

Situated on the summit of the banks on either side, this box signals trains between the Blainscough Sidings and Standish Junction signal boxes; it uses upper quadrant semaphore signals in its LNWR Tumbler Frame and controls traffic to and from Chisnall Hall Colliery, just over one mile to the west. Trains servicing the colliery must pass over an unmanned level crossing on the busy A49, on Wigan Road, just south of Coppull village. The sidings here are used to stable traffic from the colliery until transferred to Bamfurlong Sorting Sidings, south of Wigan, prior to distribution.

In the summer months working here is very pleasant, which offsets the repetitious work and boredom often experienced, but in winter I have never before worked in such bleak desolation.

Leaving this signal box and continuing towards Wigan, we pass on the right hand side, just over one mile away, a large factory with the number 57 on its chimney.

The home of those famous beans!

At one time it boasted its own sidings, having the name 'Bloomfield' after a nearby local pit, long since closed. Prior to this, the buildings (Douglas Mills) housed the Standish Royal Ordnance Factory. However, not only did this line serve the Bloomfield Colliery, but also Langtree Colliery nearby.

On the Down Fast and Down Slow lines here are Intermediate Block Sections (called Bloomfield IBSs) having upper quadrant semaphore, motorised, signals, worked from:

STANDISH JUNCTION SIGNAL BOX

A small, concealed path on Rectory Lane, Standish (near Wigan) leads to a very important junction on the West Coast Main Line. The signal box is situated in beautiful, tree-scattered, undulating countryside: an ideal spot for those interested in ornithology, although the opportunity to pursue this particular hobby here would be restricted, owing to the heavy traffic flow. Remains of the former Standish station, closed in 1949, can still be seen between the signal box and Rectory Lane bridge, and little appears to have changed around here since that date; nearby there are only a few houses, a couple of farms and the bleach works tucked in a fold of land to conceal its presence.

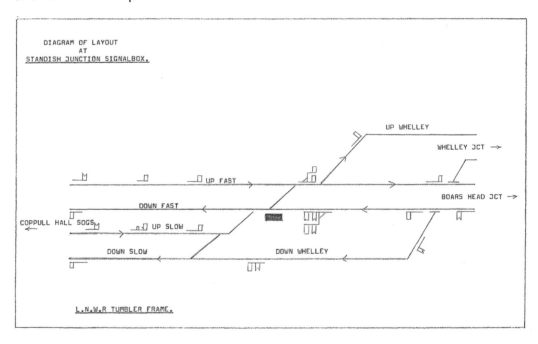

Standish Junction signal box.

In 1882 a line avoiding Wigan North Western station was built between here and Bamfurlong Junction, passing an area east of Wigan known as Whelley; hence the name adopted for this branch, used primarily by freight trains travelling via Bamfurlong Sorting Sidings, but often utilised for passenger services diverted to and from the former L&Y Railway at De Trafford Junction.

It is proving its worth during the electrification programme of the main line through Wigan.

119

Standish station with the signal box in the background, c1920.

Courtesy of Wigan World.

Approaching Standish Junction from Wigan.

Courtesy of H.G.

The junction, worked from an LNWR Tumbler Frame with upper quadrant semaphores, has been substantially altered recently, conforming to that planned under the modernisation scheme. However difficulties now arise with regard to the regulation of trains from the Up Slow line, owing to the ladder junction formation, which appears to be paramount in the future track layouts on British Railways. Signalmen working in this box must have an intimate knowledge of the local working at North Western station, otherwise havoc can be caused through poor regulation. One of the problems encountered concerns drivers' knowledge of the Whelley line route. Often a train stops, straddling the whole junction, and the driver will calmly inform the 'Bobbie':

'Don't know my way over the Whelley.'

There is no alternative but to run the train via Wigan, sometimes causing serious delay to following expresses.

Absolute Block Regulations apply on all main lines controlled from here between Victoria Colliery Sidings signal box and Coppull Hall Sidings. The Up Whelley line branches to the left from the Up Main line about 200yd from the signal box, but the Down Whelley line follows a route from Whelley Junction itself to form a burrowing junction - one of the earliest known in the history of railways - some 300yd south of Rectory Lane bridge. This line is also worked under the Absolute Block Regulations.

Most certainly the best outlook is to the east with Winter Hill rising in the distance, so the seating is arranged to gain full advantage of the view. Because the walking route is from the south, a mirror is suitably fixed to the outside wall in order to observe any gaffers approaching on the 'blind side' while one is in a reclining position; rare enough though it may be in this extremely busy junction signal box.

Approaching Standish Junction from the Whelley line. Courtesy of Wigan World.

Still travelling south, but taking the main line route, we arrive at:

VICTORIA COLLIERY SIDINGS SIGNAL BOX

In the middle of a secluded wood, on the Up line side opposite the remains of derelict buildings that once were the hub of the long worked-out Victoria Colliery, stands the signal box still bearing the same name. However today, as with Darlington's Sidings signal box, it is opened only as required. Likewise it always opens for the passage of Royal Trains and on occasions to shorten the block section between Standish Junction and Boars Head Junction.

Continuing, we arrive at:

BOARS HEAD JUNCTION SIGNAL BOX

A junction, three miles north of Wigan, was laid in 1869 from the main line to Chorley and beyond, via the village of Adlington. The signal box, in a cutting, was presumably named after the I4th-century, whitewashed 'Boars Head' inn which stands on Wigan Road. It is steeped in history and one of the oldest inns in England. In fact, it was used in days gone by as a stop-over prison, when transferring offenders from the south to appear at the Lancaster courts.

Boars Head Junction signal box. Courtesy of Winder.

The small station here closed many years ago, leaving little sign of its whereabouts, except perhaps for the artificial mound upon which the signal box **stands**: I emphasise the word 'stands', because the area around here is subject to severe mining subsidence from the nearby Victoria Colliery. In 1940, for instance, the signal box structure sank several feet, and jacks were used to replace it to its former position.

So who knows if it will still be standing tomorrow?

Of an unusual construction, the signal box looks top-heavy on its stilt-like girders, exposing the point rods and signal wires running from the LNWR Tumbler Frame down to ground level. This equipment is the cause of an eerie whistling, more pronounced in the quiet of the night, when a strong wind is blowing through the cutting on the south side. All signals are of the upper quadrant semaphore type.

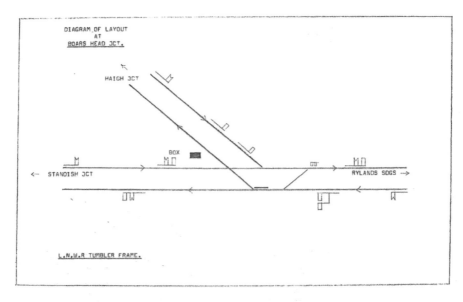

Boars Head Junction signal box.

'Mod cons' include gas lighting, a cooker and running water, but no toilet; perhaps management decided there was no need for one! However, a conveniently placed birch wood, 30yd away, littered with pages from **W2**s (fortnightly notices of signalling and engineering work to be carried out) provides adequate privacy; that is, in the summer months, but when autumn leaves begin to fall one must grin and 'bear it all'!

Traffic onto and off the branch line is light, with only a few passenger and freight trains each day. Rumours are in circulation alluding to a possible permanent closure of this line, which curves through an avenue of high trees to the Whelley line viaduct, half a mile away. Near to this viaduct, but out of sight from the signal box, is an upper quadrant semaphore Outer Home Signal, used for acceptance purposes from Adlington Junction signal box.

Haigh Junction, the one intervening signal box, has recently been closed permanently.

Passing Haigh Junction signal box. Photo by Author.

'Flying Scotsman' on the West Coast Main Line. Courtesy of Wigan World.

The armchair adorning this small, quaint signal box is a huge monstrosity, completely out of proportion and character to its surroundings: no mortise-and-tenon joints, just pieces of railway sleepers, 6in nails and plaited signal wire to support a backrest. First class coach cushions, in a beautiful shade of blue, complete this piece of furniture, weighing a ton and made entirely from plundered railway materials!

'What a versatile breed we have in the signalling grade.'

Levers releasing ground frames, or released electrically from the signal box in advance when the needle on the block instrument is turned to the 'Line Clear' position, are easily recognisable in a signal box frame, for they have a 4in-wide horizontal white-painted band encircling them. Normally, the release is activated when the catch handle is depressed, or, in some cases, when a button is pressed as well as the catch handle, but this signal box boasts the most unusual method to release a lever:

Depressing the catch handle and pressing the button as above is not enough to release the lever. One must depress the catch handle, press the button, then jump into the air like a ballerina! The vibration on impact with the floor picks up the electrical lock, positioned under the floor boards!

Talk about a 'one-man band'!

Passing the site of Boars Head Junction. Courtesy of Mick Langton.

Before we leave this signal box, I would like to relate a particularly amusing and unbelievable story.

Relaxing in front of a well stoked fire, I become aware of a locomotive safety valve blowing off, but a quick glance at the block instruments indicates that no train has been accepted, and both home signal track circuit berths are clear. Ringing the signalmen in both Standish Junction and Rylands Sidings signal boxes by telephone provides confirmation that no train has been despatched towards me.

So where is the noise coming from?

Peering into the darkness along the branch line, all I see are trees silhouetted against a starry sky. Anyway, this line closed two weeks ago, the telephone and block instruments being disconnected, and the track removed between the signal box and points on the main line only last Sunday! Still the distant hissing persists. Perhaps a train has failed on the nearby Whelley line, but this idea is discounted by the signalman at Standish Junction, so I come to the conclusion that the noise is not railway-connected. Half an hour later the clattering of hobnail boots on the metallic steps leading up to the signal box, standing in the 'V' of the junction, startles me. In walks a black-faced fireman who asks:

'Heymon, hoolungareyegonnakeepuseer?'

'Hang on a minute, lad, where are yer?' I enquire.

'Standinattharterhameonth'brarnch."

'How the heck have you got there?'

Beckoning me to the window, he retorts:

'I'lltellyehoolgiteer, seethoostworails, wecumalongem.'

Adding, *'ConwegorSpringsBrarnchnaw?'*

I think to myself, '**Oh aye, this fella's smart,**' and his name could be **Alec.**

'Sorry Alec, you'll have to go back the way you came, and travel via Chorley and Euxton Junction, or along the 'Lanky' from Lostock Junction,' I tell him.

These routes would put at least one-to-two hours on the journey time to the shed.

'NawwewannagorviWigin.' On and on he goes, until I say to him:

'Come with me.' Off we go down the signal box steps, making our way towards the junction.

Pointing the hand-lamp down, I say to him.

'Now how do you suggest I get you and your locomotive to Springs Branch?'

'THERE'S NO BLASTED RAILROAD HERE!'

He disappears into the darkness, along the branch, never to be seen again!

Continuing on down the track through the cutting we arrive at:

RYLANDS SIDINGS SIGNAL BOX

Wigan town itself is in the centre of a massive coalfield, and there are numerous collieries in its locality. Lots of books have been written about them, way beyond the scope of this volume, but the railways played their part in the development of the area, none more so than at this particular signal box.

Rylands Sidings signal box. Courtesy of Cyril Peers.

Lying between Boars Head Junction and Wigan No 2 signal boxes on the Up line side, this box controlled traffic to eight different coal mines which all deserve mention. In addition, a line ran to Rylands Mill (now the Great Universal Stores building, adjacent to Mesnes Park) and another down to the Leeds & Liverpool Canal at Crook village to enable coal to be loaded onto the canal barges.

Steaming away at Rylands Sidings. Courtesy Wigan World.

The colliery nearest to the signal box was named Elms Pit. Close to this were Gidlow Pits No 1 and 2, and further to the north-west Prospect Pits and coal yard. About a mile from here were situated the Robin Hill Drift Mine and coal yard which were opened in 1953; it closed in November 1963. Returning to Rylands, a line ran east, first to Giants Hall Colliery and the Standish coal washing plant beyond. Further east, were Taylor Pits, and close to them, John Pits, with a branch down to the canal. Giants Hall Colliery closed in 1961, along with all the associated feeder lines. An event of this nature would usually sound the death-knell of a signal box, and although the Standish coal washing plant was dispensed with, a new one was built at the Gidlow site, and many trains from surrounding collieries were sent there for their cargoes to be washed and cleaned prior to distribution.

The signal box stands opposite the Tupperware factory on the north side of Spencer Road bridge; this bridge at the moment is being reconstructed under the modernisation programme. The LNWR Tumbler Frame controls both upper quadrant semaphore and colour light signals.

On the Down Line passing Rylands Sidings signal box. Photographer unknown.

On the Down Line passing Rylands Sidings signal box. Courtesy of Wigan World.

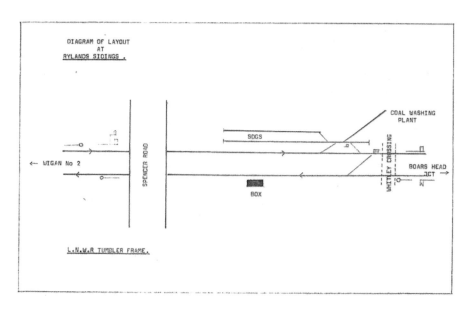

Rylands Sidings signal box.

In the Wigan area this signal box is well known for its macabre history.

Nearby, towards Boars Head Junction, a pedestrian level crossing with the name 'Whitley', adjacent to a school playing field, has been the scene of countless suicides, but thankfully I have had no personal involvement in any of them! Sadly, I must report, one of my fellow relief signalmen here at Wigan had occasion to end his life in such a way after losing his wife.

On the Down Line approaching Boars Head Junction. Courtesy of Wigan World.

A Lostock Hall to Garston freight train carrying liquid gas has arrived at Standish Junction, awaiting a margin to run through Wigan station. By chance the guard happens to be an old friend of mine from my Woodside Sidings days. Ronnie always had a good stock of 'biological' books imported from Scandinavian countries, and he requests the signalman at Standish Junction to allow sufficient time for him to stop here so he can show me his latest acquisition. Slowly, the heavily loaded train grinds to a halt, and he enters the signal box, full of excitement; whether to see me after all these years, or to show me the book, I never established, but I have

128

to inform him that he is not travelling on the Slow Road heading for Speke, and that an express passenger train is close behind his! We bid farewell and I think what a pleasant change it is to look at a book different from the usual publications which have no pictures in them!

Instead of continuing along the West Coast Main Line, may we retrace our steps to Standish Junction and look at the Whelley Branch line?

Leaving the signal box and travelling through the most charming countryside we arrive at:

WHELLEY JUNCTION SIGNAL BOX

To reach this signal box from the road one must travel down Brock Mill Lane, opposite the Wigan Infirmary, where at the bottom, surrounded by countless trees, is the mill from which it derives its name. Not too far, after passing the mill on the Down line side of the railway, stands the small signal box with an LNWR Tumbler Frame; but it cannot boast a junction anymore, because the single line to Haigh Junction has been removed, relegating it to a block post.

A block post is best described thus:

Usually placed in the centre of a long section, the signal box's main function is to signal trains, without the use of points, or if points do exist they are seldom operated.

Not often are top class relief signalmen requested to work in small signal boxes such as this, and two days are usually enough for me, mainly because of boredom. However, one adapts and settles down to enjoy the occasional rest. On the other hand there is an added pleasure, not connected to trains which are few and far between.

I mentioned earlier the public house called **Bird i' th' Hand.** A welcome is received from the other resident *in situ.* **No, it is not a two-man box!**

Bird i' th' Hand. Courtesy of Peter Worthington.

I was 'busy' doing something **(probably in a horizontal position)** when, all of a sudden and without warning, a robin flew in through the window and perched itself onto a signal repeater (see picture) at the back of the frame. Not content with just sitting there, chirping away, it began to fly to different parts of the box, and when I opened my baggin' **(sandwiches, to the uneducated: I am beginning to learn the 'lingo' a little)** it came and participated in the feast, by sitting in my hand.

Not many people I am sure have had the experience of a wild **'Bird i' th' Hand'.**

I do recall being castigated (in fun) by a Block Inspector many years ago for having a bird in the box, but I think even he would have turned a blind eye in these circumstances.

What an unforgettable experience it was!

Taking leave from this signal box, and heading on a southerly route, the countryside changes dramatically from the greenery of the meadows to the black fields of slag, the residue of the many, now worked-out collieries which once dotted this area.

It is in the middle of this landscape that we find:

ROUNDHOUSE SIDINGS SIGNAL BOX

I have never been able to establish the origin of the name given to this signal box, but can only assume that it related to one of the extinct collieries. On the introduction of diesel power, the sidings here were closed because their main use, after the demise of the collieries, was to stable coal wagons destined for the Springs Branch locomotive shed. The signal box, having an LNWR Tumbler Frame and controlling upper quadrant semaphore signals, is similar to Whelley Junction box in that it has become a block post.

Roundhouse Sidings signal box. Courtesy of P Worthington.

Unfortunately, the whole Wigan coalfield is in decline with only a handful of collieries now open.

Those at Chisnall Hall (near Coppull) and Garswood Hall (between Wigan and St Helens) have recently closed, leaving only Bickershaw, Golborne and Parkside in production, but on the brighter side proposals are in hand to begin a new opencast site at Bickershaw in the near future. These closures have a knock-on effect on railway traffic throughout North-West England and force sidings and marshalling yard staff into redundancy. The signal boxes, though, are retained because of the exorbitant cost involved in eliminating them; the signalmen, meanwhile, take advantage by putting their feet up! But, for them this is only temporary because this line is scheduled to close when the new power-operated signal box at Warrington is commissioned within the next two years.

Departing from this dismal landscape to enter, once again, the verdant fields, we arrive at:

DE TRAFFORD JUNCTION SIGNAL BOX

Named after a **'well-to-do'** family in the Wigan area, this signal box is, without doubt, the most colourful I have ever set foot in.

De Trafford Junction signal box. Courtesy of Wigan World.

The tongue-and-groove woodwork has been expertly decorated with:

WALLPAPER!

A pink, pretty floral pattern behind the stove contrasts with the dark abstract design around the door; this in turn is followed by two strips obviously left over after someone has completed their kitchen. That chosen for the wall opposite the door is more in keeping with the surroundings, having locomotives and trains of all descriptions emblazoned on it. Even the spaces between the ceiling joists are covered. An abundance of pin-up pictures adds to the overall homely, but higgledy-piggledy, environment.

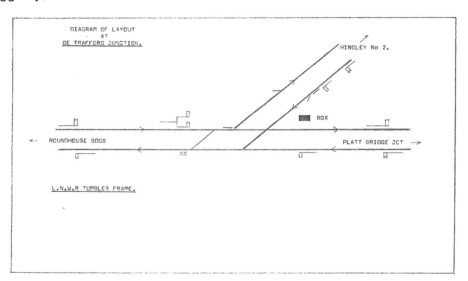

De Trafford Junction signal box.

Having an LNWR Tumbler Frame and upper quadrant semaphore signals, this junction signal box signals trains from Platt Bridge Junction (on the former LMS) Hindley No 2 (on the former L&Y) and the previously mentioned Roundhouse Sidings signal boxes. The Down line from Platt Bridge Junction has a severe upward gradient to this signal box and is a bank engine section. A train from Bamfurlong Sorting Sidings *en route* to destinations on the L&Y is drawn up the gradient by the bank engine, with the train engine banking. This may sound double-Dutch, but this method is necessary because the train must reverse here to gain access to its correct route. In addition, the bank engine now assists the train along another bank engine section to Crow Nest Junction signal box, on the Manchester side of Hindley station, before returning to Bamfurlong for further work.

Following the route of the bank engine towards Bamfurlong we arrive at:

PLATT BRIDGE JUNCTION SIGNAL BOX

This signal box is isolated on top of a high embankment overlooking the main road running between Wigan and Warrington. It is of the LMS Standard type and controls both upper and lower quadrant semaphore signals.

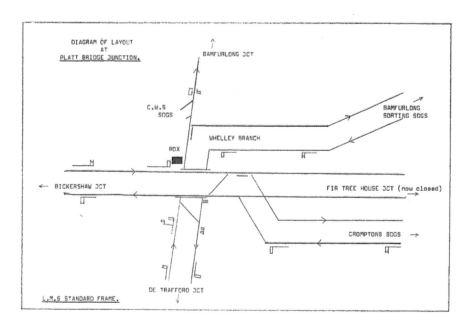

Platt Bridge Junction signal box.

It signals trains between Crompton's Sidings and Bickershaw Junction signal boxes on the Eccles Branch, which opened in 1864, and between Bamfurlong Sorting Sidings and De Trafford Junction signal boxes on the Whelley Branch line running at right angles underneath the former.

The Up and Down lines to Ince Moss Junction via the quaintly named Firtree House Junction, (with not a tree within miles) closed recently, in readiness for the modernisation, and the track has been lifted.

A facing junction from the Up Whelley Branch line leads to Bamfurlong Sorting Sidings signal box, and from this a further junction, along a single line passing Bamfurlong Screens Sidings on the right, leads to a trailing connection onto the Up Fast line at Bamfurlong Junction. On this single line is a ground frame, released from this signal box, to control traffic into the Co-operative Wholesale Society Glass Works Sidings a few hundred yards away.

Passing Standish Junction. Courtesy of Ron Couchman.

Platt Bridge Junction signal box. Courtesy of Wigan World.

At one time, this was indeed a very busy signal box, but today few trains pass over this unusual junction.

Delving into the archives, I found some interesting literature about signalmen working in:

BAMFURLONG SORTING SIDINGS SIGNAL BOX

This signal box is found on the western side of the **'flying junction'** embankment, at the bottom of the gradient leading up to Bamfurlong Junction one mile away, the most southerly end of the 'Whelley'. Whilst it still boasts two geographical junctions, the traffic dealt with has declined over the past few years.

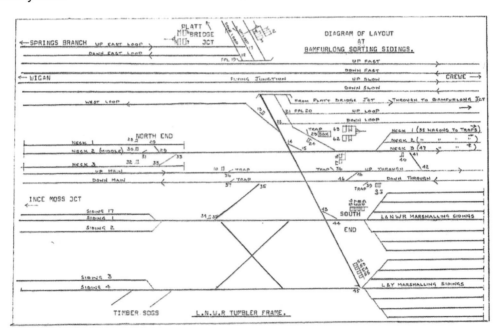

Bamfurlong Sorting Sidings signal box.

I would like to look at the discussions which took place at Railway Staff National Tribunal level in July 1938.

This lengthy report covers many aspects of signalmen's work and conditions at the time, so allow me to take an extract from it to illustrate the vast changes that have occurred in the short space of thirty years:

Report of the proceedings before the Railway Staff

National Tribunal in regard to claims in connection

with the Signalmen and Traffic Regulators on 21st, 22nd,

23rd and 26th July 1938.

The Chairman of the Tribunal.

Sir Arthur Salter, K.C.B, D.C.L, M.P.

Representing his Members.

Mr John Marchbank.

General Secretary of the National Union of Railwaymen.

BAMFURLONG SORTING SIDINGS SIGNAL BOX

Another goods box to which I would call your attention is a Class 2 Box Bamfurlong Sorting Sidings, Springs Branch L.M.S. Railway.

It is rated at 62s.6d per week. The box opens at 5am on Mondays and remains open until 6am each Sunday. It is staffed by three signalmen working eight-hour turns except in so far as the first turn on Monday is concerned. This turn is from 5am to 2pm.

The equipment of the box is as follows: 22 point levers; 30 signal levers; 2 locking bars, making a total of 54 working levers. There are four North Western Tell-Tale Type Permissive Block Instruments and one N.14 Single Needle Absolute Block Instrument; also two Circuit Telephones and one Control Circuit telephone. The ground staff comprises the following: one Class 3 Inspector; two Class 1 Yard Foremen; two Class 1 Goods Shunters; and four Class 3 Goods Shunters.

WORK MORE SEASONAL

The box has been Class 2 Goods ever since the classification of boxes was arranged in 1922. Until recently the box was reputed to be particularly heavy and complex to work, but during recent times, presumably owing to the shrinkage of the South Lancashire coal trade, the intensity of the work has tended to become seasonal. That means to say, the fewer wagons in summer time, and the consequent better timekeeping of freight trains tends to prevent congestion in the sorting sidings, and keeps traffic moving evenly. What appears to have added to the even flow of traffic is that the company have, during the last eight years, concentrated upon the timing of freight trains to produce this even flow, which, together with the elimination of traffic passing unnecessarily through the sidings, has had the one purpose and result, namely, avoidance of all possible congestion and delay. However, about 80 freight trains are timed to work at the sidings in the 24 hours.

GOODS BOXMAN REVIEWS LEVERS

In a normal passenger box, frame locking is a valuable check to a signalman. By it he may rely, after having pulled a particular signal lever, that all the point levers in his frame are correctly set for the passage of the train. In this manner a signalman, in dealing with a train travelling from one particular road to another road may, before the train traverses the road, check his levers at any time - as he constantly must - and assure himself that the route is correctly set by seeing that the correct signal lever is over in his frame. If the correct signal is over, then the road is right. The goods box signalman pulls his signal, and to see that he has set his route correctly he must mentally review every lever he has pulled and every lever appertaining to the particular route. In a passenger box such a happening would be a major error, but in the box I am speaking of the signalman has the one signal which reads from four roads to three roads and he bears the responsibility of auditing himself, as it were, every time he sets up a route without the helping correction of either adequate frame locking or adequate signalling system. It means that, as in most goods boxes, he must not only exercise the mental power of setting the road, but must bear the mental strain of examining every lever which bears on the particular route.

PRIMITIVE CHECK

Reverting to the taxation of the signalman's memory, the signalmen at this box have a rather primitive method of keeping check on the state of the Necks. It is of the utmost importance that the signalman should remember the state of the Necks. If a neck is occupied by anything at all he must not forgetfully turn another train into it or even give permission for an engine to be put into it from the other end. To help keep a check they have a number of empty '20 cigarette packets'. They turn the packet inside out and inscribe on such packets in bold print words such as:-

'Neck No I Blocked', 'Neck No 1 engine and van', 'Crossing engines', 'Blocked'.

This size of packet fits very nicely on the handle of the levers and although the method is, as I have said, rather primitive, the signalman, when working in the dark, dares not dispense with the idea.

(A primitive idea it may be, but the signalmen in Wigan No 2 signal box still use **'Woodbine'** packets to remind them of the traffic situation in the sidings, 25 years after this report.)

They work with an inadequate signalling system and with the minimum of protective device. Their work is not straightforward. Their memory is fully taxed. Lacking protective devices, they must carry out their duties with unusual care. They have to contend with two sets of ground staff. They are really in control of the 'clearing house' between two sets of marshalling sidings and the running lines. In giving illustrations of trains accepting signals not intended for them, I mentioned cases of mishaps. Although this box is not notorious for mishaps, they do occur, but it is with pride that men refer to the fact that they have spent so many months in the box without mishap. I ought to state that the company has dealt very leniently with men when mishaps have occurred at this box, and in only one case can I find evidence of suspension from duty. I could go on at considerable length in giving information as to the various types of boxes; the different experiences of men engaged therein, and the instruments about which these men have to possess a complete knowledge, but I hope I have given you sufficient to enable you to appreciate the exacting nature of the work. From what I have described, it will, no doubt, go home to you with great force what I referred to in connection with the work of relief signalmen.

All the grades concerned must understand the regulations in connection with the working of the traffic they have to deal with, and here it will become obvious to you that a good memory is of supreme importance in the work of the signalling grades: however, I will not detail the work further. I have endeavoured in the course of my statement so far to give you an outline of the development of signalling. From what I have described, you will doubtless agree with me that the inventors in the matter of railway signalling do not stagnate. They are continually developing their ideas with a view to making signalling of trains more fool-proof. They are succeeding in removing some of the disabilities of the heavy manual work involved in the pulling and pushing of levers. Electricity or power of every description is being used in connection with the work. However, all this is designed to meet the developments in railway transport. Speedier trains, increased services, longer trains and the general requirements of the public demand the introduction of methods of operation which will assist in satisfying all these requirements. However, they also do something else. You will see from the figures I have given you that there is a reduction in the number of signalmen employed.

This is a grade that is not particularly affected by depressions in traffic from the point of view of redundancy of men. It only affects them in the matter of wages, because, as you will have learned from what has been described, the wages of signalmen depend upon the work performed and the number of marks allocated for such work. The railways have to be kept open, whatever the volume of traffic. Accordingly, I think it is reasonable to argue that the reduction in the number of signalmen is due primarily to the new methods which have been introduced. Indeed, I think I am on safe ground when I state that railway companies' signal engineers will agree that the developments which are taking place will still further diminish the number of men required to man signal boxes. Excellent examples are provided by what has been done on the S.R. Here electrification has proceeded apace and it is continuing. Increased passenger services are the natural result. But what of the men who man the signal boxes, responsible for controlling this traffic?

I have accepted the fact that these developments tend to ease the manual side of signalmen's duties, but it is not difficult to see the increased mental responsibility that results. I have said there is no uniformity. There is not, neither can there be in the light of developments. One of the most recent signal boxes open on the L.N.E.R. at Hull is described as the most up-to-date method of signalling on the railways. Indeed, we are again reminded that there are now no technical limits to achieving almost anything desired in signalling. It is truly said that the area of control of one signal box can in theory be extended indefinitely. However that may be, the work of the signalman, always a very important factor in railway work, is increasing. I have reminded the Tribunal that the intention is to establish fool-proof apparatus, but with mechanism that appears to be almost impossible. At least, the experience of signalmen can give an answer to the suggestion that their responsibility is lessened. I have quoted an instance which shows that the signalman even in those excellently arranged signal boxes must be ever alert because upon the signalman may depend the lives of hundreds of people.

One slip and the consequences are serious. The multiplicity of devices in actual use must strike you as a taxation upon the minds of men called upon to understand them. Indeed, it will not come as a surprise to you that instances are known of experienced men failing after several months' tuition to qualify for working in some of these newer boxes.

The key to all power boxes is the diagram.

Men have to maintain a constant watch on this diagram, to keep track of all the movements made within the sphere of their particular box. This is specially the case where junction working away from the sight of the box is in operation. This kind of work is one of the features of power boxes. Concentration of signalling is over a wider area than formerly, the work of several boxes being concentrated into one. Can it be reasonably argued that this reduces the responsibility of the men employed in such boxes? The result of these newer methods materially shortens the headway between trains and makes for greater acceleration. When shunt operations are made, it is supremely important for the signalman to observe them, so that at the actual moment of clearance, routes can be set to enable further movements to take place. The application of the signalmen's mind to the diagram, the watching of tracks for the purpose of effecting quick movements, the observation of point indications, the intent listening for a thousand and one movement orders given by the ground staff below and given through loud speakers, often amidst the noise of engines, may be described as the reverse of comfortable. Then again, the type of diagram may be floodlit; you will readily appreciate that a certain amount of eye strain must accrue. This is a serious question for railwaymen because eyesight failure will mean loss of position; it may mean serious reduction in wages and in some cases dismissal.

I am glad to say not many instances of that kind occur because companies generally endeavour to find a post for such men. However, serious loss in wages accrues; that may vary probably as much as 20s per week reduction, owing to a failure of that kind. It might be assumed that there is little physical strain in the newer type of boxes, but men have to be on their feet continuously for eight hours. I do not think it will be disputed that there is some exertion. Furthermore, opportunities for meals are not specifically provided. It is not an unusual thing (and I have mentioned this already) for men to take home food that they have brought. I mentioned that men will bring sandwiches. These are handy because men are able to eat them in the course of their duties.

(The situation with regard to taking meals is still the same today, and instances occur often when signalmen do not have time to eat their sandwiches.)

To continue:

As I have already stated, in our view, that is not good for the health of the men. That is the experience of many men in these very busy boxes, and helps to show the strength of the union' submission that the maximum working day should be six hours in such busy boxes.

(Allow me to have another go! I have worked in some very busy signal boxes, but the eight-hour turns of duty still exist.)

I have stressed the position so far as automatic, semi-automatic and power-boxes are concerned. I do not pretend for one single moment that what I have given you in the way of illustrations may be regarded as typical of the work of all signalmen. For the reasons I have mentioned elsewhere, they cannot be so regarded because of the different construction of signal boxes, the different layout, the nature of the traffic, and so on. However, what has to be borne in mind in connection with the work of signalmen is the fact that they are key-men to the satisfactory working of traffic.

Do not misunderstand me in that respect. I do not assume that signalmen are alone responsible, because each unit in the service is essential to efficiency in railway transport. However, from the time the engine emerges from the locomotive shed, or a set of coaches proceeds from the siding, or wagons are removed from sidings and goods trains begin to pass, signalmen have the responsibility in some way or other for their movements. Generally, signalmen work alone. They are confined to a signal box for the whole of their shift of duty. In the more busy centres, as you will have observed, there are signal boxes where more than one man is on duty but these are comparatively few in number. No-one can rightly gauge the mental responsibility of men in such heavy boxes. In theory it is argued in some quarters that the work of the men in these boxes is less difficult. The men concerned will tell you a different story. Now, I have tried as nearly as humanely possible to give you a picture of the position.

It is not a simple matter to do this. Practical experience is often the only true way to ascertain realities, and if you bear in mind what I have stated as to the difficulties of experienced men learning the work in these heavier boxes, you will understand that it is no joy-ride. Signalmen as a body are an important section of our railway service. In their hands are placed the lives of many millions of passengers and millions of tons of goods. Speed is the key-note of transport today. It is so with the railways, and signalmen play their part in the scheme of things designed to produce that efficient state of railway transport which is evident to anyone who studies railway timetables.

Signalling is a very interesting study and its development proceeds.

(It is a pity that I never experienced the density of traffic dealt with by the signalmen here in 1938, but I can visualise what it must have been like. However, as described earlier, the decline in the freight traffic within the Wigan area has affected the working of this particular signal box the most.

The lifting of the Sorting Sidings and Pemberton Corner leaves a rutted landscape in their place, and where many railway staff were employed only the signalman here remains, surrounded by the residue from old mines. Overall, it is a thoroughly dismal scene.

Signalman Ray Burgess at Bamfurlong Sorting Sidings signal box.

Not far along the East Loop line towards Wigan is:

CROMPTON'S SIDINGS SIGNAL BOX

This signal box no longer controls any movements into the sidings after which it is named, because they have been recovered. However, it still controls the southern end of Springs Branch Locomotive Shed and has upper and lower quadrant semaphore signals worked from the LNWR Tumbler Frame.

The line from Springs Branch to Manchester via Eccles has recently closed and all traffic timed to run on this route is now diverted via Lowton Junction. The signals at Platt Bridge Junction have been taken down, but the signal box there remains to signal trains on the Whelley line only.

An incident occurs here that warrants a mention in relation to the installation of track circuits, but first I should like to digress a little, to recall two collisions in this area: one between Bickershaw Junction and Platt Bridge Junction signal boxes, the other near Ince Moss Junction. Both of them were caused by a lapse of concentration on the part of the signalmen, and almost certainly because there were no track circuits.

Result of the collision between Bickershaw and Platt Bridge junctions.

Photographer unknown.

In the case of the Bickershaw collision, a locomotive was allowed to travel to the starting signal to await acceptance from Platt Bridge Junction. Unfortunately, the signalman on duty at Bickershaw Junction, for some unknown reason, forgot about this engine and accepted and offered on to Platt Bridge Junction the following parcels train which received clear signals. The parcels train collided with the locomotive, travelling at a much slower speed in the advance section. Both became derailed, but none of the train crews were seriously injured.

The Ince Moss incident occurred in a block section between Springs Branch No 1 and Sharpe Street (St Helens) signal boxes.

The intermediate boxes were being switched out of circuit, as is usual at weekends.

In the early hours of a Monday morning the signalman at Sharpe Street signal box in St Helens accepts a light engine running from Preston to Liverpool from Springs Branch No 1, but it stops on the curve near Ince Moss Junction because the driver is unfamiliar with the route and requires a pilot for the rest of his journey. The engine is unseen at a stand by the signalman in No 1 signal box because the Springs Branch Yard Master's administration block obstructs the view in that direction. Sharpe Street signal box stands not far from a main road overbridge, and the signalman, although he does not see the engine, thinks that it has passed his signal box and sends the Train out of Section to Springs Branch No 1 signal box.

It must be assumed something passed over the bridge to give him this impression.

However, he is immediately offered, and accepts, the 2.10am Wigan to Liverpool train from No 1 signal box, and this train collides with the still-stationary engine. Unfortunately, the fireman on the engine should have protected it by walking back to No 1 Signal Box in accordance with the rules, but failed to do this. However, at the enquiry the signalman at Sharpe Street box was subsequently blamed for this accident.

These two accidents, which would have been avoided had track circuits been installed, clearly demonstrate the need for constant vigilance on the part of the signalman.

A similar incident occurred on the Whitehouse triangle at Preston some years ago.

Here, the West Coast Main Line traverses the Preston to Southport line running beneath. The signalman in Whitehouse West Junction signal box sets his crossover road for an engine to reverse, but he assumes, wrongly, that an engine passing over the bridge above was the one he was dealing with, and he replaces the crossover road. Shortly after he accepts a passenger train, and this collides with the engine, still stationary in advance of the crossover road.

I return to the incident here at Crompton's Sidings. Whether the installation of track circuits would have averted what could have been a terrible accident is open to conjecture.

A small upper quadrant semaphore signal, 50yd in advance of the signal box, allows locomotives to clear the points for disposal on the depot.

Result of derailment at Crompton's Sidings signal box.

Courtesy of Wigan World.

Early one foggy morning, an unbelievable set of circumstances arises through a Wigan-to-Manchester parcels train, timed to travel via Lowton Junction, being erroneously described as a light engine for Springs Branch shed by the signalman in Wigan No 1 signal box. I happen to be on duty here and, quite rightly, clear the signal as usual, but for some unknown reason the driver takes the signals at Springs Branch No 1 for the closed Eccles line.

None of the signalmen in the intervening signal boxes at Wigan and Springs Branch notice that the locomotive is hauling a van and is now proceeding towards Platt Bridge Junction.

The engine passes my box and I can see it isn't a light engine at all, but a train with one van.

I cannot contact anyone, because both Platt Bridge and Bickershaw Junction signal boxes are closed, with the semaphore signal arms removed. The driver, as if by divine providence, decides to stop his train on the approach to Howe Bridge to query the missing signals. I receive a telephone call from this driver who has made his way to a local public house, informing me of the situation he is in. I arrange with him and the guard the correct way to solve this very unusual incident, and agree for him to set back to the signal box, and proceed along the right route via Lowton Junction.

Little does he realise that this action undoubtedly saves his life, together with the lives of the fireman and guard, because the bridge passing over the main road 20yd ahead of his train has been dismantled!

Which I only found out about several days later!

Looking over the West Coast Main Line in a westerly direction can be seen:

SPRINGS BRANCH No 1 SIGNAL BOX

(The Cattery?)

This signal box, worked by two signalmen on each turn, has an LNWR Tumbler Frame controlling upper quadrant semaphore signals. It controls traffic between Bamfurlong Junction and Springs Branch No 2 signal boxes, on the Up and Down Fast and Slow lines under the Absolute Block conditions. A junction to the north diverts traffic from the Up Slow line towards Ince Moss Junction, St Helens and further west, and vice versa. The Up and Down East Loop lines, from Springs Branch No 2 and Bamfurlong Sorting Sidings signal boxes, are worked under the Permissive Block Regulations, as is the line from here to Crompton's Sidings signal box, via a junction on the East Loop lines.

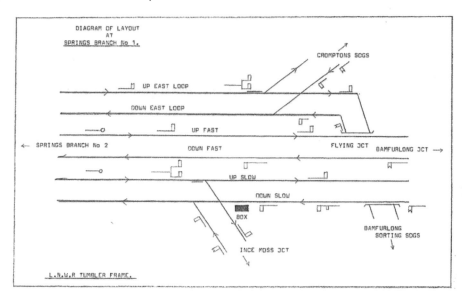

Springs Branch No 1 signal box.

At one time it was possible to run trains from Crompton's Sidings across a junction onto the Down Slow line, but this has now been replaced with plain line. Just prior to this remodelling I recall the incident when a coal train, running out of control, sliced through the centre of a car train travelling at speed on the Fast line, spilling the contents of both and making a thorough mess.

Springs Branch No 1 signal box, c1910.

Courtesy of Dave Houghton collection.

141

The signal box is situated in the 'V' where the main line, running south to north, converges with the Liverpool line curving sharply from the west. Nearby is a large brick building used as the administration centre for the Springs Branch area. The overall outlook is dismal; it is typical of a mining area, with large and small slag heaps placed at random everywhere. Visibility is restricted on the southern side by Taylor's Lane overbridge whilst in the other direction railways occupy most of the view.

One of the cats in Springs Branch No 1 signal box.

Courtesy of James MacKenzie.

The structure of this signal box has been badly affected by mining subsidence, falling at least a foot from north to south, making it hard not to break out into a trot when operating the levers from the Wigan end. The sloping floor does not seem to bother the signal box pets (notice the plural) as there happen to be no fewer than 13 cats roaming around, from the smallest of kittens to the old great-grandma, who is at the moment curled up on her favourite spot behind the block instruments, away from the general melee in which her offspring are engaged.

Occasionally one gets kicked accidentally, making it scamper to a safe haven behind the lever frame. In spite of their numbers, the regular signalmen feed them, supplementing their usual diet of Springs Branch rats and mice!

Passing Springs Branch No 1 signal box. Courtesy of Mick Langton.

The 'Royal Train.' Courtesy of Mick Langton.

Looking north, and to the right, about 300yd away, can be seen:

SPRINGS BRANCH No 2 SIGNAL BOX

This signal box stands between the Up Fast and Down East Loop lines, adjacent to the large locomotive sheds. It signals trains between Wigan No 1 and Springs Branch No 1 signal boxes under the Absolute Block Regulations on the main lines and Permissive Block on the East Loop lines.

Springs Branch No 2 signal box. Courtesy of Lawrence Thorpe.

It contains an LMS Standard Frame and the signals are a mixture of upper quadrant semaphores and colour lights.

Recently, the quadrupled lines between this signal box and Wigan were altered, the Slow lines being severed near to the box and merged with the Fast lines to form the new Up and Down Main. Behind the signal box there is a connection from the Down East Loop line into the northern end of the locomotive shed, and the Ince Wagon Works a mile or so east.

It is here that redundant steam engines are being broken up. They stand in continuous lines, buffers-to-buffers, rusting away, casualties of a progress that is not altogether welcomed by old railwaymen because so much character has been lost with their passing.

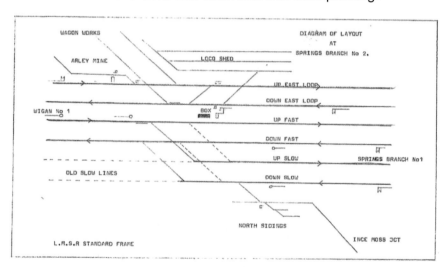

Springs Branch No 2 signal box.

Opposite the signal box is North Sidings, with one running line through to Ince Moss Junction, worked under Permissive Block Regulations. Completing the layout is a connection from the Up East Loop leading to the Arley Mine, but this is now closed.

144

Courtesy of Mick Langton.

Passing Springs Branch Shed on Up Fast line.

Courtesy of Mick Langton.

Electrification work is well under way, with stanchions being erected every Sunday, and as the permanent way re-laying, remodelling and grouting trains finished their work, the overhead equipment trains can be positioned without hindrance. All this activity is not new to me, having witnessed the same throughout the Liverpool to Crewe section, but such mammoth operations require expert planning and co-ordination by everyone involved. In charge of these operations are six inspectors, five of them former top class relief signalmen, two from Wigan and three from Winsford, the sixth being a former passenger guard, again from Wigan. These lads earn a great deal of respect and assistance from all the signalmen in the area during this arduous period, and the enthusiasm generated is second to none, despite the fact that within 12 months the majority of these signalmen, some with many years' service in the grade will be made redundant.

Springs Branch Shed at night. Courtesy of Mick Langton.

On 10th December 1972, Liverpool Central station and the signal box controlling it was permanently closed, and one of the signalmen there (Ron C) had become redundant prior to this date and was offered, under the conditions of service, a vacancy in the same category as his box. He chose Springs Branch No 2 box, which was Special Class 'A', and double-manned. Like myself, he, and others to follow, were not greeted with enthusiasm by the resident signalmen in this area because we were treated as outsiders and seen as pinching the work to which they thought they were entitled. Whilst, I was ex-LMS, he was an ex-Cheshire Lines-ite.

At this time I lived in Orrell, and he in the village of Halsall, between Liverpool and Southport. On early turn I travelled the few miles to Wigan on the bus from Orrell Post, when to my surprise one morning a car stopped and, lo and behold, Ron was the driver. He offered me a lift, then dropping me off outside North Western station, continued to Springs Branch. We were actually on the same turn of duty, but he had left there before I gained promotion to that of a Special Class Relief Signalman, so never had the opportunity to work alongside him and lost contact.

'Lion' heading for Rainhill at Springs Branch, 1980.

Courtesy of Mick Langton.

146

'A wet day in Wigan.' Courtesy of John Harrison, railway artist.

'Wigan Springs Branch.' Courtesy of John Harrison, railway artist.

Leaving this signal box, and retracing our steps, we pass No I signal box, proceeding around the curve towards St Helens to arrive at:

INCE MOSS JUNCTION SIGNAL BOX

This is well known to all railwaymen through North-west England as the dumping ground for train-loads of refuse collected from re-laying operations, demolition sites, and even over-ripe bananas from Garston Docks for over 40 years. The word 'Moss' in the title gives a false impression of the actual surroundings here, because extensive opencast-excavations, now exhausted, have left the countryside looking more like that seen by Neil Armstrong on his historic journey, except that water filling the workings has created large artificial lakes, abounding in fish, the home of several angling and yacht clubs.

Ince Moss Junction signal box. Courtesy of Wigan World.

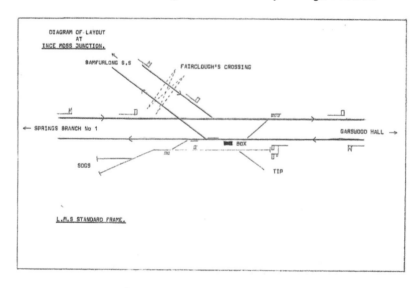

Ince Moss Junction signal box.

This signal box with an LMSR Standard frame is comparatively new, replacing an earlier one which was severely damaged by mining subsidence. It stands between the Up line running from St Helens to Springs Branch and the Tip road behind. The main lines between the above points were first opened in 1869. Later, two geographical junctions were laid controlled from this box. One, as mentioned earlier, the line via Firtree House Junction no longer exists, leaving only the Up and Down Goods lines to Bamfurlong Sorting Sidings, worked under the Permissive Block Regulations, with upper quadrant signals. An hourly passenger service runs each way between Liverpool and Wigan throughout the day, but freight traffic is minimal owing to the closure of the local collieries.

Firtree House Junction signal box. Courtesy of Wigan World.

A new private level crossing has been installed on the Goods lines between here and Sorting Sidings, to give road lorries access to a site where breezeblocks for house-building are made from the residue of mining activities. George, a retired coal miner provided by the firm to operate the barriers, works under the authority of the signalman in this signal box. His day is made when he signals a train conveying HRH the Duke of Edinburgh over the crossing, in transit from Lowton Curve to St Helens. Until the late 1950s, quadrupled lines existed from here to Carr Mill Junction, situated overlooking the A580 East Lancashire Road, on the outskirts of St Helens. The old slow lines were retained for a short time to stable condemned coaching stock, near Garswood station, but eventually they fell into disuse and finally were lifted.

The next signal box along the line was Garswood Hall Colliery Sidings, situated, again on the Up line side opposite the **'Three Sisters'** slag heaps, but closed, as was the pit, in September 1968. On the site of this dominant landmark the local council were later to build a racing track using materials from the levelled mounds; it was on this track that my son was to win some races riding his motor-cycles.

Author's son Tony on his Yamaha 250cc TZ.

Further on, towards St Helens on the Up line side stood Bryn Junction signal box, controlling the lines from the LMS to Pemberton Junction on the Lancashire & Yorkshire Railway, but this closed in April 1959, the lines being lifted and the signal box abolished. Continuing on, out of the Douglas valley, the railway line curves in an 'S' fashion through a delightful countryside setting until we arrive at the small village of Garswood. On the eastern side of the station platforms stands:

GARSWOOD STATION SIGNAL BOX

Garswood Station signal box. From the Tony Graham collection, courtesy 8D Association.

This tall signal box between the quadrupled lines, two of which are no longer used to run main line traffic, only signals trains with its LNWR Tumbler Frame and upper quadrant semaphore signals between Ince Moss Junction and the quaintly named Pocket Nook Junction, under Absolute Block Regulations.

The signal boxes at Carr Mill and Gerrards Bridge junctions have been abolished, the latter being replaced with a ground frame to service Messrs Pilkington's glass works at Cowley Hill. As mentioned earlier the old slow lines are now utilised to stable condemned coaching stock, and this is a particular local eyesore.

Gerrards Bridge Junction signal box. Photo by Les Fifoot.

One of the regular signalmen here turns out to be a stick-in-the-mud type, probably because he has worked here too long. Behind the stove, two pokers and a homemade toasting fork hang on nails, and curving scratch marks they have made on the walls suggest that this signal box, like many others, has not seen a paint brush in years. However, on relieving this signalman one day, he gives me the run-down on the current traffic position, a duty taking place in every signal box at relief times.

'One on the Up, and one on the Down!'

He then castigates me for not replacing the utensils on the correct nails three weeks ago.

Oh well, it takes all kinds to make a world, but in the event of my returning here, I remember his instructions. **Large Poker, Toasting Fork, and then Small Poker!**

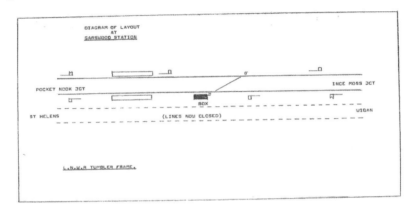

Garswood Station signal box.

Not far from here as the crow flies is:

BAMFURLONG JUNCTION SIGNAL BOX

Located at the southern end of the Whelley Branch avoiding line, the junction controlled from this signal box has been altered to a ladder formation, from the Down Slow to the Up Fast line. The signals are upper quadrant semaphores, the distant signal being colour-lit, worked from an LMS Standard Frame, and trains travelling via the Goods lines, either to the Liverpool direction via Ince Moss Junction, or over the Whelley, are diverted from the main lines, north of the signal box, after first crossing a bridge over the Worsley Branch of the Leeds & Liverpool Canal. The single line running from Platt Bridge Junction to the Up Fast line, as noted earlier, is seldom used, and Bamfurlong Screens (a large group of sidings with connections onto this line) once used to stable coaching stock for local passenger services, have closed completely.

Bamfurlong Junction Signal Box. Courtesy of Cyril Peers.

This signal box is one of the few in the area that have box lads in their complement, and one here now, transferred from a guard's position after being knocked off his push-bike going to work, is quite proficient.

After I pass out for the signal box, he thinks he knows more than I, which he quite obviously does so I, being diplomatic or just plain lazy, let him get on with it!

The view from here is fantastic, with Wigan and its dominant church visible on its knoll in the centre of the valley in the distance. Looking east, the remains of buildings at Maypole Colliery stand stark against the sky, reminding one of the terrible underground explosions that occurred there some years ago, killing so many men and young boys. In spite of this reminder, the overall landscape is pleasing to the eye, especially when long boats make their leisurely way along the still waters of the canal between Wigan and Manchester, contrasting with the express trains speeding over the 'flying junction' between here and Springs Branch No 1 signal box.

Cross Tetleys signal box was the next one to the south, but this has recently closed and the block section now extends to Golborne Station signal box some two miles away.

Train crews working slow freight trains from Carlisle to Crewe, and vice versa, are almost invariably relieved here, a small cabin being erected alongside the signal box for their sometimes long wait, which can be counted in hours, rather than minutes.

(Do you know, there are some good jobs on the railways?)

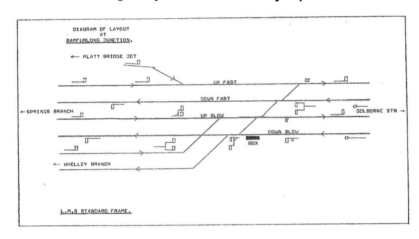

Bamfurlong Junction signal box.

At one time two signal boxes were situated at Golborne, but today only one exists:

GOLBORNE STATION SIGNAL BOX

Anyone entering this small signal box for the first time cannot fail to notice how busy the signalman is. Overlooking Tanners Lane, it has 26 levers in an LNWR Tumbler Frame, with a mixture of upper quadrant semaphores and colour light signals, and it controls traffic on the quadrupled lines between Golborne Junction and Bamfurlong Junction signal boxes.

All signal boxes are classified by the amount of work undertaken and the number of levers operated during a 24-hour period, in accordance with the 'Marks System'. The lowest class of signal box is 5, followed by 4, 3, 2, 1, Special `A', Special 'B', and finally Special `C'.

In the Wigan area, for instance:

Wigan No 1 signal box is Special 'B'

Springs Branch No 2 Special 'A`

Wigan No 2 Class 1

Standish Junction Class 2, then this signal box Class 3, which is definitely underrated in comparison to others nearby.

Scotch Express passing Golborne Station signal box. Photo by Author.

Leaving the West Coast Main Line for a moment, I should like to mention the line between St Marys, Lowton and St Helens, on the former Great Central Railway, which came under Dr Beeching's axe in the early '60s, but the rails were never lifted. A few years later the Shell Petroleum Company built a large storage depot at Haydock, requiring a railway connection. This was achieved by the installation of a single line from the former LMS line near Golborne station, to link up with the Great Central at Edge Green Lane. Buffer stops were placed at the St Helens end, one mile west of Ashton-in-Makerfield old station, resurrecting the route, now renamed the **'Chord Line'**.

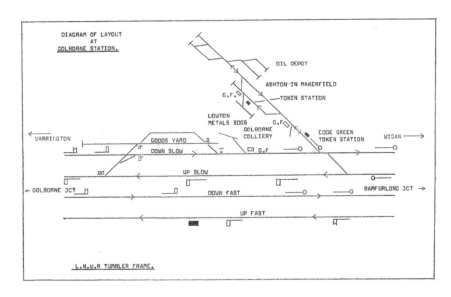

Golborne Station signal box.

Half a mile from the main line junction, near Edge Green Lane overbridge, the driver obtains a single line token, authorising passage of his train to Ashton-in-Makerfield. Not far from this token is a sidings connection to Golborne Colliery, worked from a ground frame released by this signal box. All empty wagon trains destined for the colliery must be disposed of by using this route. After passing the wooden semaphore distant signal and the old platform (also of wooden construction) at Haydock Racecourse, a pair of spring-loaded facing points divert traffic to the left into Ashton-in-Makerfield station platform, at the end of which is situated the western end token hut.

153

D J Norton with the wooden semaphore stop signal.

Another ground frame here allows access into Lowton Metals Company Sidings. The final section of the line to Haydock Oil Terminal is worked under 'One Train Working Regulations'. All traffic movements throughout are controlled from Golborne Station signal box.

The loading of each train to enter onto this single line is given to the signalman, who records it in a special register, thereby compiling a complete record of traffic on hand at each location. The signalling on this line may appear to be complicated to others than signalmen, so I have a little challenge to advanced students of railway signalling practices, and 'Whizz Kids'. **(This is an affectionate title for Traffic Apprentices who go under the pseudonym of railwaymen, after two years of swotting to gain a smattering of knowledge, when, in practice it takes many years to reach this level of proficiency)**

To them I direct the following question.

What is the maximum number of trains that can be allowed onto the 'Chord Line', within the normal signalling guide lines?

All fully-loaded coal wagons from Golborne Colliery are shunted, via a ground frame on the Down Slow line, into the goods yard opposite the signal box, from where Target 81 trips them to Parkside for further handling. Again the number of wagons is recorded by the signalman.

The colliery-owned locomotive has running powers on the main line, authorised by the Ministry of Transport, but only from the ground frame into the northern end of the goods yard; but on occasions it does travel back from the sidings, along the Down Slow line, when everyone keeps their fingers crossed, because if it became derailed questions would be asked!

Absolute Block Regulations apply on all main lines and the 'Train Approaching' bell signal (1-2-1) is sent to the advance signal boxes, on the receipt of 'Train Entering Section' from the one in rear.

The 'Train Approaching Signal', must not be confused with the 1-2-1 signal heralding the approach of a bowler-hatted gentleman!

Signalmen, for one reason or another, stop trains as milkmen break bottles! Such is the time I forget to clear the signals for a Birmingham-bound express passenger train travelling along the Up Fast line. I only realise the aberration when I see it approaching under the main road bridge, bringing it nearly to a stand at the home signal. As it passes the signal box, going at a speed of at least 30mph, but accelerating, I notice someone's head popping out of a coach window, and I give a friendly wave, which is reciprocated. I think how nice it is to be recognised by a member of the public, and consider the incident closed. Half an hour later, though, I receive a telephone call, 'This is Mr So-and-so, speaking,' **(What else could he do on a telephone?)** 'could you tell me why the Birmingham express was stopped at your signal box?' Quick as a flash, I reply, 'The signal wire came off the pulley wheel under the signal box.' **(Do not forget that I have been in this game for a long time!)** I again consider the incident closed. **It is not!** For next day, for some inexplicable reason, I stop the same train; the same head pops out; I give the same friendly wave; the same telephone call follows, and so as to not break the sequence I make the same excuse. However, I have misgivings as to the outcome of this particular episode. This calls for action! That would not baffle the likes of **Sherlock and the Doc,** but as for Mr So-and-so, we shall soon find out!

Under the signal box I go, and make marks on the pulley wheel to suggest that the wire has slipped!

Sure enough, as expected, an immaculately dressed gentleman enters the signal box (the 1-2-1 having already been sent) and, quick as a flash, I say, **'Hey, you're the bloke that waved to me from the Birmingham express. Do you live around here?'**

'That is correct, signalman, I am Mr So-and-so, but I actually live in Crewe.' I weigh him up, and think, **'Typical pen-pusher!'** I go on to say, 'I've had trouble with the signal wire slipping off the pulley wheel, but the Signal Lineman is on his way to fix it.' **The plot thickens!** 'Come on, and I will show you.' To those not acquainted with the lower part of an old signal box like this, one must picture a setting for a horror movie, with large undisturbed cobwebs hanging everywhere, the skeletons of their makers still attached. Armed with an oil-filled hand-lamp **I, being a gentleman** make sure he precedes me into the gloom, where lubricating oil on the cranks and pulley wheels has spread and solidified with age. I invite him to inspect the troublesome wire. The Signal Lineman arrives, and our learned friend, oil on his shoes and trousers, hair dishevelled, streaked with silver **(because he did now duck)** diagnoses the problem to the in-the-know lineman. **We exchange winks, and this time, the incident really is closed!**

We get a lot of problems in this area owing to vandals and thieves, and they have stolen signalling cable on the Haydock Chord line, putting all electrical equipment out of order. In circumstances of this nature, trains can still run over the line, under Single Line Working conditions, with an inspector or relief signalman acting as Pilotman. I am acting as Pilotman, first taking an oil train up to the depot at Haydock, and then returning with the empty tank train on the adjacent line. At first it is quite a novelty, but later it becomes an utter bore, waiting for train crews to perform their duties and wangle half an hour here and there to boost their overtime!

Thick fog blankets the ground, and I notice a track circuit failure on the overlap of the Down Fast Intermediate Block Home Signal, but I am getting relieved by the night turn signalman. Not wishing to leave him in this situation, I volunteer to investigate the cause. Imagine my horror when I discover a 3in gap in a broken rail! Hastily, I make for the telephone on the IB Home Signal but, hearing a train approaching (on which line I do not know, but certainly not on the Down Fast Line anyway) I freeze in the 6ft between the Down Fast and Up Slow lines. Suddenly, out of the fog looms an express passenger train on the '**DOWN FAST LINE**' A series of bumps indicate that the train has become derailed, and I visualise the express spread-eagled across the tracks, as I slither over the uneven ballast, the displaced stones breaking the eerie silence. Arriving at the broken rail, nothing, and the train has gone! As I retrace my steps once more to the telephone, another train speeds past on the same line. Contacting the signalman, I give him a piece of my mind, going home thoroughly disgusted with his efforts.

Did you manage to answer the question of how many trains can be allowed onto the 'Chord Line?'

Please refer to the signal box diagram. The maximum number of trains, believe it or not is FIVE.

TRAIN No 1.

Driver obtains token at Edge Green.

Replaces token at Ashton-in-Makerfield.

Extracts Staff (type of token) at Ashton-in-Makerfield then travels to the Oil Terminal.

Returns to Ashton-in-Makerfield, being diverted to the left-hand road, via spring-loaded facing points.

Replaces Staff into instrument.

TRAIN No 2.

Driver obtains token at Edge Green.

Replaces token at Ashton-in-Makerfield, having taken the left-hand line, via the spring-loaded facing points, passing Train No 1 on the adjacent line.

Extracts Staff, then proceeds to the Oil Depot.

TRAIN No 3.

Driver obtains token at Edge Green.

Replaces token at Ashton-in-Makerfield, having taken left-hand line, via the spring-loaded facing points.

Ground Frame release is given, and the train is shunted into Lowton Metals Sidings, after which the Ground Frame is locked.

TRAIN No 4.

Driver obtains token at Edge Green.

Replaces token at Ashton-in-Makerfield, having taken left-hand line, via the spring-loaded facing points.

This train stands here, with Train No 1 still on the adjoining line.

TRAIN No 5.

Driver obtains token at Edge Green. Travels to Golborne Colliery Sidings to stable a train of empty wagons.

The engine working this train returns to Edge Green and the token is replaced into the instrument, allowing Train No 1 to leave Ashton-in-Makerfield.

Of the many times I have been employed at this signal box, the situation described above has occurred only once.

Leaving this work-house and continuing in a southerly direction for approximately 1½ miles, we arrive at:

GOLBORNE JUNCTION SIGNAL BOX

The Wigan Branch Railway's connection at Parkside was laid in 1832, followed by the Lowton West Curve in 1847, forming through lines from Wigan to the south and east. Golborne Junction signal box, ¾-mile west of Lowton Junction, along with Winwick Junction, came into being when the 2½-mile-long Winwick Branch was opened in 1864, by-passing Newton-le-Willows and Earlestown stations and the two severe curves on that route. All express passenger train services between Wigan and Warrington, and vice versa, are timed via this new line, relieving the congestion on the Liverpool to Manchester considerably. Today it retains the title the **'Winwick Branch',** although it forms part of the West Coast Main Line. Drivers and Guards must acquaint themselves with the diversionary route via Lowton because it is often used in cases of emergency.

Golborne Junction signal box. Courtesy of Dave Lennon.

In the distance, the Pennine chain forms a backdrop to the beautiful countryside here, and the abundant wildlife is a pleasure to watch, that is, when the frequent traffic flow diminishes temporarily. Behind the signal box is a large house in its own grounds, at the moment up for sale. I often wish that I could afford to buy it, but the pittance collected from the railway for my loyalty makes it only a dream.

Golborne Junction lever frame. Courtesy of Dave Lennon.

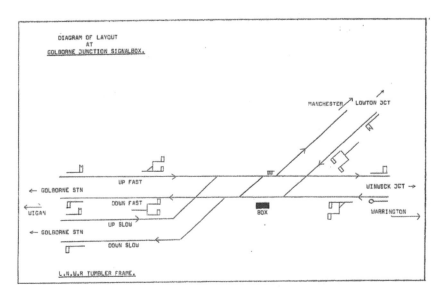

Golborne Junction signal box.

On the night turn the white back lights on the signals twinkle like stars against the blackness, indicating they are at danger. When a signal is cleared, this small bright light is obscured by a metal plate attached to the semaphore arm. **The dull illumination from Parkside No 1 signal box, seen across the fields, vanishes just after midnight: a sure sign the signalman is saving paraffin.**

Looking from the signal box to the right, around the curve can be seen:

LOWTON JUNCTION SIGNAL BOX

Lowton Junction signal box. Courtesy of Wigan World.

When the Lowton curve was laid from Parkside No 2 (now Newton-le-Willows) signal box in 1847, thus completing the triangle, this junction bore the name Preston Junction, this later being changed to the present name. It is locally known as the 'Royal' signal box, undoubtedly owing to the numerous photographs of His Majesty King George VI, Queen Elizabeth, Princess Elizabeth (later to become our Queen) and other members of the Royal Family alighting from trains at the station nearby. These photographs are pinned all over the walls, and even cover the Special Instructions to Signalmen (rules unique to this signal box, in addition to the mandatory general issue) but the Signalmen's Inspector does not object. In fact, every time he visits the signal box, a quick glance through them is a must.

Signalling trains under the Absolute Block Regulations between Newton-le-Willows and Golborne Junction signal boxes and that at Parkside Junction, around the east curve, this signal box operates both upper and lower quadrant semaphore signals from its LNWR Tumbler Frame. Overlooking Southwood and Parkside roads opposite the 'Bulls Head Hotel' (definitely out of bounds for signalmen) one may wonder at the reason for such a high structure, when the railway runs past far below. Obviously, it was due to the cuttings on each side restricting visibility, but little consideration was given to the signalmen having to climb the 30 steps or more, especially when humping buckets of coal for the stove! However, signalmen being members of such (I reiterate) a versatile breed, one has devised an ingenious method of making the task easier. A pulley wheel is attached to the outside wall, and a piece of rope stretches to ground level. After filling the bucket, a modicum of brute force is required to raise it up to window height. As consolation for all this effort, one gets a good view of Golborne Junction signal box and the main line traffic passing it.

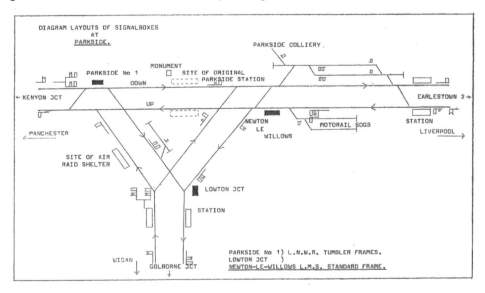

Locations of signal boxes in the Parkside area.

Leaving this signal box and taking the West Curve, we arrive at:

NEWTON-LE-WILLOWS SIGNAL BOX

This signal box stands on the Up line side of the Liverpool to Manchester Railway, and has an LMS Standard Frame controlling upper quadrant semaphore signals. In addition to signalling trains on the West Curve, it controls traffic into Parkside Colliery Sidings, the mine having been sunk recently, and most of the coal extracted is transported by rail to Fiddlers Ferry Power Station, between Widnes and Warrington. To the right of the signal box are two sidings which have fallen into disuse, but the implementation of Motorail trains has resurrected them. During the week several of these trains run to destinations as distant as Newton Abbot and Stirling. On the western side of the station, a few hundred yards to the right, a man-made embankment runs for a mile across an area known as **'The Mesnes'** (pronounced 'Mains') to Earlestown, which is situated atop a 1½-mile-wide ridge running from the north to south.

During Single Line Working, signalmen must be extra careful when signalling trains in the wrong direction, because in many circumstances there are no signals to prove the lie of the points, with visual observation being the only check. An incident occurs at this signal box that illustrates this point. A train is travelling over the single line in the wrong direction and becomes derailed at the switch diamonds (points) under the M6 motorway bridge, causing a tremendous amount of damage. The signalman claimed that the Pilotman travelling with the train gave the wrong information when withdrawing the Single Line Working to resume normal train running, but the signalman had to take the blame.

On the eastern side of the Parkside triangle is:

PARKSIDE No 1 SIGNAL BOX

Most certainly, after Edge Hill, the name Parkside must rank among the most famous in railway history, but for entirely different reasons.

On Wednesday 15th September 1830, the 31-mile railway line from Edge Hill, Liverpool to Manchester opened with great pomp and ceremony, seven trains leaving Crown Street station consecutively, the first travelling along the southernmost line, hauled by locomotive **'Northumbrian'**, driven by George Stephenson. The other six left on the adjacent track, led by the renowned **'Rocket' (winner of the Rainhill Trials the year before)** followed by the train hauled by **'Comet'.**

Aboard these trains were many dignitaries, including the Prime Minister (the Duke of Wellington); Lord Melbourne; Mr William Huskisson (MP for Liverpool) and Robert Peel (who, later, as Prime Minister, brought about the introduction of policemen). The forerunners of the modern day railway signalmen were, in fact, policemen, and like his 'Peelers' were called 'Bobbies', a name still in use today.

Facilities were made available here at Parkside, halfway between the two conurbations, for the locomotives to take on water, and hundreds of people turned up at the small countryside station to witness the spectacle. Little did they realise that their day would be marred by the tragic accident that befell Mr Huskisson. One of his legs was crushed when he was struck down by the train drawn by 'Rocket', and although taken by the 'Northumbrian' (detached from its train for the purpose) to Eccles for medical attention he later died of his injuries.

Parkside Junction signal box. Photo by J A Sommerfield, courtesy of Martin Bott.

Passing the Huskisson Memorial at Parkside. Courtesy of P Norton.

Spruced up in readiness for Royal Duties at Lowton Junction.

Courtesy of Wigan World.

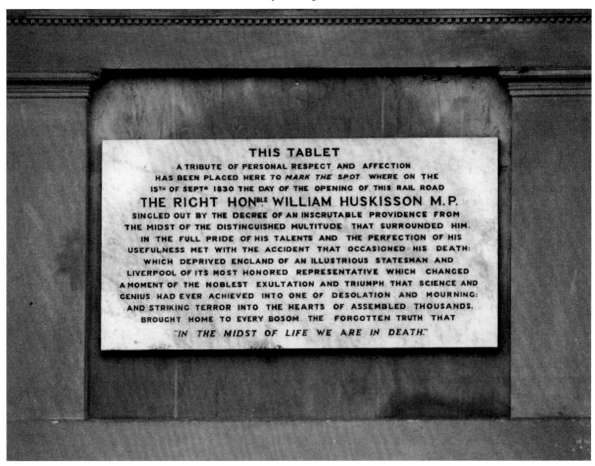

THIS TABLET

A TRIBUTE OF PERSONAL RESPECT AND AFFECTION
HAS BEEN PLACED HERE *TO MARK THE SPOT* WHERE ON THE
15TH OF SEPTR 1830 THE DAY OF THE OPENING OF THIS RAIL ROAD

THE RIGHT HONBLE WILLIAM HUSKISSON M.P.

SINGLED OUT BY THE DECREE OF AN INSCRUTABLE PROVIDENCE FROM
THE MIDST OF THE DISTINGUISHED MULTITUDE THAT SURROUNDED HIM.
IN THE FULL PRIDE OF HIS TALENTS AND THE PERFECTION OF HIS
USEFULNESS MET WITH THE ACCIDENT THAT OCCASIONED HIS DEATH:
WHICH DEPRIVED ENGLAND OF AN ILLUSTRIOUS STATESMAN AND
LIVERPOOL OF ITS MOST HONORED REPRESENTATIVE WHICH CHANGED
A MOMENT OF THE NOBLEST EXULTATION AND TRIUMPH THAT SCIENCE AND
GENIUS HAD EVER ACHIEVED INTO ONE OF DESOLATION AND MOURNING:
AND STRIKING TERROR INTO THE HEARTS OF ASSEMBLED THOUSANDS.
BROUGHT HOME TO EVERY BOSOM THE FORGOTTEN TRUTH THAT

"IN THE MIDST OF LIFE WE ARE IN DEATH."

The tablet on the memorial at the site of Parkside station.

Little is left of the original station, but in the undergrowth on the eastern side of Parkside Road bridge can be seen the narrow sandstone steps leading down to rail level. Opposite these, on the site of the accident, stands a monument serving as a reminder of its place in history.

Travelling on the railway at this time was an unknown and frightening experience, which can be judged from a passenger's account of the journey from Manchester to Liverpool.

A few minutes after seven we started, not very fast at first, but in less than five minutes, off we went like a shot from a gun. No sooner than we came to a field, it was a mile behind us. But this was nothing in comparison with meeting a long train from Liverpool. I was never so frightened in my life, and I shrank back horrified into my seat. I did not think the train was more than 2 seconds in passing. We were going at a full speed of 34 miles per hour. It's hard to explain the rapidity of moving. Several other trains passed us, but as I was aware of their approach they no longer surprised me as at first. The first 17 miles we did in 32 minutes.

I am much disappointed in the view of the countryside, the railway being cut through so many hills, you have frequently for miles only clay mounds on each side of you. Consequently, no splendid prospect can attract your attention, even if the railway is on a bridge or elevation above the usual tract of land. You are not charmed by the diversity of prospect which is to be met in ordinary stage coach travelling, that has a decidedly superiority of this new work of man.

I was one and a quarter hours going this 33 miles, the latter part of the journey being performed at a slow speed of 20 miles per hour. Previous to entering Liverpool you go through a dark, black, ugly, vile tunnel, 300 yards long, which has all the horrors of banishment from life, such as one I never want to go through again, unless my time is as precious as it was the other day.

In 1832 the Wigan Branch Railway Company built its railway from a junction connected to the Liverpool and Manchester Railway, here at Parkside, to Chapel Lane in Wigan. Close to this junction stands an ancient round water column, but not one of the originals in use at the time of opening of the line.

Parkside No 1 signal box (renamed Parkside Junction) after the renewal of Parkside No 2 and Newton-le-Willows Station signal boxes (the new box being named Newton-le-Willows) signals trains on the main lines between Kenyon Junction No 1 and Newton-le-Willows signal boxes, and on the branch line to Lowton Junction, under Absolute Block Regulations. The frame is of the LNWR Tumbler Frame type, and all signals are upper quadrant semaphores. The eastern curve of the triangle runs through a secluded cutting to Lowton Junction, and it is here during the Second World War that the Royal Trains were stabled on the occasions when His Majesty King George VI and Queen Elizabeth visited North-West England. An air-raid shelter was built alongside the railway track to accommodate them and their retinue, but I hardly think it would have been used. Still, it stands today unseen from the road, another reminder of days long past.

The signal box - or 'studio', would be more appropriate - has many paintings and pencil drawings on the wall and shelves, the artists being two relief signalmen who often work here. One is chiefly interested in landscapes, the other portrait work, and an indication of the standard reached is recognised when an exhibition is opened in the Wigan Library showing their work.

This picture was taken by the Author on 11th August 1968.

It is the last steam passenger train on Britain's standard gauge railway.

It had stopped here at Parkside in deference to William Huskisson MP, who was struck down by 'Rocket' on 15th September 1830 and died of his injuries later that night.

Hundreds of people attended the ceremony that day, and only recently I was made aware that among the people was none other than Ron Couchman (accompanied by his wife, Val), a signalman I met while I was working in Wigan No 2 signal box, and he in Springs Branch No 2. I lost contact with him in 1972, but he went on to much higher accomplishments than I, being the Area Manager at Wolverhampton, Birmingham New Street and Warrington, before finally retiring from Manchester Piccadilly station.

On the Down platform at Earlestown station. Courtesy of Ray Burgess.

Mausoleum of William Huskisson MP in St James Cemetery, Liverpool.

Courtesy of Liverpool Echo.

We now leave Parkside, and by way of 'The Mesnes' arrive at:

EARLESTOWN

In 1831 the Warrington and Newton Railway company forged a south-to-west link with the Liverpool & Manchester Railway at Newton (now Earlestown) Junction. Later a line was laid from the southernmost junction - a branch line, leading to the Haydock Collieries – and it ran directly north, passing over the Liverpool to Manchester route at right angles on the same level. The complexity of the railway here merited the building of five signal boxes.

Courtesy of 8D Association.

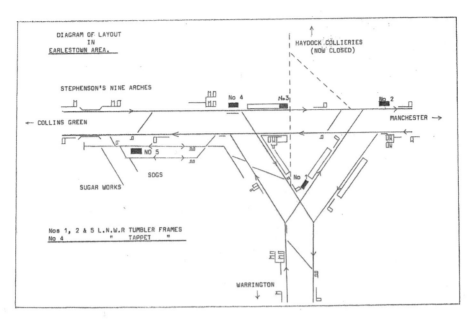

Locations of signal boxes in the Earlestown area.

EARLESTOWN No 1 SIGNAL BOX

This signal box is situated between the Up Manchester platform and the Haydock Collieries single line, at the highest point of a 1 in 84 gradient from Winwick Junction, 1½ miles away, and is dwarfed by the large gasholder nearby. It controls the southernmost junction, signalling trains under the Absolute Block Regulations to No 4 signal box, at the western tangent, No 2 to the east, and to Vulcan Bank signal box on the south side. Trains running on the single line to the Haydock Collieries line are signalled with Single Stroke Block Instruments. All the signal boxes at Earlestown have LNWR Tumbler Frames installed, with the exception of No 4, which has a Tappet Frame controlling a mixture of upper and lower quadrant signals. There is no regular passenger train service to the Liverpool line now, the St Helens to Warrington service having been recently withdrawn, but often, when work is taking place between Edge Hill and Weaver Junctions, this becomes the diversionary route. At Vulcan Bank, on the left, half way between Earlestown and Winwick Junction, is situated the Vulcan Foundry, connected via a level crossing to the main line which is under the control of Vulcan Bank signal box. Scores of steam locomotives were built here, both for British-owned railway companies and many other countries throughout the world, and those not possessing the standard wheel gauge were transported by road to Liverpool Docks for shipment. Hundreds of **Stanier 'Black Five'** locomotives were built at various locations, but this foundry holds the distinction of turning out the first one of the class **(No 5020).The engine depicted on the back cover of this book, was built here in 1935.** In addition, the very first **'Deltic'** locomotive was built here, which I was to witness on its first trial run on British Railways at Widnes when it became derailed in front of the signal box I was working in at the time. Owing to the demise of steam locomotives at the present time the foundry is engaged in the manufacture of marine engines.

Of the signal boxes at Earlestown, this one is probably the easiest, and I notice my opposite number at Wigan, Bramwell, works here on a regular basis which substantiates this, thereby avoiding the slogging at No 4.

Vulcan Bank signal box. Courtesy of Warrington Library.

At the Manchester end of the station platform stands:

EARLESTOWN No 2 SIGNAL BOX

The signalman working in this box is responsible for regulating freight traffic running in front of those carrying passengers, so a good deal of telephone work is involved, but the recessing of these trains is carried out at other signal boxes, because the layout here consists of only the junction leading from the Manchester direction to the south and west. About 1840 a junction was laid here, leading to the north-west, connecting with the Haydock Collieries line, but there are no visible signs remaining of the course it took.

Referring to the diagram of Earlestown, it will be noticed the crossover road controlled from this signal box is 'in rear' of the junction, which is unusual, but it is authorised to run trains from the yard at No 4 signal box wrong line to enable them to regain access to the right line, under normal signalling regulations. It was while working in this signal box I discovered three old square-shaped stone sleepers, along with a short stretch of fish-bellied rail in its chair.

On closer examination these proved to have been originally laid down by George Stephenson in 1830, and such was my interest in them that I approached the management asking if I could have them. After receiving this permission I donated them to the Ironbridge Gorge Museum in Shropshire, as they wished to put them on display.

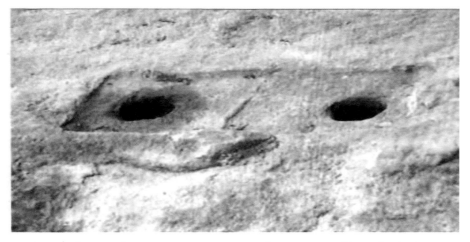

One of George Stephenson's sleepers at Earlestown. Photo by Author.

A small piece of fish-bellied rail found at Earlestown. Photo by Author.

Chair and piece of fish-bellied rail. Photo by Author.

The artefacts shown on this and the previous page can be seen in the Coalbrookdale Museum in Ironbridge, Shropshire.

So if you visit this museum, you will recall who found them buried in the thick undergrowth and, further, they may even have my name on them.

Some of these original sleepers have been incorporated into the buildings at Huyton station.

Towards the station platform on the Liverpool line stood:

EARLESTOWN No 3 SIGNAL BOX

The operation of this signal box is unusual in that it controls slotted signals in No 2 and No 4 signal boxes respectively, and also a signalman does not work in it; duties are carried out by a porter from the station who is not obliged to have a knowledge of all signalling regulations.

Referring back to Huyton Quarry Station signal box, and the duties of a Porter/Signalman, in most instances more time is spent working in the signal box, but here at Earlestown the opposite is true..

167

Earlestown No 3 signal box. Courtesy of P Norton Collection.

Slotted signals are introduced at locations where the signal boxes are closely spaced, as is the case here at Earlestown, with the distance being less than ½-mile between Nos 1, 2, 3, and 4.

Normally, the levers in No 3 signal box are operated to the 'Off' position, but the signal arms remain at danger until the signalman in either No 2 or No 4 pulls the corresponding lever in his box.

A majority of slotted signals installed on the railways appertain to distant signals, and not stop signals, as is the case here.

In the event of a train approaching to pass over the right angled crossing to or from the Haydock Collieries line, the levers would be put back, thus maintaining the protecting signals to danger. (The Haydock Collieries line, along with this unique signal box, finally closed on 17th February 1959.)

Train on Haydock Colliery line passing over the main line.

No 2 signal box can be seen in the background.

Photo by Alex Appleton.

168

At the end of the platform, adjacent to the overbridge is:

EARLESTOWN No 4 SIGNAL BOX

The **'Slogging Box'** is the best way to describe this particular signal box, and considering that most of the levers in the frame control points and signals close-by, above the normal physical exertion is necessary to operate them; but one must take the rough with the smooth and not be jealous of Bramwell at No 1 having an easy time.

I just wonder at times if he pays the Signalmen's Clerk.

In 1854, the **LNWR** acquired land nearby for building a factory to make and repair wagons, on a site west of the station on the Up line side. This signal box controlled the connections to the sidings, but in 1964 rationalisation forced its closure. Plain line replaced the points, leaving little evidence to suggest that the factory was ever railway connected. It also controls the original junction between the Liverpool to Manchester and the Warrington to Newton railways, which follows an extremely sharp curve from the west to south.

Push-and-pull train propelling into Earlestown station. Courtesy of Arthur Chester.

This curve was the subject of a dispute among the early railway companies, resolved only by the opening of the Britannia Bridge across the Runcorn Gap. In spite of this newer route from Liverpool to London, the junction here remains, one of the oldest in the world. Two loop lines run towards No 5 signal box from connections on the main line and also the curve. These facilitate the regulation of traffic travelling in the Liverpool and St Helens direction.

Permissive Block Regulations apply on these particular lines.

On the Down line side at the other end of the Goods Yard can be seen:

EARLESTOWN No 5 SIGNAL BOX

Situated ¾-mile from Earlestown station, towards Liverpool and between the Down line and No 1 loop, is No 5 signal box. It controls, in addition to the main lines and loops from No 4 signal box, leads into the Goods Yard and Warehouse sidings and connections into a private sidings; these are owned by a sugar refining company which takes its name from the valley it overlooks. One hundred yards away from the signal box are **'Nine Arches'**, George Stephenson's viaduct that passes over the Sankey Navigation Canal.

George Stephenson's 'Nine Arches'.

Courtesy of Warrington Library.

The viaduct is represented in many contemporary prints, and it remains much the same as it was then, though blackened with age, in the midst of beautiful unspoilt countryside.

My first visit here gave me the impression I was in a beachcomber's paradise, with literally thousands upon thousands of cockle, mussel and oyster shells strewn in the vicinity of the signal box. Useful as they are in giving adequate warning of persons intent on violating the signalman's privacy, by the tell-tale crunch, I could not understand why so many, many miles from the sea they should be here. The mystery is solved when I discover that one of our long service relief signalmen relishes the succulent innards then discards the non-edible parts at random, within throwing distance, onto the railway tracks.

Leaving 'Nine Arches', heading for Liverpool.

Courtesy of P Norton Collection.

170

Following the completion of a 6am to 2pm shift at Standish Junction, I am resting at home when the telephone rings. I am requested to book on duty at 9pm at this signal box for the night turn of duty. Normally, after midnight, traffic running along this line is minimal, so I accept, assuming that I will have an easy night.

Astride my Suzuki 'Hustler', I run into dense fog nearing the intersection of the M6 motorway and the East Lancashire Road. Eventually, I arrive at the signal box and find that there is no telephonic or telegraphic communication with anyone. Visibility is nil, and I hear a faint rumbling, but I cannot distinguish the direction from which it is coming, until, a few minutes later, I am joined by a fireman from a train which is standing at the Up line home signal. I am advised that all trains to and from Liverpool direction are being diverted via Earlestown, owing to a mishap on the Runcorn section.

Not having timetables for that particular section, it is impossible to know what is coming, a case of **working in the dark!**

In the event of the 'failure conditions' that exist here at present **Time Interval Working is instituted**.

This enables trains to enter into an advanced section if there is no communication between signal boxes.

Basically, before a second train is allowed to proceed, the normal running time is used as the criterion.

The driver of the train is cautioned past the starting signal at danger into the advanced section, but the following train must not be allowed to proceed forwards until the normal running time has elapsed, in addition, allowing for the train having been stopped at the home signal of the advanced signal box.

One can imagine the experience of not knowing when or whence a train is approaching, the only intimation being a member of the train crew coming to the signal box as there are no track circuits to rely on. This situation, coupled with the lack of sleep, forces me to sit in the cold at the top of the signal box steps in an effort to stay awake. In the early hours I actually fall asleep in the sitting position, only to be awakened by the vibrations of someone stepping onto the bottom of the steps, which in the eerie quietness resembles a violent earthquake!

The Sankey Canal, which is now disused, runs parallel to the Sankey Brook and was opened in 1757 to transport coal from the St Helens coalfield down to the River Mersey at Warrington. The coming of the railways did much to relegate this mode of transport to one used mainly for pleasure, although it took 100 years for the transformation to take place. The railways, on the other hand, have been in existence for 150 years, and vast changes have been made, especially in connection with signalling practices.

Today, we are entering the field of electronics, and where once signalmen pushed and pulled levers, they are learning about the operation of electrical apparatus. This technology is a far cry from the earlier days of the railway policemen, but things go wrong!

Minor faults occur often, causing nothing more than delay to traffic.

'Wrong side' failures of any equipment, however, are taken very seriously and are followed by thorough investigations to establish the cause. Such is the recent case involving a Newcastle to Liverpool express passenger train at Bold Colliery Siding signal box, between this signal box and St Helens Junction. The signal box at Bold Colliery is comparatively new and controls electrically-operated points from the main line into the colliery sidings. All signals are in the 'Off' position for the above-mentioned train, travelling along the main line towards St Helens Junction. The mechanical locking in the lever frame prevents the signalman from operating the points yet, as the train is approaching, and without explanation, the points turn and the train is diverted into the colliery sidings, in full view of the astounded signalman. The train is derailed, demolishing a signal post in the process. Edge Hill and Springs Branch cranes are required to attend, and Single-Line Working is brought into operation during the re-railing procedure.

Bold Colliery Sidings signal box.

Photo from the Tony Graham collection.

Incidents such as this – derailments, and the like - usually awaken the **'pen-pushers'**, snug in their offices, who make a beeline for the dust-covered rule books, thumbing through to find out whom to blame.

This is similar to what occurred at the Newton-le-Willows incident.

At first, it is bandied about that signalman's error is the cause, but when this is refuted, the innocent driver of the train is thought guilty.

It doesn't matter who is innocent or guilty to these people, as long as they 'find a baby'.

The electrical wiring connecting signal boxes and trackside equipment is laid within wooden trunking, and it is here that the cause of this particular incident is found. A nail securing the trunking cover has penetrated the wood and pierced a wire leading to the points, causing a short circuit which enables them to move to the reverse position.

So, no-one is 'nailed' after all, as the person responsible for knocking the nail in is unknown!

Imagine the thick-head in the office reporting the matter to his superior: 'We know who did it, and have managed to nail it onto a nail!'

Warrington to St Helens local train in Earlestown platform.

Photographer unknown

This completes the list of signal boxes I work on the former LMS.

A few miles on the other side of St Helens we find the

THE FORMER LANCASHIRE & YORKSHIRE RAILWAY.

RAINFORD JUNCTION SIGNAL BOX

The Signalmen's Inspector informs me that Token Working is to be implemented between Rainford Junction and Fazakerley station in north Liverpool next Monday, and that I am to go to Rainford and train the resident signalmen on the rules and regulations and operation of token instruments. He is not aware that **I have never set foot in Rainford Junction signal box, or in fact, worked with token instruments** connecting two signal boxes in my life! However, one must learn, so not wishing to lose face, off I go and bury my head in the appropriate regulations.

The author above the steps of Rainford Junction signal box. Courtesy of Joe Gerrard.

Edward Tyer patented the Electric Tablet Instrument in 1878, providing an efficient and safe signalling system for use on single-line railways. In 1921 a serious head-on collision occurred on the Cambrian Railway at Abermule, between Montgomery and Newtown, in Mid Wales. Unfortunately, 17 persons perished, owing entirely to violations of rules and regulations governing Electric Tablet Working. At the subsequent enquiry, recommendations were issued that all Electric Tablet Instruments should be installed within the controlling signal boxes and not at other locations as was the case at Abermule. In 1941 I had occasion to meet the mother of one of the victims in this train accident, and this meeting came to my mind on my first visit to Rainford Junction signal box, as I shall explain.

Lever frame in Rainford Junction signal box.

Photo by Terry Callaghan.

Electric Token instruments are reminiscent of the chocolate machines, coloured red, once seen outside many sweet shops, although somewhat larger. One of these machines is installed in each signal box controlling the entrance to the single line and contains a stipulated number of Tokens/Tablets.

The following system is adopted to release a token from the machine:

A train is offered to the next signal box by means of the bell code, using a plunger positioned on the instrument fascia, and as he accepts it the signalman at the other end of the section depresses an identical plunger on his instrument. A needle gives a visual indication that the token can now be removed.

The token resembles a large key, and it is the driver's authority to travel over the single line.

Token machine in Rainford Junction signal box. Photo by Terry Callaghan.

Scabbard with token. Photo by Terry Callaghan.

Another token cannot be removed from either instrument until the one extracted has been replaced in one or the other. Many single lines throughout the country are worked using Tyer's instruments, and on each section the tokens have different configurations, so you can imagine my surprise when I discover that the instruments to be used on the Rainford Junction to Fazakerley section originated from the Cambrian Railway at Montgomery! Normally, a scabbard fastened to the end a hoop is made available for the token to be inserted then handed to the driver of a train about to enter the single line, but in this instance none is forthcoming. So to save my energy, running up and down the signal box steps, I devise a method in the form of a stick to which I mount the token. As the train is passing slowly, the driver grabs the token and off he goes. For a train coming from the Liverpool direction it is necessary for the signalman to leave the box, cross over the lines, and collect the token from the driver. It is then placed it in the machine in readiness for the next time it is required.

Handing the token to driver of a train heading for Liverpool at Rainford Junction.

Notice the token scabbard is on the end of a stick: the

method I introduced when the single line was instigated.

Photo by Terry Callaghan.

At one time Rainford Junction was an important intersection, linking the L&Y Railway with the LNWR, running from Gerrards Bridge Junction via the village of Crank to Randle Junction and Skelmersdale beyond, thereby forming a triangle, with the latter, between Randle Junction and Bushey Lane Junction, passing over the L&Y ½-mile south-west of the station.

It was here at Randle Junction that crews working trains from Garston were relieved, because LNWR staff did not have route knowledge to travel over the L&Y Railway. L&Y staff travelled only as far as this junction, in the opposite direction, for the same reason.

Today, a very different picture presents itself.

All that remains here at Rainford Junction are the Up and Down lines from the Wigan direction, merging to form the new single line through to Fazakerley.

Rainford Junction of old. Photographer unknown.

The line to the left led to Randle Junction on the LNWR, whilst the line coming in on the right ran from Bushey Lane Junction to the west. The bridge in the background carried the line from Randle Junction to Bushey Lane Junction and, beyond, to Skelmersdale.

Houses have been built where the line deviated towards Bushey Lane Junction in the west, but behind the signal box the curve leading to Randle Junction is unaltered and derelict. At Fazakerley, a prefabricated railway track depot is situated, and trainloads of the completed sections are transported all over the North-West of England for relaying operations. Because of their extreme width, restrictions and special conditions, such as blocking the opposite line when running them, apply to these particular trains.

Between Rainford Junction and Orrell, traffic passes through the 959yd-long Upholland Tunnel, where the opposite line must be blocked before a **'pre-fab'** train is allowed into the section. Old track being transported back to the depot has many more restrictions than the new material as it tends not to be loaded as neatly.

Unfortunately the signalman here in this picture has to collect the token from the driver by hand, possibly because there is no stick long enough to reach the train from the signal box.

Photo by Terry Callaghan

Relief signalmen must work at any signal box in which they have been passed proficient by the inspector. Some are busy, others are not. This line is closed on Sundays except for engineering or Signal and Telegraph work. Such is the time that I am requested to work 12 hours, from 6pm one Sunday night. Relieving my mate, I settle down ready to tackle anything! At 11pm I ring the signalman at Fazakerley signal box to have a chat, but it is obvious to me that I have upset his somnolent interlude, so I apologise and hang up!

This telephone call is the full extent of my night's work: no bells; no trains; nothing!

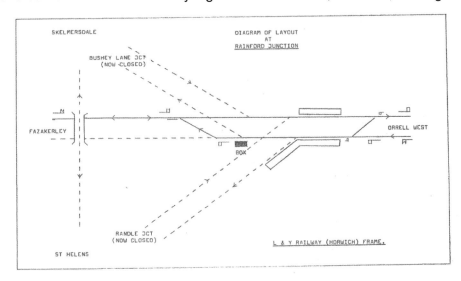

Rainford Junction signal box.

Three weeks pass and I am requested to repeat the same turn of duty. 11pm arrives, but I decide not to attempt to be sociable with the signalman at Fazakerley, and I complete my night's work just staying awake and brewing up? **(Do you really believe this?)**

Fazakerley Sidings West signal box.

A few days later, and an audible alarm indicates a malfunction on the Up line distant signal. As there are no trains in either section I decide to investigate the cause. Two hundred yards past the station overbridge on the Wigan side, I observe three men silhouetted against the night sky; two of them are on the embankment, the other up a telegraph pole cutting the wires. Returning to the signal box, I find all telephonic and telegraphic communication has been completely lost, so proceed to the public phone box nearby and report the matter to the police.

I duly report the matter the next day and receive a letter in acknowledgement, as follows:

FR.

British Railways London Midland Region

Rail House
Lord Nelson Street
Liverpool 1 L1 1JP.
051-709 8292 Extn. 2343.   R. H. N. Hardy Divisional Manager

Mr. A.J. Cook,
Relief Signalman
WIGAN.

y/r
o/r   WA/A.15/3.   Date 5th May, 1970.

Dear Mr. Cook,

BETWEEN WIGAN WALLGATE & RAINFORD JUNCTION. COMPLETE
BLOCK AND TELEPHONE FAILURE. 15.3.70.

I have been advised that when you were on duty at Rainford
Junction Signalbox on Sunday, 15th March, you became aware at 20.35 hours
of a complete block and telephone failure between your signalbox and
Wigan Wallgate Signalbox and you suspected that wire was being stolen.
After leaving your signalbox and making investigations, your suspicions
were confirmed when you observed two men on the embankment rolling up wire;
then you immediately reported the incident to the Police.

When the Police arrived you accompanied them and the men,
who were rolling up the wire, observed the police approaching and ran away,
out-running the officers. Then you yourself gave chase and caught
one of the men and handed him over to the Police who charged him with
stealing the copper wire.

I wish to take this opportunity to thank you for your
alertness, your prompt action in notifying the Police, and for chasing
the thieves and apprehending one, resulting in the recovery of the wire.
Your initiative is highly commendable and I shall be pleased if you will
accept the enclosed cheque for the sum of £10 as a token of appreciation.

I should also like to say that a record of the circumstances,
and a commendation will be made on your service record.

Yours sincerely,

R H N Hardy, Former Shed Master at Edge Hill, wrote a book **'Railways in my Blood'**.

178

This is the first signal box I have worked on the L&Y, the lever frame being built at their works at Horwich, near Bolton. The few signals left are of the upper quadrant semaphore type, and the signalling is under the Absolute Block Regulations between here and the next signal box:

ORRELL WEST SIGNAL BOX

The Lancashire and Yorkshire Railway was built in 1848 across undulating terrain, and reaches its highest point in West Lancashire on the eastern side of Upholland Tunnel. From here the line falls on a 1 in 91 gradient as far as Wigan Wallgate station. At Pemberton Junction a deviating line passes over a man-made embankment to Hindley where it re-joins the main line east of Wigan. These geographical differences gave rise to it being called the 'Switchback Railway'.

Orrell, famous for its Rugby Union Football Club was also, of more relevance to this work, the home of the first steam railway locomotive in Lancashire, built in 1812 and used at Orrell Colliery, itself long since closed. I live in Orrell in a railway-owned cottage built in the 16th century, long before the railway was laid through a cutting at the bottom of the garden. The cottage near Orrell station in Church Street, must rate as one of the oldest in the district. **It has now been demolished.**

Orrell West signal box is situated in a small cutting just outside Upholland Tunnel, and it controls traffic into a coal yard on the Up line side. The lever frame, an L&YR type, is connected to upper quadrant semaphore signals. Two signal boxes were built at Orrell, the one east of the station having only recently been closed permanently. It controlled the exit from a loop line running from Winstanley Colliery signal box, itself now demolished.

A feature of the L&Y was the number of running loop lines laid. Freight traffic would be regulated into them, awaiting the passage of a passenger train, and would then be allowed to travel only as far as the next loop line, in a leap-frog fashion. Today this method of working is seldom seen, mainly owing to pit closures in the area.

Referring to the naming of signal boxes, it will be noticed that the LNWR adopted a numerical system when building signal boxes close to one another, whereas the CLC used the Cardinal Points. The Lancashire & Yorkshire hierarchy obviously could not make up their minds, because here at Orrell the cardinal points were used, but only a few miles away at Hindley they bear numbers!

Unfortunately, I do not often get the opportunity to work this signal box, but when I do it is very beneficial to me because (1) I have not far to travel, and, most importantly (2) I get paid travelling time from Wigan!

The next signal box along the line towards Wigan is:

PEMBERTON JUNCTION SIGNAL BOX

At one time this signal box, east of the station and overlooking the Douglas valley, controlled two geographical junctions, but now it can only be described as a block post signalling trains under the Absolute Block Regulations between Orrell West and Wigan Wallgate signal boxes, with upper quadrant semaphore signals, from an LMS Standard Frame.

One of the defunct junctions formerly diverted traffic towards Bryn Junction on the LMS but, as mentioned earlier, this line closed in April 1959. The second, built in 1889, served two purposes: first, it becomes a diversionary route (by-passing the busy station at Wigan); and secondly, it was later used by coal trains destined for Westwood Park Power Station, one mile away. Today, the line is no longer used, and Hindley No 3. at the eastern end. and Westwood Park signal boxes have been demolished.

Approaching Pemberton Junction signal box from Liverpool. Photographer unknown.

After training this signal box I am called upon to work here on only one occasion, unlike the next one along the line, which is:

WIGAN WALLGATE JUNCTION SIGNAL BOX

When I was promoted to Relief Signalman, Special Class, at Wigan, the Signalmen's Inspector required me to train only Wigan No 1 and Standish Junction signal boxes in order to qualify for the rate of pay for the job, as mentioned earlier.

This signal box, worked by two men on each turn, is the next in importance in the Wigan area, but it is at my home station, and remuneratively is not worth my while training it, there being no travelling time payments unlike the 40 others I might cover. I make up my mind to train as many of these as possible, thereby lessening the chance of me being requested to train this signal box.

The Signalmen's Inspector is adamant in attempting me to train this signal box, and when I am spare (not very often) his first thought is to request me to report for training. I duly accept, by adding, **'Give me three continuous weeks to learn it then, boss'.**

As instructed I report for the agreed three weeks' training. **(He's got me!)**

After two days of learning, the telephone rings and the Signalman's Clerk tells me to go home and report for duty at Golborne Junction signal box for the night turn at 10pm. This pattern repeats itself many times until the inspector gives it up as a bad job! **(I know it is!)**

Original signal box at Wigan Wallgate Junction.   Courtesy of Wigan World.

'Ooch I, Mon.'

'Flying Scotsman' passing under the West Coast Main Line.

Courtesy of Cyril Peers.

Wigan Wallgate signal box. Courtesy of Cyril Peers.

Thus, of all the signal boxes in the Wigan area I manage to elude this one, much to my financial advantage. Nevertheless, I have a fair knowledge of the traffic dealt with here because, as a signalman in Wigan No 2, I had a panoramic view of all the area it covered and, between you and me, I could have trained it in about a week, but the inspector didn't know that!

Wigan Wallgate station from West Coast Main Line, 1964. Photo by Author.

The two platform and bay lines are sandwiched between the Up and Down Through lines which extend from the LMS main line overbridge to the east side of Wallgate road bridge. A small siding with a turntable road and excursion platform lies between the high main line embankment and the Down Through line; it is chiefly used to stable coaching stock during the night and permanent way material trains. Directly opposite, with connections from the Up Through line, are the Fish Sidings.

The excursion Platform was often used to stable Bertram Mills' Circus trains, and it was entertaining, from our vantage point in Wigan No 2, to see elephants and other animals being de-trained.

In the centre of the bifurcation, west of the main line, stands Wallgate signal box, built at the same time as No 1 and No 2 signal boxes. It is of similar design, containing identical equipment *i.e.* an NX Panel, Colour Lights and Floodlit Ground signals

Signalman Cyril Peers in Wigan Wallgate signal box. Courtesy of H.G.

Prescott Street Locomotive Shed, between the Liverpool and Southport lines, closed on the advent of diesel power, but today the site is being used as a storage depot for overhead line equipment and wiring trains in connection with the West Coast Main Line electrification scheme. Where once the sky was filled with columns of smoke from the locomotives, there now rise gigantic piles of grey-painted steelwork. Across from the depot, on the Up Southport line side, are three sidings running parallel, used principally for stabling and servicing DMUs.

Wigan Wallgate signal box, 2014, from a similar position to the previous picture.

Courtesy of Cyril Peers.

'Royal Train' on the through road at Wigan Wallgate.

Courtesy of Mick Langton.

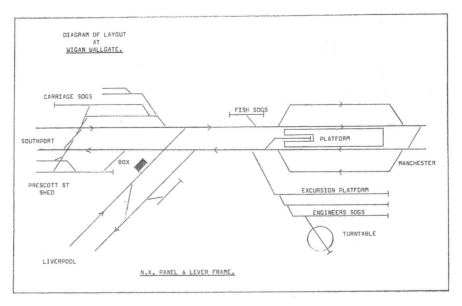

Wigan Wallgate signal box.

Towards Southport on the Up line side is:

DOUGLAS BANK SIGNAL BOX

This signal box is aptly named, being situated close to the River Douglas and the Leeds & Liverpool Canal, threading their way westwards through charming countryside.

The distinctive lean of the structure away from the railway is due to an embankment slip, and it becomes more noticeable when one walks uphill to answer the block instrument. Pulling the levers can be quite hazardous too because of the tendency to let go too soon after they are fully over, and continuing the natural backward momentum. This can be arrested only by crashing into the nearest obstacle, be it the stove or handy ambulance box, hanging on the back wall!

Douglas Bank signal box.

Courtesy of Lawrence Thorpe.

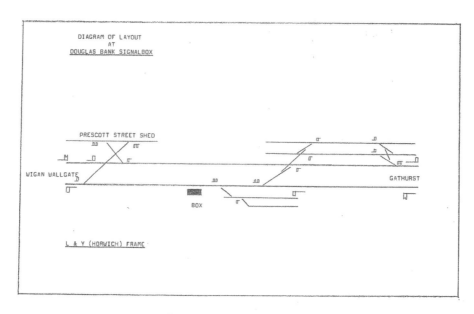

Douglas Bank signal box.

Several signalmen have received minor injuries whilst working in the **'Leaning box of Wigan'**, and it should be noted that the management do not pay danger money at all! It controls, in addition to the Up and Down lines, the western connections of the old locomotive shed at Prescott Street, signalling all the electrification traffic.

Absolute Block Regulations apply, and the upper quadrant semaphore signals are controlled from an L&Y Standard Frame.

The next signal box along the line, again in the Southport direction, is unique and must claim a rightful place in railway history. It is:

THE SIGNALBOX THAT NEVER WAS!

No signalmen ever trained or worked this signal box. In fact, there are no points or signals to operate. The mystery of the 'signal box that never was' will now be revealed!

Negotiations took place between representatives of British Railways and the well-known 'beans' processing firm, mentioned earlier, who have premises in the Kitt Green area of Wigan, with a view to a railway connection from the factory to the Southport line between Douglas Bank and Gathurst. Agreement was reached that British Railways would finance and build the signal box containing an LMS Standard Frame, provided that the firm paid for the connections and the line leading to the factory.

Up went the brick-built signal box on the Down line side, in readiness, but that was all! The plans never materialised and the signal box was demolished before it even opened. Its name:

BRANCKERS SIDING SIGNAL BOX

Branckers Siding signal box. Courtesy of H.G.

Continuing along this line we arrive at:

GATHURST STATION SIGNAL BOX

It is similar to Lowton Junction signal box in so many ways, even down to the pulley-wheel method of raising coal to the operating floor level. This signal box, 3 miles from Wigan, stands high above the canal and river valley amidst countless trees which form a landscape of great beauty, even though the massive M6 motorway viaduct intervenes in the distance.

Basically a block post, it does control a ground frame allowing traffic, chiefly gunpowder, into a privately-owned quarry to the east. The next two signal boxes that once stood further along the line - Appley Bridge East and West - have recently been closed permanently.

The Douglas valley is bounded by Billinge and Parbold Hills, and between these is:

PARBOLD STATION SIGNAL BOX

Parbold village, opposite Ashurst Beacon, is situated in the valley where the terrain levels into the plain that stretches 11 miles to Southport and the sea. It was on this section of line that the first DMUs were tested prior to being introduced into regular railway service. The station signal box controls level crossing gates in the centre of the picturesque village. In addition, two Automatic Half-Barrier crossings and three Red/Green Miniature Light crossings are located in the section to Burscough Junction. Level crossings equipped with Automatic Half-Barriers are operated by approaching trains activating treadles and, providing there is no emergency or a need to work the barriers manually, the signalman works normally.

Parbold Station signal box. Courtesy of Lawrence Thorpe.

The barriers are raised to a vertical position allowing road traffic through whenever the section is clear, and telephones are *in situ* for the use of the public to enable them to contact the signal box if the need arises. Level crossings equipped with miniature Red/Green warning lights can have gates or barriers, which are operated by rail users, but do not always have telephones installed.

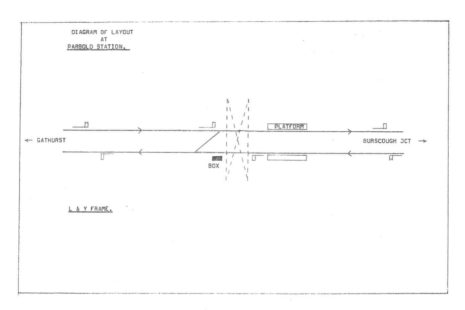

Parbold Station signal box.

An interesting feature on this line is that there are five different types of level crossings within a space of two miles:

1 **Manned level crossing, with block instrument indications**

2 **Controlled from a signal box**

3 **Automatic Half-Barriers**

4 **Occupational crossing (used by farmers)**

5 **Miniature Red/Green warning light crossing.**

Snow on the early turn at Parbold station. Courtesy of Lawrence Thorpe.

On the crossing controlled from the signal box a nasty accident occurs, which is worthy of mention; but first I must set the scene. The minor road passing the signal box, linking the two sections of the village on either side of the railway, is connected to the main Wigan to Southport road 200yd away. There being a 'plutocratic fraternity' living here, most are car owners, which accounts for the heavy usage of the crossing. Railway traffic is light, with only one or two freight trains running daily between the half-hourly passenger services.

The block section from Wigan Wallgate to this signal box is 7 miles long when the intervening signal boxes are switched out of circuit. Freight train running times vary, and one tends to guess when to open the gates so as not to stop them. Many times I have pulled off the signals for a train, only to watch a build-up of road vehicles occupied by irate and impetuous drivers.

The wheel for opening and closing the gates in Parbold signal box.

Courtesy of Lawrence Thorpe.

In one particular incident the signalman here has a freight train approaching, with all the signals in the clear position. Several minutes pass, and the sound of an ambulance's siren attracts his attention. Glancing at the clock, he considers that he has time to allow it through by replacing the signals to danger and opening the gates. Unbeknown to him, a mini-car close behind the ambulance follows the ambulance onto the crossing.

The train crashes through the gates and collides with the car, carrying it 100yd down the line before finally coming to a stand. Out of the mangled wreckage steps the lady driver who, miraculously, survives this horrendous experience.

The next signal box along the line towards Southport is Burscough Bridge Junction.

Burscough Bridge Junction signal box. Courtesy of Ron Couchman.

Signalman Denis Crombleholme, at Burscough Bridge Junction signal box.

Courtesy of Ron Couchman.

Only a few miles to the west of Burscough is Southport station.

It is probably one of a few in the world that can boast four trains leaving the station platforms at the same time, because of the complexity of the track layout.

Southport station. Courtesy of Ron Couchman.

Parbold Station signal box is the last one on this line towards Southport covered by Wigan relief signalmen, so we will now go to the eastern extremities of the area in the Manchester direction.

Crow Nest Junction Signal Box (administrated from Manchester) is now the Fringe Box to the Warrington power signal box.

Crow Nest Junction signal box. Photo H.G.

Crow Nest Junction old signal box Photographer unknown.

Old Crow Nest Junction. Courtesy of Ron Couchman.

HINDLEY

This area of the former L&Y has been altered drastically, with numerous tracks abandoned.

HINDLEY No 1 SIGNAL BOX

This signal box, on the Manchester side of the station, is fairly new, having an LMS Standard Frame controlling upper quadrant semaphore signals and signalling trains between Crow Nest Junction and Hindley No 2 signal boxes, under Absolute Block conditions.

I work only two turns of duty in this signal box before it finally closes.

Towards Wigan, on the other side of the station is:

HINDLEY No 2 SIGNAL BOX

This signal box, out in the wilds, at one time boasted two signalmen and a box lad on each turn of duty, and it has over 80 working levers in an L&Y Standard Frame.

Hindley No 2 signal box.   Courtesy of Cyril Peers.

Passing Hindley No 2 signal box. Courtesy of Wigan World.

Now, it controls traffic only on the Up and Down lines, and via a junction to De Trafford Junction on the LMS. I would have enjoyed working here in its hey-day with the quadrupled lines and numerous sidings, but now the repetition bores me.

Nearer Wigan once stood:

HINDLEY No 3 SIGNAL BOX

Mentioned earlier, this signal box has recently been demolished. It controlled the junction diverting traffic onto the now-closed Westwood Park deviating line, but I never had the opportunity to train this signal box, though I do work in the next one along the line:

INCE STATION SIGNAL BOX

Purely a block post, this signal box stands on the station platform signalling trains between Hindley No 2 and Wigan No 1 signal boxes, and it is not one of my favourites.

This completes the signal boxes under the Wigan administration and, to end this chapter, a few amusing anecdotes. On lines where traffic is light, it is difficult at times to keep awake throughout the night.

Such is the case with a young signalman who is overcome with the desire to sleep, knowing that a block bell or telephone ringing will arouse him. He does not bargain for the stationmaster, after an evening on the binge, deciding to make an out-of-hours visit to the signal box. Being a humanitarian **(as all bosses are?)** he leaves the signalman prostrate on the locker without disturbing him, though he signs the Train Register as proof of his presence. Making his way to the next signal box along the line, he rings **'Dream Boy'**, and enquires what he is doing.

'I am reading the Block Book, Sir,' comes the reply,

'That's very good,' says the stationmaster, adding:

'Just take a look at your Train Register.'

'Good Night, I will see you tomorrow!'

Some stationmasters go to the extreme, spying on signal boxes in an attempt to catch the signalman breaking rules and regulations. Our monastic occupation is bad enough without intrusions of this nature; however, such actions sometimes backfire on the 'rubberneck'. One such incident concerns a signalman who, in the gloomy twilight, observes the stationmaster lurking among the cabbages in a farmer's field opposite the signal box intent on violating his privacy. Like a good protector of someone else's property, the signalman calls the police.

Several cars arrive at the scene and the stationmaster is apprehended. One can imagine the feeble excuse he offers to the police officers, who duly take their captive to the signal box for identification.

'I've never seen him before in my life,' says the signalman.

With that, the stationmaster is frog-marched into custody to the obvious delight of other signalmen hearing about it! Reprisals were forthcoming, as might be expected, but no further reports are received of trespassers on the farmer's field!

Lostock Junction signal box. Courtesy of Mick Langton.

CHAPTER ELEVEN

FROM LEVERS TO BUTTONS

1972-80

WARRINGTON POWER SIGNALBOX

Three officials sit behind a large polished mahogany table piled high with reams of paperwork, together with a wooden block with rows of holes drilled into it, a small box of pegs and a telephone.

'Good morning, Signalman. You are here today for us to consider your application for a position in Warrington power signal box,' says the one sitting in the centre.

'I am Mr So-and-so,' (Oh! Another!) and *'This is Mr So-and-so,'* and '*Yes*!' another!

After these introductions he goes on to inform me I am eleventh in order of seniority.

'In front of you is a block of wood with a hundred holes in it; a box containing a corresponding number of pegs, and a telephone.'" Continuing:

'During the interview you must place the pegs into the holes, and if the phone rings, answer it.'

'What kind of game is this?' I think to myself.

'The object is to test your co-ordination when carrying out more than one task at the same time,' I am told.

'Could you please tell us details of your railway career?'

'I started as a signal box lad in Edge Hill No 13, etc. etc.' and in no time at all I have filled all the holes, so I begin to take the pegs out.

'The signalling in the new signal box is under Track Circuit Block Regulations, and we are going to ask a few questions about them.'

All three begin to fire questions at random, as I start refilling the block.

'Thank you signalman. We will let you know of our decision.' **(The phone did not ring.)**

Two weeks later I receive a letter instructing me to report for training at Warrington Central station. Walking up the sloping road adjacent to Central station, two large buildings face me, each bearing huge signs relating to the Cheshire Lines Committee Railway. In the smaller of these, a room has been provided for the 13 Signalmen and six Controllers to learn the theory of panel-operated power signalling. Around three walls of this large room is a facsimile of the panel at present being installed in the signal box at Warrington Bank Quay station.

My first impression is that I will never learn this lot!

Two inspectors have the unenviable task of training us for this new concept in railway signalling. One of them, Norman, I know very well because he worked as a relief signalman at Wigan a few years ago; Ron, the other, I met on several occasions supervising movements of exceptional loads travelling by rail.

Hundreds of buttons, 1in in length, cover the 7ft-high panel fascia upon which is drawn a coloured diagram of the area controlled (on a grey background), each button corresponding to a signal location, though not to scale. The panel is of the NX type, with Entrance and Exit buttons.

(An entrance button is depicted by a black arrowhead pointing in the direction of travel, whilst an exit button carries an outlined clear arrowhead.)

When an entrance button is pressed, an intermittent white flashing light indicates that the electrical apparatus is prepared to function. When the exit button is then pressed, a row of white lights appears on the diagram indicating the route selected. All points connections within the given route are set automatically to their correct position and proved electronically before the signal will clear.

Individual Point Switches **(IPSs)** are placed along the top of the panel, and any signalman of small stature must stand on tip-toe to reach them. Point switches have three indications; **to the left 'N'. (normal), to the right 'R'. (reverse), and central position 'OOC' (out of correspondence).**

When an intermittent white light flashes in the 'OOC' position it indicates a malfunction, either physical or electrical, which requires immediate attention, for no trains can pass over the points involved unless they have been clipped and scotched.

A fault of this nature can cause serious delay to train movements.

Provided no route is set, IPSs can be operated for testing purposes, etc.

We begin by setting routes, with imaginary buttons, and playing with imaginary trains on the paper diagram, going through all the functions as if they were on the proper panel.

New terminology, such as Remote Control Systems and their overrides, Swinging Overlaps, Opposing Route Selection, Comprehensive Approach Locking, Route Oversetting, and much, much more, must be learnt in great detail during the training period.

After a few weeks confined to the classroom, practical training commences at Derby power signal box, on a panel similar in design to, though somewhat smaller than, the one at Warrington. I myself cannot see the benefit of this exercise, owing to the different geographical location, but staying in a POSH hotel for 6 days breaks the monotony of pressing buttons at St Mary's (somewhere in Derby).

Warrington power signal box controls a vast area stretching from Bank Top, Coppull, in the north, to Preston Brook in the south, a distance of some 30 miles; added to this are the Chat Moss route from St Helens Junction to Astley and all the associated feeder lines, making a total of 64 miles of 'geographical' railway. **(The total track mileage is some 125 miles.)** A major part of the training programme is familiarisation with the traffic density and movements at different locations covered by the new panel.

Having worked in every signal box north of Winwick Junction, my task is easier compared to, say, the two signalmen coming from Birkenhead who have no knowledge of the area at all.

Fringe signal boxes on the extremity of the power box area include:

Preston power signal box

Weaver Junction

Wigan Wallgate

Crow Nest Junction

St Helens Shaw Street Station

Rainhill Station

Astley Level Crossing

Norton Station

Sutton Oak Junction

Arpley Junction.

A visit was arranged to all of the above locations.

Preston power signal box. Courtesy of Ray Burgess.

Weaver Junction power signal box.

Courtesy of Ron Couchman.

Panel in Weaver Junction power signal box.

Courtesy of Ray Burgess.

Crow Nest Junction signal box. Courtesy of H.G.

Lever frame in Crow Nest Junction signal box.

Courtesy of H.G.

St Helens Shaw Street signal box.

Photo by Anthony Flusk, courtesy of 8D Association.

Rainhill Station signal box.

Photo by Nigel Mundy, courtesy of 8D Association.

Astley Level Crossing signal box. Courtesy of H.G.

Old and new signal boxes at Norton station.

Courtesy of Dave Lennon.

Sutton Oak Junction signal box. Photo by David A Ingham

Arpley Junction signal box. Photo by David A Ingham

Norton Level Crossing signal box. Courtesy of Ray Burgess.

The signals at Norton Crossing signal box, between Weaver and Acton Grange junctions, are controlled from this signal box; but the small signal box here actually controls the gates for the crossing.

My first view of Chat Moss, on the Liverpool to Manchester main line, was from 2,000ft on the end of a parachute, after jumping from a United States of America C82 Flying Boxcar aircraft in 1950, and I recall the landing adjacent to the railway line, quite close to Astley Level Crossing. It was very difficult traversing the large morass of soft, damp peat, with all the paraphernalia of an airborne soldier, and I fully understand the formidable obstacle that Chat Moss provided when the pioneers reached it in 1829/30, because one sinks at least 8in with each step taken. To build this railway, many tons of cotton bales and wattles were deeply buried before a foundation strong enough to support the weight of a fully laden train was successfully completed.

The training programme allows for signalmen to travel in the driver's cab on any train throughout the power signal box area, and one can hear and feel the change from consolidated track to that running over the springy moss.

Of the signalmen training, two, as already mentioned, originate from the Birkenhead area, two from Wigan, two from Winsford, and the rest from signalmen's positions in the Warrington area.

I spend three weeks' familiarisation at each of the following signal boxes:

Warrington No 1

Warrington No 2

Walton Old Junction

Winwick Junction, and **Acton Grange Junction.**

Winwick Junction signal box. Photo by Dave Lenon.

In addition, I walk through the sections taking notes of signal locations, gradients and any item that could possibly assist me in my future duties.

Returning to Acton Grange Junction for a moment.

It was here a few weeks ago that a freight train broke into two portions, the rear one running back towards Weaver Junction, before becoming derailed at catch points 200yd from this signal box. The signalman, rightly, sent the 'Train out of Section' on seeing the tail-lamp of this train, and accepted 1S06 20.20 Euston to Inverness express passenger train. Although the emergency regulations were carried out, the express could not be stopped and the luckless driver was killed in the ensuing collision.

'Winwick Junction' by John Harrison, railway artist.

Occasionally, messages are sent requesting attendance at the classroom for more theory, general discussions, and inquisitions to assess the level of learning. During the training period only one visit to the new £4,000,000 signal box, built by the Westinghouse Company, is allowed, because hundreds of technicians are engaged in installing the vast amount of electrical equipment.

After six months of brainwashing, two examinations follow. The first is in front of our tutors who, I must say, worked hard throughout. A measure of their success can be judged by the fact that only one signalman failed to complete the course, not, I hasten to add, because of his lack of signalling ability, but simply because he could not adapt to modern signalling techniques after a lifetime spent 'bashing levers about'. The second examination at Liverpool, in front of the 'big-wigs', is not as severe as the first; understandably so, because Ron's and Norman's reputations are at stake. However, it is bad enough!

The big day is imminent; next Monday actually, but first, one more day in the classroom. At 2pm precisely, information is received that the Ministry of Transport Inspectors have postponed the opening of the power signal box for six weeks! This, after gearing up to it and, to make matters worse, I am requested to visit Winwick Quay signal box on the way home because I will be working 12 hours early turn next week.

WINWICK QUAY SIDINGS SIGNAL BOX

Monday morning arrives, and after one hour's training I am in the middle of it.

Winwick Quay Sidings signal box. Courtesy of Ron Couchman.

Trains, trains and more trains; my enthusiasm wanes, the Train Register begins to lose its importance, so I devise a way of excusing myself from this chore, by writing across the page:

NO FURTHER BOOKING. PEN RUN OUT OF INK [!]

'That's another job out of the road.' ('These new Biros do run out of ink sometimes!')

Three weeks are spent in this workhouse - another on the long list of signal boxes in which I have worked - but a welcome change is nigh.

Report to Pocket Nook Junction signal box, St Helens, next Monday morning for 12 hours of duty.

POCKET NOOK JUNCTION SIGNAL BOX

The only time I have seen this signal box has been through the window of a passing train, but mine is not to reason why! I remember a few years ago, being on the carpet, for doing such as this!

Pocket Nook Junction signal box. Courtesy of Robert Humm collection.

However, I am three weeks working in this boring place, and that's enough for me. Six weeks have passed. Let us hope there has been no further postponement and the power box will soon be in operation.

Installation of the vast array of electrical equipment is achieved in three different ways:

First, by direct wiring in the Warrington area.

Secondly, to five Remote Control areas *viz.* Earlestown, St Helens Junction, Parkside,

Bamfurlong and Garswood.

These are so wired that the signalman can bypass the normal control system, by operating the Remote Control Override Switches (RCOs); Alternative Route Selection Switches (ARSs) are used in conjunction with the RCOs at junctions during an equipment failure.

At Wigan the **Time Division Multiplex System** is adopted - **the third method** - and the signalman can select one of two signalling controls, wired up to the remote control cabin south of North Western station, adjacent to Chapel Lane Goods Yard. **(This control system is far superior to that in other locations, where Remote Control Overrides are installed.)**

In addition, three indication systems transmit to the signal box panel the exact location of trains in the area.

Great care must be taken before altering these controls, because any signal in the 'Off' position is automatically replaced to danger when the switch is operated.

In the event of a failure in the electrical equipment, the Alternative Control Switch can be operated, and normal working resumed.

The Remote Control Override Switches are entirely different because, once the switches have been operated, the indications on the panel cannot be relied upon, and hand signalmen must be employed at strategic junctions to observe the passage of trains. This causes heavy delay to traffic until the necessary men are in position.

Signalmen Eddie Moseley and George Bowen on the panel in

Warrington power signal box. (September 1972.) Photo by Author.

The big day is imminent, AGAIN

Yes? Warrington power signal box is to be opened in three stages, instead of the planned five.

The first covers an area from Preston Brook to Acton Grange Junction, a distance of only a few miles, on straight track. For two weeks the observation of track circuits and of descriptions stepping from signal to signal - and supping tea - are the main occupations. Seeing trains passing the signal box at speed, under the control of the existing manual signal boxes, seems strange, and soon becomes boring!

However, things are soon anything but boring! The second stage has begun in a chaotic way.

Acton Grange to Golborne station, Rainhill to Astley, and all connecting lines between these points come under the control of the power signal box, and this is only the beginning. Two weeks later, the third and last stage is implemented in utter chaos, which continues for a long period.

Over 40 manual signal boxes have been closed, making more than 160 signalmen redundant under this scheme. The complement of 13 signalmen working in this signal box has been increased to 15 in the past couple of weeks. (Still not enough?)

In fact, these 15 signalmen are theoretically doing the work of 160 men for a paltry £38 basic pay per week, per man.

One of the signalmen sums up the operating of the panel to a member of management thus:

'You can train monkeys to press buttons. All we want in here is to be given bloody bananas, and we'll look like them!'

How right he is, but the truth of the matter is that if we had been given bananas, no time would have been allowed to eat them.

It is 40 years since the RSNT advocated meal breaks in large signal boxes, but from its inception the management here has disregarded our efforts to negotiate on this matter, treating the signalmen as if they were animals, rather than human beings.

These signalmen have been selected on seniority to open the power box in September 1972.

Back Row. Left to right:

Jim Kennedy	Charlie Robinson	Henry Houghton	Eric Mills	George Bowen	Eddie Chadwick
Winsford	Warrington	Wigan	Warrington.	Winsford	Warrington

Middle Row. Left to right:

Billy Baines	Frank Brocklehurst	Norman Carter	Ron Woods	Jimmy Topping
Birkenhead	Warrington	(Tutor)	(Tutor)	Warrington
		Wigan	Southport	

Front Row. Left to right:

Bill Wolstenholme	Tony Cook	Johnny Jackson.	Eddie Moseley
Birkenhead	Wigan	Warrington	Warrington

The panel is divided into three sections for operating purposes, with one signalman to each panel section.

The South panel controls the lines from Preston Brook to Winwick Junction, on the West Coast Main Line (WCML); Norton Station to Acton Grange on the Chester line, and Walton Old Junction to Arpley Junction on the Manchester Low Level line, including the marshalling yards at Walton Old Junction and Arpley.

The Middle panel controls an area from Winwick Junction to Golborne Station on the WCML, and Rainhill Station to Astley, including Earlestown and Parkside junctions, on the Liverpool to Manchester line.

The North panel includes from Bamfurlong Junction to Bank Top at Coppull on the WCML; Crow Nest Junction to Wigan Wallgate on the former Lancashire & Yorkshire Railway; Springs Branch to St Helens Shaw Street Station and the branches to Bickershaw Colliery and the Haydock Oil Terminal.

A massive electrical failure occurs in the Wigan area, 14 miles from Warrington, creating havoc among the train services. After several hours an investigation proves that rats have taken a liking to the rubber on the electric cabling!

On Christmas Day the railways shut down, but it is necessary to book staff on, for security reasons, at this establishment. Feeling a little bored on my own, I decide to operate the Remote Control Override Switch at Bamfurlong. Normally, after two minutes, pre-selected routes set up automatically, in a set sequence, but five minutes pass without any of the usual visual indications being received in the signal box, so I return the switch to normal and forget about it.

On Boxing Day the trains begin to move again, but, only as far as Bamfurlong Junction, because none of the routes are working and traffic begins to queue up. The Chief Signal and Telegraph lineman investigates, and reports that someone has operated the RCO switch.

I feel my face redden, but, admit that I am the culprit? No way!

The equipment is supposed to work, is it not?

I recall the signalman on my turn, at Standish Junction, maintaining that, from the viewpoint of safety, power signal boxes, being so far apart, could not compare with having a number of manual operated signal boxes on a section of line. Having worked in both fields now, I tend to agree with this statement, and an incident occurs in the Wigan area that proves it.

Working in a power signal box does not involve merely pressing buttons, as the casual observer may think.

Many unseen activities take place, miles away, with only a telephone for communication.

Without telephones, a power signal box is absolutely unworkable, and it is important to adhere to telephone discipline otherwise they can be extremely dangerous places; several minor accidents have been caused because of the lack of such discipline.

I now relate the incident at Wigan, but first one must understand that not everyone is proficient when it comes to using the telephone.

Signalmen in power signal boxes get many cryptic calls which must be deciphered.

A train conveying high octane fuel from Stanlow Oil Refinery to Scotland has just passed the signal box adjacent to Bank Quay station, on the Down Fast line. An express passenger train has left Crewe *en route* from Birmingham to Glasgow, but the distance between them allows for the tank train to run forward onto the Preston power signal box area before diversion is necessary. I am working on the North Panel and observe the Stanlow train approaching on the diagram and passing Golborne Junction. **(One can judge the speed of a train travelling over track circuits, with a little experience.)** This particular train is maintaining a good headway in front of the following express, which is indicated on the South Panel.

On average, the number of trains on each panel at any given time is six: so my reaction to receiving the following message by telephone can be imagined!

'STOPTHATTRAINTHEREISSUMTHINKWRUNGWITIT!'

First, I must establish the origin of the phone call, then which train, and on which line it is travelling. *'IamringingfrumSprings,'* **Before the next part has been uttered, the signal prior to North Western station has been placed at danger:**

'Brarnchthetrainisapprawchingwigin.' The driver observes the signal changing aspects, and brakes immediately; but is unable to stop and runs past the signal.

This does often happen, and no blame is attributed to the driver in circumstances of this nature.

The Scottish express is now approaching Golborne Junction, and the signalman working on that panel can see the situation on mine, so he decides to divert it to the Down Slow line to Bamfurlong Junction to enable it to overtake the tank train, via the Goods Loop at Springs Branch; but, again, the sudden change in the signal aspects means the driver of the express is unable to stop in time.

For a few moments we are in limbo, awaiting information by telephone regarding the situation at both points.

None of us in the power signal box are aware that two disasters of major proportions have been averted in so short a space of time, at two different locations.

At Wigan one of the tanks is only half an inch above the running rail, and in an extremely dangerous condition. Emergency services are called and the police evacuate people from nearby houses for fear of an explosion, which could cause widespread damage and loss of life.

Such an explosion most certainly would have occurred, had the train entered the station platform.

Firemen on the scene spray neutralizing chemicals onto the vehicle which is now being shunted into Chapel Lane Goods Yard, an operation taking a full two hours. Sandbags completely cover the tank before the residents are allowed to return to their homes and normal working is resumed.

Meanwhile, six miles to the south an even more alarming situation has developed. The Glasgow express has come to a stand on the upwards curve, 20yd short of the junction at Golborne. The signalman instructs the driver to propel his train behind the signal to enable it to be diverted onto the slow line.

'Signalman, I cannot move backwards or forwards,' says the driver, adding:

'THERE IS NO JUNCTION AT GOLBORNE.'

'It's all been ripped up, and my train is in danger of becoming derailed!'

The emergency services are also called to this scene, as platelayers install tie-bars to stabilise the damaged track, an operation which takes some considerable time. Extraordinarily, there are no visual indications on the panel to suggest that anything is amiss in that area. Eventually, both trains continue on their journeys, but the question remains:

How, and why, did it arise?

The M6 motorway traverses the Winwick Branch, approximately ½-mile south of Golborne Junction. It is here that the drama begins to unfold as the Stanlow train passes. Unbeknown to the driver and guard, a vehicle becomes derailed in the centre of the train and is dragged towards the junction. A combination of the train's speed and weight transfers tremendous pressure onto the permanent way, completely destroying it, but somehow the trailing vehicles remain on the rails and, remarkably, the one causing so much destruction re-railed itself approaching the East Lancashire Road overbridge.

This accounts for the broken springs on the tank vehicle seen by a locomotive fireman at Springs Branch, the caller on the telephone.

Who knows what the consequences might have been if I had not received that telephone message? Later, I receive a letter of commendation for my prompt action, but I consider that to make decisions of this kind is an integral part of a signalman's work.

This incident, I feel sure, is what my colleague at Standish Junction had in mind when he made that statement.

It was shortly after this episode that I was recommended to be inducted as a leader for the British Railwaymen's Travel Club **(BRTC).**

This involved taking parties of 38, made up of railwaymen and their wives, by train to Germany, Holland, Austria, Switzerland and Spain to name but a few, though my favourite destination in Europe was Sorrento, in Italy. The idea behind having a leader was to ensure that the party reached their destination; that they were looked after during the vacation, taken to places of interest, and then brought safely back home to London.

As one can imagine problems do arise; things do not always go to plan. In one particular instance I met the party at Victoria station in London, but the railwaymen in France had called for strike action to commence at midnight that day. Bearing in mind all sleeping cars and seats on the trains are booked before the holiday, I ring the head office of the BRTC at Skegness and am given the following instructions:

'Take your party to Belgium, and take pot-luck from there.'

It sounds easy, but railwaymen apply for tickets to travel through specific countries to reach their intended destination, and in this case **through France and Italy only**.

So off we sail to Ostend and arrive at the railway station where I contact an inspector who finds all the party seats, though he is unable to supply sleepers. A small 'backhander' to him on behalf of the gang is accepted with thanks.

Travelling through Belgium without tickets does not cause any trouble, but in Switzerland, well, the ticket snapper has other ideas and demands that the party pay their fare. I tell him we are all '*Chemin de fer* **employees'** and are forced to travel through his country because of the strike in France. But this doesn't do me any good, nor does he accept my pleas and threatens to evict us all from the train at the next station, which is Berne **(where we have to change trains anyway!)** if he is not paid.

I think to myself, *'How do I tackle this fella?'*

Taking him to an empty compartment I ask him to how much he wants to be paid. Getting out a piece of paper he writes down **38 x Blah, Blah, Blah!**

'Okay. It's a lot of money,' I say. *'Will you accept a pay to bearer?'*

He answers in the affirmative.

I promise to pay the Swiss Federal Railways 6000 Blah! Blah! Blah! In payment for my party of 38 to travel through Switzerland on behalf of the BRTC. Signed, AJC.

He accepts this without question.

That is another problem solved! What a versatile breed we signalmen are!

Arriving in Berne, I tell the station inspector we are heading for Naples, to which he replies, *'The only train going to Italy tonight is terminating at Milan.'*

'Avanti, platform 10.' I tell the party.

Arriving in Milan, there is a train ready to depart for Naples, and on it we get. It is 2am when we get to Naples station, and I ring the **Hotel Vesuvio** in Sorrento, requesting that they send a bus for us. We arrive there only about four hours later than we would have done travelling by the normal service through France.

This area is ideal for sightseeing: Capri, Mount Vesuvius, Salerno, Amalfi, Monte Cassino, Rome and Pompeii. On the tour this year we have a driver, Richard, from Wolverhampton accompanied by his wife, Barbara. He fought here during the Second World War, and wants to return to a particular crossroads in the new town of Pompeii to re-kindle his memories. Whilst there, Barbara tells me her boss is none other than Ron C, the former signalman at Springs Branch No 2 signal box - mentioned earlier - and now the Area Manager at Wolverhampton. (So that is where he finished up!)

'Isn't it a small world?'

Do you know I could write a book about my exploits with the BRTC (later to become the British Transport Travel Club) but it will have to be put on the back-burner, I'm afraid, because I have enough on my plate writing this one. However, there is one particular story I would like to relate to you which will definitely bring a smile to your face.

At one time two widows of railwaymen were in my party to Sorrento, which I gathered together after breakfast on the first morning and told they could all have a day off to explore the town, and that I would arrange trips to the various places mentioned above, during their stay.

These two ladies asked me what I would be doing that day. Anyone who has been abroad on holiday could not have missed a Japanese party, with their leader holding up his umbrella, shouting, **'Follow me!'** in Japanese, of course. Well, I used similar tactics, but held up my trilby, (made of straw) which I tend to wear out in a very short time, through the endless doffing of it to the ladies! I told these ladies I was going into town to part-exchange my hat **with a hole in it.** They asked if they could come with me, and I agreed. *'Io parlare l'italiano, pochissimo?'* Arriving at the shop, these hats **(costing £1, or 1500 Lira)** were hanging up on a line, and I said to the lady owner, *'I am interested in buying a hat from you, but could you give me something in return for this one?'* She apologised, with an emphatic l'italiano, **'NO!'**

'Okay', I said, and walked away. She followed me and agreed to a sale, and I got my new hat for **15 bob!** It was a joy to see the faces of these two ladies, standing with their mouths agape, not believing what they had witnessed.

Back to work now!

Every signalman is aware of a **'moving track circuit'**. In the event of a description not being received, a train will occupy each track circuit in the normal way, and consequently the title **'moving track circuit'** is adopted in these circumstances. I observe a track circuit become occupied leaving platform No 2 at Wigan North Western station, followed almost immediately by the next. Contacting the station supervisor, he informs me that in this platform is the station **350hp diesel shunt engine**, and that the driver is sitting next to him having a cup of tea.

Further track circuits drop, indicating that something is definitely moving towards Springs Branch along the Up East Loop line. The supervisor rings, telling me the engine has left the platform, minus **ONE DRIVER,** who has now left his tea, and is in hot pursuit of his runaway steed! Unfortunately, the locomotive has too large a start; however, a quick call for the intervention of an agile driver at Springs Branch brings the episode to a harmless end.

A small portion of the electrical relays at Warrington power signal box.

One would consider in an establishment of this nature, with all the signalmen having many years of experience in the grade, that they are quite capable of maintaining the high standard attributed to a signal box such as this, but:

'THERE'S TROUBLE I' TH' MILL!'

The introduction of Controllers into power signal boxes proves to be an excellent idea for traffic and liaison purposes; but after six months they are re-graded to Supervisors. A vacancy arises, and one of the many qualifications listed, **'Supervision of Signalmen',** causes consternation amongst us. So now we have a situation whereby a signalman may be supervised by someone who has never worked in a signal box in his life. This is totally unacceptable **(and rightly so)** to men with a minimum of 25 years in the signalling grades. Bitter verbal altercations ensue as a result of this senseless and unnecessary gradation, orchestrated by a **'gaggle of quill-shovers'',** creating tension and a bad atmosphere in the general running of this important and busy signal box. But that is not all; a far more unsavoury situation occurs concerning the manning levels of the signal box.

Initially, the 15 signalmen attempted, through the Machinery of Negotiations, to have the establishment increased to 18 signalmen owing to the excessive overtime being worked to cover sickness, undoubtedly caused by the high levels of strain and stress. Eventually, two more posts of signalmen were created, one short of the desired complement; but still the overtime continues, and this against the principles laid down by the National Union of Railwaymen.

The outcome of these negotiations turned out to be a farce, as can be judged by an article in the press at the time. I quote:

'UNION CHIEFS OPPOSE MANNING FIGHT.'

Warrington signalmen are being summoned, three at a time, to the headquarters of the National Union of Railwaymen in London to see the General Secretary or his representative. The men claim that they are being threatened with disciplinary action unless they agree to drop their claim for an extra man in the signal box and return to so-called 'normal' working. So far they have not given any assurance to the union and say that all their actions over the claim for an extra man have been entirely in accordance with the union's rules and regulations.

The 17 signalmen at the Warrington power signal box have always maintained that an extra man was necessary. They were promised a review in 1974, which was only finally carried out in 1978, and they have still had no news about the extra man. An extra man would make a big difference, the signalmen say. At present they have to work long hours of overtime with high levels of strain and stress

OVERTIME

Six weeks ago they began limited action – 48-hour week (which includes normal overtime) but they refused to work in place of men who were sick or for any other breakdown, so some of the signal panels went unmanned, **being left on Automatic.** For the last six weeks a number of trains in the Warrington area have either been cancelled or diverted. The public has not been told the real reason by British Rail. The men point out that union policy is to put pressure on management to fill vacancies rather than work excessive overtime. So what, ask the men, have they done to displease the union hierarchy to such an extent that they are now facing expulsion from the union and the loss of their jobs?

The men are also anxious about a separate claim - for re-classification. Euston signalmen were upgraded to the top grade last May when they threatened industrial action. The Warrington signalmen, who have always been on the same classification, applied for parity in July last year.

(A sum of £6 or £7 is involved.)

FROZE

But, last November the NUR executive froze all re-classification claims and since then the men have made no progress with their claim. Work study schemes have proved that the Warrington signalmen have a work-rate similar to their colleagues in Euston and should therefore be re-classified. But it seems that the union leadership, far from backing the men on this issue or the manning shortage question, would prefer to join with the management in forcing a group of workers to '*toe the line*', or be sacked.

In other words they used:

'SLEDGE HAMMERS TO CRACK NUTS.'

In 1980 the signalmen at Warrington succeeded in their claims for re-classification, and another signalman was added to the complement shortly after. Unfortunately, this whole episode exposed a great deal of corruption, but that is another story!

Let me digress a little to a much more interesting subject:

THE ROYAL ENCOUNTER.

An innovation introduced with modern power signal boxes is that of **Hot Axle-box Detectors. (HADs)** HAD sensors are placed at strategic points throughout the area of control, and a visual display unit in the signal box records the number of axles on a train. These sensors are capable of detecting up to nine single axle boxes running hot, but will not indicate whether one is on fire, which does happen from time to time. In connection with signalling, the following rules must be adhered to:

If the HAD is activated the train must be stopped at a nominated signal and examined by the train crew. On confirmation of a hot box, the train may proceed at 10mph to detach the vehicle into the nearest siding.

In certain circumstances false readings occur, and in these circumstances the train is allowed to travel forwards at 20mph for further examination by Carriage and Wagon staff to ascertain whether the vehicle is safe to continue on its journey.

Hot Axle Box Detector.

Members of the Royal Family frequently travel on the West Coast Main Line, as mentioned earlier, and tonight Her Majesty the Queen and the Duke are travelling to Balmoral Castle at the start of their summer vacation. The HAD sensors situated at Preston Brook transmit that No 9 axle-box on the left-hand side in the direction of travel of the Royal train is running hot; so, in accordance with the rules and regulations, I stop the train at Acton Grange Junction.

I notice the bosses, who swarm like bees to witness the train passing, vanish like a flock of sheep in a snowstorm as it comes slowly to a stand!

I am contacted by way of the Signal Post Telephone (SPT) by an inspector travelling on the train:-

'Do you realise you've stopped the Royal train?'

'Of course, I am well aware of this fact,' I reply, adding, *'Would you please examine the 9th axle on the left-hand side in direction of travel?'*

'There is nothing wrong with this train.' He assures me, adding,

'Do you realise we have the Queen on board?'

'Yes! I am well aware of this fact,' I repeat, *'and when you see Ma'am, just mention it was Tony Cook who stopped her train, just in case I get an invitation to Buckingham Palace at a later date.'*

Repeating my request, he reluctantly examines the vehicle, to return a few minutes later confirming his own prognosis.

'Come on, let's get going.' he orders.

'May I speak to the driver, please?' I ask.

'What for? I am Inspector So-and-so.' (Surely I've heard that name before, somewhere?)

Not the same chap, though, perhaps it's his brother, because there do appear to be quite a lot of 'So-and-sos' working on the railways!

'Yeah! And I am the signalman in Warrington power signal box.'

I instruct the driver to travel at 20mph to Warrington Bank Quay station for further examination of the suspect vehicle, where I am again subjected to more didactic verbosity from this inspector.

He must think my name is *'Joe Soap'*, but rules are rules, and I mean to carry them out correctly, especially when the safety of my sovereign is involved!

The Carriage and Wagon examiner passes the vehicle fit to travel. The train leaves 30 minutes behind schedule, obviating the need for the party to roam about the platform in their **pyjamas!**

Her Majesty. Photo by Author.

For my devotion to duty, and sticking to my guns, my colleagues in the box bestow on me a temporary Honorary Knighthood - though, I am still awaiting for the invitation to make it permanent!

It is hard to comprehend that we, the signalmen, in an establishment such as this would have to deal with a lever frame, but the management were still in the Ice Age when they designed this particular signal box. They decided to incorporate **Ground Frames** (with levers) throughout the area, for emergency use only! A good idea? But, they did not bargain for the time it took to call people out to operate them, causing catastrophic delays to traffic.

Winwick Junction ground frame. Courtesy of Ray Burgess.

Recently, we managed, through the Machinery of Negotiations, to have three extra signalmen added to the complement for the sole purpose of Personal Needs Breaks (PNBs). This enabled the signalmen working the panels to be relieved for meal and toilet breaks. I am the PNB man on duty when a Scotland-bound express passenger train fails completely at Winwick Junction at 02.00hrs, and the driver requests assistance by providing a fresh locomotive.

Armed with a Bardic hand lamp**, I head to the junction and work the ground frame under the auspices of the signalman on the central panel, but it still takes over an hour to complete the exercise! So much for modern technology.

[A Bardic hand lamp, complete with battery and bulb, replacing the use of paraffin.**

An absolutely brilliant idea from a member of the management team!]

Not so that clever fella, Mr S, who advocated the asinine idea of using levers being controlled by power operated signal boxes?

They say, 'It takes all kinds to make a world, don't it?'

212

'Caledonian' at Warrington Bank Quay station.

Courtesy of Arthur Chester.

'Mid-Day Scot'. Courtesy of Lawrence Thorpe.

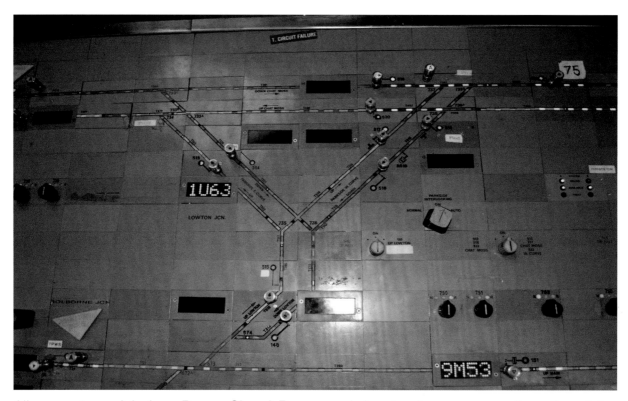

Allow me to explain how **Power Signal Boxes** work by showing you a small section of the **Middle Panel** in this box.

The diagram in the picture is approximately one square mile. Starting at the very top, the two horizontal lines feature the original Liverpool to Manchester Railway opened in September 1830, Liverpool being to the right.

From the Liverpool direction the junction leads to and from the Parkside West Curve along to Lowton Junction, whilst opposite to this is on the Manchester side is the Parkside East Curve.

It will be noticed that the tracks are divided into different coloured segments, each one being an individual track circuit with its own unique number. A row of **WHITE LIGHTS** signifies the route is set on that particular section of track for an approaching train; the **RED** lights indicate the presence of a train. i.e. **9M53, (a freight train)** is in transit on the Winwick Branch, this section forming a part of the West Coast Main Line. Meanwhile **1V63, (an express passenger train)** is standing at Signal WN 513 (which is showing **RED**) to await passage onto the Up Chat Moss Line. **WN 518** on the Down Chat Moss Line is showing **GREEN**, with an illuminated **(A)** button to its right which signifies that it is being worked automatically with the passage of trains. It was close to this signal that William Huskisson was struck down on the day that the railway opened.

Immediately to the right of the A button is WN 521 at **RED**. This is a ground signal, the **Black Arrowhead** indicating that it is solely an **ENTRANCE** button. This particular signal can be operated for two separate routes, via **739a** and **739b** to the Up Chat Moss Line, or via **739b and 739a, and 738** to the Down Parkside West Curve, with signal **WN 516** being the exit button for that particular route (the arrowhead being clear). R 516 is a repeater of **WN516**, to assist drivers because of restricted visibility of the main signal. **(Each button on the signal box panel can be easily distinguished, whether it be an ENTRANCE, EXIT or BOTH.)**

The **BLACK SWITCHES** can be manually operated by the signalmen for testing or emergency purposes. Points **750 and 751 are both in the REVERSE position, whilst 753 and 755 are in NORMAL.** If a fault occurs on the points, the centre light will flash intermittently and no train would be allowed to travel over them, unless they are manually clipped by a hand signalman.

As stated earlier there are 5 Remote Control Areas and there Overrides on the panel here, and you can see the **Yellow Switches for the ones at Parkside.**

You will have to excuse me for not attempting to describe how these systems work but, to put it bluntly, one has to be a Philadelphia lawyer to understand the complexity of the rules appertaining to their use. This also goes for Swinging Overlaps, Opposing Route Selection, Comprehensive Approach Locking, and Route Oversetting.

Unfortunately, the management do not employ lawyers in Power Signal Boxes, and the only thing you cannot expect from them is an increase in remuneration, so we the signalmen here have to smile and say CHEESE while they PUSH PENS!

The part of the panel I have just described is the small portion under the clock on the left of the signalman, so you can judge how much equipment is installed, and the area that is covered by the whole box. Bear in mind that we, the original signalmen, had to learn everything about the operation of what you see with only one visit allowed to the premises in six months. *(The signalman on duty happens to be the Author, photographed in September 2015 on a visit for the first time since retiring in 1994.)*

As previously mentioned, the centenary celebrations commemorating the opening of the Liverpool & Manchester Railway were held at Wavertree, Liverpool. The 150th anniversary celebrations are to take place on the stretch of railway used in the Trials at Rainhill in 1829. Contractors are erecting scaffolding on either side of the line stretching from Rainhill station to Lea Green. It will hold the seating for the thousands of people that are expected to attend. Bold Colliery Sidings are only occasionally used today for traffic destined for Fiddlers Ferry Power Station, on the banks of the River Mersey near Warrington, so these have been selected to stable all the locomotives during the three-day festival. For days, the locomotives to be included in the cavalcade are making their way, either assisted or under their own steam, in readiness for the big day. As seems to happen on all notable occasions, something goes wrong. **'Rocket'**, the locomotive aptly chosen to lead the procession, unceremoniously becomes derailed in the sidings and is slightly damaged. She is able to take part in the cavalcade, although this is only possible with the assistance of **'Lion'**.

At the end of this chapter we have a list of all the participating locomotives at the festival.

Allow me to digress a little and look at the Low Level Line running through Warrington. The line commences at Ditton Junction and runs parallel to the River Mersey for most of its length.

On 1st February 1853 the St Helens Canal & Railway Company opened the line which reached Whitecross, in the centre of Warrington, erecting a terminal station.

Arpley Junction signal box.   Courtesy of Dave Lennon.

Underneath a Tappet Frame signal box.

Courtesy of Dave Lennon.

Signalman Ray Dutton in Arpley Junction signal box. Photographer unknown.

Meanwhile, the Warrington & Altrincham Railway, later renamed the Warrington & Stockport Railway, reached the town at Wilderspool. This company also built a station, linking up to the SHCR by way of a bridge erected over the River Mersey. Also passing through Warrington is the famous Manchester Ship Canal, and to enable its construction the railway, which blocked its path, had to be diverted to allow the work to commence. On 8th July 1893, the deviation line was opened, with a new station being built at Latchford, the old one now redundant. In 1956 Wilderspool Level Crossing, on a busy road south of the town - a bottleneck for road users - was replaced with a new overbridge. Arpley station closed on 15th September 1958 and passenger train services ceased running along this line on 10th September 1962. Freight traffic finally ceased running towards Manchester on 7th July 1985, the high level bridge being made redundant. Arpley Junction signal box is still open, servicing the massive Fiddlers Ferry Power Station, a few miles to the west.

Just to digress, my son Tony, who worked as a manager of a motorcycle shop adjacent to Earlestown station, asked me one day if I could get him a job on the railways, and using my influence I secured him a position as a signalman, working at Crosfield's Crossing signal box, in Warrington. Crosfield's is a large firm making soap and chemicals, etc.

After twelve months or so he said to me:

'I couldn't work in this job as long as you,' and off he went to achieve a higher accolade than I could ever reach, being elevated to the position of Chief Pilot of an airline based at Liverpool John Lennon Airport!

Crosfield's Crossing signal box. Courtesy of Dave Lennon.

Absolute Block Instrument.

Courtesy of James MacKenzie.

The Author's son in the Cockpit of 'Concorde' - with me as his co-pilot (?)

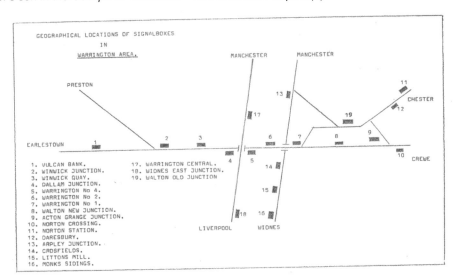

Locations of signal boxes in the Warrington area.

44686 5MT 'Caprotti' in Up Slow platform.

Warrington Bank Quay station. Photo by Harry Arnold, MBE.

Engines in the 1980 cavalcade:
ROCKET
NOVELTY	LION	SANS-PAREIL

(Lion is the only surviving locomotive which worked on the original Liverpool & Manchester Railway.)

LNWR	0-6-2	'Coal Tank'	1054	Webb
MR		'Spinner'	673	Johnson
L&Y	0-6-0	'Saddle Tank'	752	
LNWR	2-4-0	'Hardwicke'	790	Webb
NBR	0-6-0	'Maude'	673	Holmes
MR	4-4-0	'Compound'	1000	Johnson
LMS	0-6-0	'Goods'	4027	Fowler
LMS	0-6-0	'Jinty'	7289	Fowler
LMS	2-8-0		13809	Fowler
LMS	4-6-0	'Black Five'	5000	Stanier
WLLR	0-6-0	2ft Gauge		
LMS	2-6-0	'Mogul'	46521	Ivatt
LMS	2-6-0	'Mogul'	43106	Ivatt
LMS	4-6-0	'Jubilee' (Leander)	5690	Fowler
LMS	4-6-2	'Princess Elizabeth'	6201	Stanier
LNER	2-6-2	'Green Arrow'	4771	Gresley
LNER	4-6-2	'Flying Scotsman'	4472	Gresley
LNER	4-6-2	'Sir Nigel Gresley'	4498	Gresley
GWR	4-6-0	'Hagley Hall'	4930	Collett
SR	4-4-0	'Cheltenham'	925	Maunsell
SR	4-6-0	'Lord Nelson'	850	Maunsell
SR	4-6-2	'Clan Line'	35028	Bulleid
LMS	4-6-2	'Duchess of Hamilton'	46229	Stanier
BR	2-10-0	'Evening Star'	92220	
BR	2-6-4	'Standard'	80079	

Derailed 'Rocket'. Photo by Mick Langton.

Walton Old Junction. Courtesy of Arthur Chester.

Warrington No 2 signal box.

P Norton collection.

Warrington No 1 signal box, 1972.
(New power box in the background.)
Photo by David A Ingham

Warrington No 4 signal box. Courtesy of P Norton collection.

The old signal box at Acton Grange Junction.
Photo by David A Ingham.

New signal box at Acton Grange Junction

Courtesy of D Lennon.

On Acton Grange Viaduct. Courtesy of P Norton.

On Acton Grange Viaduct. Courtesy of P Norton.

Ditton to Timperley train at Slutchers Lane station

Photo by Les Fifoot

Single Line Working at Norton station.

Photo by Roy Gough.

Latchford Old Line to the right. Deviation Line to the left.

Photo by Robert Callaghan.

'Right Away' at Slutchers Lane, Warrington.

Photographer unknown.

Building the Manchester Ship Canal, 1891.

Latchford old station is to the left.

Courtesy of Warrington Library.

On the Manchester Ship Canal at Warrington,

Latchford Swing Bridge is behind the boat.

(Note train on High Level Deviation Line.)

Courtesy of Ron Couchman.

CHAPTER TWELVE

THE PREMIER RAILWAY

1980-84

WARRINGTON CENTRAL STATION SIGNAL BOX

Management, in their divine wisdom, consider that I am better suited to bashing levers than pressing buttons!

The old and new signal boxes at Warrington Central station.

Courtesy of Dave Lennon.

'Pull the Home board off,' says my mate Albert. Yet again, new terminology to learn in this LMS Standard Frame signal box, working both upper quadrant semaphores and colour light signals. This line opened in 1873, run by the Cheshire Lines Committee and a few miles south of the Liverpool to Manchester line, connects same two cities and still bears a lot of its original charisma after all these years. Conversations in the early 1950s regarding the 'Premier Railway' baffled me somewhat, but now I see, first-hand, the enthusiasm of the staff and their courteous attitude towards the public and colleagues; so different from other areas in which I worked.

The signal box, on the east side of the Down line platform, was built in 1972 replacing a dilapidated structure close-by. I believe the new building and frame originally stood at Platt Bridge Junction, Wigan, in which I actually worked in a few years ago.

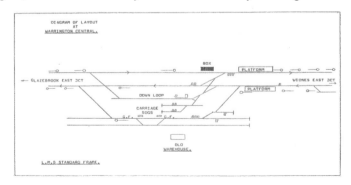

Warrington Central Station signal box.

Passing Warrington Central Station signal box.

Photographer unknown.

On the Cheshire Lines at Farnworth station.

Courtesy of 8D Association.

Widnes North station (formerly Farnworth).

Photo by Terry Callaghan.

Lever frame in Warrington Central signal box. Courtesy of H.G.

(It will be noticed that the handles of the levers are different.)

The smaller ones are operated electronically, and are therefore easier to pull over, whilst the larger ones are manually operated and require a certain amount of brute force to get them fully over. It is very unusual to have this many different coloured levers in a signal box, so I will explain each one as seen in the picture.

1   Red Levers are Stop Signals, which can be electronically or manually operated, depending on the distance from the signal box.

2   Red and Yellow Levers control the entrance to an Intermediate Block Section.

3   Black and White with Chevrons pointing DOWN operate an emergency Detonator Machine on the down line, whilst those pointing UP are for the UP line machine.

4   Red and Yellow Levers with White Horizontal Stripes indicate an Intermediate Block Section signal released electronically when a train has been accepted by the signal box in advance.

5   Black Levers are for points.

6   Blue Levers are for locking points (these being either Rods or Bars depending on the distance from the signal box).

7   Blue/Brown Levers are Remote Ground Frame Releases.

8   Blue/Black Levers operate Remote Points with Locking Rods.

9   Yellow Levers operate Distant Signals.

10 White Levers are disused.

The following are not applicable in this signal box:

11 Brown Levers (in signal boxes controlling level crossings with gates).

There are four: two for locking the gates and two controlling pedestrian wicket gates.

12 Green Levers operate Shunting Gongs and are installed in some goods signal boxes.

This signal box stands opposite a gigantic warehouse; empty, decaying, in a sombre state, bearing the names:

GREAT NORTHERN RAILWAY,   MIDLAND RAILWAY,

and the

GREAT CENTRAL RAILWAY.

These are moulded in concrete under the eaves, to remind us of its former glory.

Luckily, a preservation order has been placed on it as its historical significance is undeniable. Traffic on this line is light in comparison to others around Warrington, consisting chiefly of DMUs or 'Sputniks' (as they were affectionately christened on their introduction which coincided with advances in Russian space technology) plying between Liverpool and Manchester monotonously, which quite frankly, bores me.

Television-watching is strictly prohibited in signal boxes, as previously mentioned, and until a few years ago the Block Inspectors even frowned upon the presence of newspapers. Today this is accepted as the norm, and I happened to pick up the local rag which read:

'LOCAL SIGNALBOX BROKEN INTO!

NO APPARENT DAMAGE DONE, BUT

THE SIGNALMAN'S TELEVISION SET WAS STOLEN!'

Good gracious me! If this signalman were identified, he would be for the high jump!

Tapestry work interests me, so off I go to the local shop for expert advice on the subject and finish up with a 5ft x 4ft masterpiece. It takes twelve months to complete, with well over 170,000 stitches. I suppose the management could object to my pastime, so I **'needle'** them by keeping up with the rules and regulations (which are continually being updated) to such an extent that I have a particular rule altered on one occasion. Not to be outdone the management **sowed** as well (their seeds) and had the audacity to request me to train a future signalman on the rules and regulations. I remember the help I received from Reggie in Pighue Lane signal box, and thought, 'why not follow in his footsteps?' I was pleased that my pupil passed his examination with flying colours; this gave me great satisfaction, knowing that I had given my time to help him. The management took further advantage of my good nature by sending a young **'whipper-snapper'** of a management trainee for me to train.

In he walked, and guess what his name was? Yes, **Mr So-and-so!** He settled down very quickly, delving into the books, but what struck me most was his cavalier attitude**.**

He thought he knew everything!

This aside, he did pass his examination, and went on his merry way.

Warehouse at Warrington Central station. Photographer unknown.

45305 on special approaching Warrington Central.

Photo by Martin Peers.

Nearing Warrington Central station. Photo by Martin Peers.

The Garston to Liverpool Railway opened on 1st June 1864 and terminated at Brunswick station. This line was incorporated into the Cheshire Lines Committee Railway on 5th June 1865. On 2nd March 1874 this line, nearly 2 miles long, was extended to the present Liverpool Central station, passing through five tunnels. The first of these, starting from Central was called St George's, followed by St James 1, 2, 3 and 4. It was between St George's and St James No 1 tunnel that St James station was built. As well as the signal box at Central (worked by a signalman and a box lad) another was erected with 17 levers at St James station.

On 15th October 1913, a serious crash between two trains occurred here at St James causing the deaths of seven people. In the enquiry that followed, the cause of this accident was found to be that the signalman allowed the box lad to operate the block instruments, and owing to a misunderstanding between them the signalman allowed the second train into the occupied section.

On 1st January 1917 St James station closed to passengers, Brunswick station having already been closed to passengers on 2nd March 1874.

Platforms of former St James station. Courtesy of Liverpool Echo.

A detailed study of St James station, with other interesting information about the area, compiled by Paul Wright can be found on the 'Disused Stations' website.

It was while reading this story about this train accident that I recalled a Relief Signalman, with whom I had worked in Edge Hill No 13 signal box in 1948, had lost his life in one of the above-named tunnels. He transferred from his relief job to work as a regular signalman in the box at Lime Street. One night after finishing an afternoon shift, he walked over to Central station to catch his train home and, for some inexplicable reason, put his head out of the moving train and caught it on the buttress on one of the tunnels.

Liverpool Central station, looking up Ranelagh Street. Courtesy of Ron Couchman.

Central station is sited at the crossroads of Church Street, Hanover Street, Bold Street and Ranelagh Street, at the top of which is the famous Adephi Hotel, with Lewis's department store opposite. Whilst the Adelphi Hotel remained untouched, Lewis's store was completely gutted by fire when hit by incendiary bombs during the Blitz. It remained in this state for many years, but was rebuilt, and a statue, **'Liverpool Resurgent'**, by Sir Jacob Epstein was unveiled in 1956, high up on the facade commemorating the centenary of Lewis's store and rebirth of Liverpool after the war. I can vividly recall passing the empty shell of the building on a tram going to work in the British Home Stores in Lord Street in 1944, and witnessing the unveiling of the statue, which attracted thousands upon thousands of people for many years after.

'Liverpool Resurgent' by Sir Jacob Epstein.

At the top of Bold Street stands St Luke's Church, close to the site of the former St James station. Like Lewis's store it was reduced to a shell after being hit by incendiary bombs. It remains in this state today, unaltered, nature having taken it over for perpetuity. Liverpool Corporation chose to keep it this way as a memorial to the resilience of the people of Liverpool and to those who perished during this turbulent period.

More in keeping with this work and in relation to the birth of the railways, the tomb of William Huskisson, who lost his life at Parkside on the opening day of the Liverpool & Manchester Railway, is situated in the grounds St James Cemetery adjacent to Liverpool's Gothic, Anglican Cathedral, less than a mile from this location.

St Luke's Church, at the top of Bold Street, Liverpool.

The interior of St Luke's Church after bombing on 6th May 1941; the 'May Blitz'.

It remains in this condition today as a memorial to those who lost their lives in the war.

(Liverpudlians call it the 'Bombed out Church'.)

Courtesy of Liverpool Echo.

Hunts Cross power signal box. Courtesy of James MacKenzie.

The railway lines between Liverpool Central and Garston stations closed to passengers on 17th April 1972, and all traffic was diverted and transferred to Lime Street station, via Allerton Junction, over the Hunts Cross Chord; official complete closure took place from 10th December 1972. However, it received a new lease of life when the Link line was built under the city of Liverpool, joining the old Lancashire & Yorkshire Railway at Sandhills with the CLC leading from Central station.

Liverpool Central station. (Note the 'Scammel' in foreground)

Courtesy of Ron Couchman.

In addition, two new interchange stations, one at Moorfields and the other at Central were built to connect with a single-bore tunnel on the Wirral line. This link line continues along the original path of the CLC railway to Garston, on third-rail DC electrification. All of the old stations are refurbished, and a new footbridge is planned for Garston station, situated at the southern end of Liverpool.

Liverpool Central station. Courtesy of Ron Couchman.

The last train to leave Liverpool Central station,

10th December 1972. Courtesy of Ron Couchman.

Back to Warrington Central.

A train in the sidings opposite the signal box is loaded with the footbridge, and is ready to follow the last passenger train to Liverpool, but the guard informs me that form BR 29973 has not been issued.

This form authorises movement of a train conveying an 'exceptional load' and indicates restrictions relating to the route that it takes.

Many signalmen will verify the existence of a book **(which is yet to be published?)** but which certain persons expect one to work to, in order to cover up their own or others' inefficiencies. This may sound double-Dutch, so I will explain. **I refer to the 'Sunday Rule Book'; no, not the Bible.** During the week, signalmen must strictly abide by the rules and regulations but, come Sundays, management tend to ignore them; **in their eyes, to keep the job moving?**

To illustrate this with an example, I refer back to this bridge train. The guard, quite rightly, refuses to travel without the form. One would think that the appropriate action to take is to supply one as soon as possible; but no, this would take too long and expose the person responsible.

So out comes the fictitious tome. *'Let's do this, to get the job moving,'* pleads the inspector.

To get the job moving the signalman would violate two, and probably more, regulations.

I say, *'Sorry, we can't do that.'*

Flipping a few imaginary pages, another outlandish suggestion is made; again, not in accordance with the rules. When all is exhausted, it is decided to ask for a form to be delivered post-haste, which is what should have happened in the first place.

Signalmen hold a very responsible position and should never be coerced into violating rules and regulations by anyone, because they would almost certainly **'carry the can'** if anything of a serious nature occurred; the instigator, meanwhile, being protected by a web of intrigue and subterfuge!

The 'North Sea Gas' project has resurrected the sidings here after little use in these past few years. Trainloads of pipes are received and transferred onto road vehicles for distribution to places far afield but, owing to routing difficulties, the work is being transferred to Dallam Sidings on the West Coast Main Line, north of Bank Quay station. Once more the sidings are closed, this time, sadly, forever.

The largest army stores depot in Europe is situated at Burtonwood air base, three miles from Warrington, and its railway sidings are connected to the main line via a ground frame controlled by Widnes East Junction signal box, the next along the line from here towards Liverpool. To service the depot, authority is given for Wrong Line Working from Warrington Central.

Absolute Block regulations apply between Glazebrook East Junction and this signal box, also to Widnes East, but on the latter section of line are two Intermediate Block sections, very unusual, by normal standards.

In the early hours of this morning heavy rain floods Sankey station, and I receive a report of sleepers (the railway type) floating between the platforms. All trains are stopped, and I notice irate passengers begin to alight at the home signal, half a mile away, and advance towards me like an army in attack, gingerly stepping over signal wires and other railway booby traps. Discretion being the better part of valour, I defend myself against any verbal flak that may come my way by mingling with some platelayers, viewing the scene at the bottom of the signal box steps!

Cows, horses and sheep on the line are commonplace to signalmen, but a chap walking along the track, shouting up to the signal box, *'Am I on the right line to London?'* is slightly more unusual.

'Yeah, keep going pal, only another 190 miles to go!'

Numerous fatal accidents occur on our railways and, so far, in 35 years I have been involved with only one, this being the passenger found at Woodside Sidings after falling out of a train. Here, in the space of two weeks I have dealt with three. I mention this fact to illustrate that signalmen's duties have many facets, not all of them pleasant.

Glazebrook East Junction signal box. Courtesy of A Gardiner.

Diagram in Glazebrook East Junction signal box. Courtesy of A Gardiner.

Digressing once more, I wish to refer to a large political demonstration in London, which is to end with a lobby of MPs at Westminster. One of the relief signalmen is determined to attend, but holidays and sickness deplete the signalling staff, so he decides to wire off sick, to be doubly sure. Of course no-one is any the wiser; that is until headlines on the television news show the procession meandering through the streets of London. In front, holding the banner is none other than our intrepid friend! The scene is watched by millions, including - you know who - Mr S!

This little escapade cost our colleague a few days' unpaid leave. **'Be sure your sins will find you out.'**

After four years working here, the powers that be consider that I am better suited to pressing buttons than bashing levers about.

Oh, I wish they would make up their minds!

Signalmen Stan Seddon (left) and Joe Holt ('Dover Joe')

working in Glazebrook East Junction signal box (old diagram).

Courtesy of Val Seddon.

On Monday I transfer to Edge Hill, Liverpool but - before I go - let me return to the large warehouse opposite the signal box, to rectify an omission in the text. On the west and east sides of the building, in giant letters, are the words, **'CHESHIRE LINES'** which also appear on the south frontage. No-one can doubt the overpowering visual effect these have over the other railways' names alongside, as if to say:

'This is the Premier Railway'.

Well! I second that: **It is 'THE PREMIER RAILWAY'** and I have worked on it!

Liverpool Central station cat. Courtesy of Ron Couchman.

A few photographs of the old Liverpool Central station:

Diagram in Liverpool Central Station signal box.

Courtesy of Ron Couchman.

Waiting to leave Liverpool Central station.

Courtesy of Ron Couchman.

One out and one in at Liverpool Central station.

Courtesy of Ron Couchman.

CHAPTER THIRTEEN

THE NOSTALGIC RETURN

1984

EDGE HILL POWER SIGNAL BOX

After 37 years on my travels, sorrow fills my heart as I observe the contraction that has taken place at this once hustling and bustling railway centre of Edge Hill, Liverpool.

It was because of this that I decided to embark upon writing this book, remembering all the railwaymen I met and worked with all those years ago.

The Author standing on the original steps leading down to Crown Street railway station.

Courtesy of Joe Gerrard.

Amid the desolation I stand under the crumbling Moorish Arch viewing, on the left, the worn steps used by the first railway travellers now leading nowhere up the grimy sandstone wall.

The famous 'Moorish Arch' at Crown Street, Liverpool.

From 1831 Bury Print.

Engine shed, workshops and offices are denuded, leaving only scratches etched by navvies' picks as reminders of ages long past. Behind me are the stark entrances to the three juxtaposed Crown Street Tunnels, illustrated in many nineteenth century prints; now clear of smoke, they echo no more to clanking wagons and squealing brakes, awaiting an uncertain future. Remember what they were like, and the diverse methods of working the traffic through them, primitive though they may seem today, were, nevertheless, effective and stood the test of time.

The three juxtaposed tunnels at Crown Street, Liverpool.

Courtesy of Liverpool Echo.

Loaded coal wagons hauled chiefly by **'Saddlebacks'** or **'Super D'** locomotives were taken through the left-hand tunnel into Crown Street Coal Sidings for stabling in readiness for several local distributors to unload. There the similarity with other railway operations ceases, for the empty wagons were shunted from the same yard into the right-hand tunnel by a tractor, fastened to which is a sleeper, positioned at buffer height, to facilitate disposal.

It was through this particular tunnel, several hundred yards long, that the first passenger train left the station in Crown Street Liverpool *en route* to Manchester in 1830, but because of its restricted headroom, locomotives were unable to enter it, and the coaches were first hauled through it by ropes to enable the engine to be attached for the forward journey. Passenger trains ceased to use this tunnel six years later when the terminus at Lime Street was opened.

Obviously, nobody at this time had the foresight to invent No 1 lever, later to be found in Edge Hill No 13 signal box!

The 'Glass House' in Wapping cutting. Courtesy of Liverpool Echo.

Park Lane Goods signal box. Courtesy of Liverpool Echo.

An unorthodox system was adopted for the nearly two-mile-long Wapping Tunnel, leading downwards to Park Lane Goods Yard, adjacent to Wapping Docks in south Liverpool.

A 'Caledonian Railway' brake van, christened the 'Glasshouse' because of the all-round fitted windows, was dropped down into the tunnel on the Down line and stopped short of a pair of catch points, then the 20 wagons shunted onto it. Once accepted by the signalman at Park Lane signal box - itself unique, because it was inserted into the cutting wall, and any slightly obese signalman would have difficulty gaining entry because of the restrictive nature of the entrance! - the guard would set the points and release the brakes on the van and, using the sanding equipment, control the speed of the train. On arrival at Park Lane all shunting movements were carried out using capstans.

'Saddlebacks' or **'Super Ds'**, especially loaded with blind coal to reduce smoke and fume emissions, stood beneath a vent in the tunnel roof, whilst the capstan operators shunted the wagons onto them for the return trip to Wapping Bank Head.

The Author in the office, at the entrance to Crown Street Tunnel.

(Occupied by his Railway Foreman Uncle 'Ozzie' for 50 years.)

Courtesy of Joe Gerrard.

It is hard to comprehend that something really happened here 157 years ago that changed man's thinking so dramatically; and, on a more personal note, that my uncle spent his entire railway career in this very cutting.

241

The three juxtaposed tunnels.

From an 1831 print by Bury.

Crown Street Tunnels today in 2015. Courtesy of Liverpool Echo.

The Western end and only tunnel in operation today.

Courtesy of Liverpool Echo.

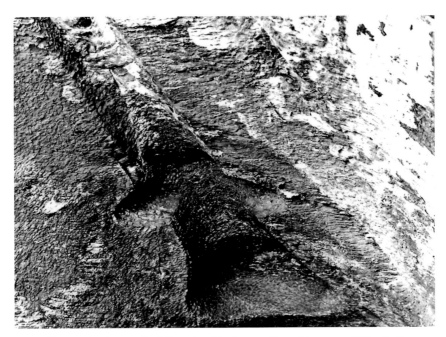

Gouge in the roof of the shed to house the chimney of 'Rocket'.

Courtesy of J Gerrard.

The sound of an electric locomotive hauling a passenger train through Edge Hill station awakens me from my reverie, bringing me, once again, back to reality.

Edge Hill, the oldest passenger station in the world, and still in use, remains much as it was when first built in 1836, the masonry looking decidedly cleaner than the blackened sandstone of the Lime Street cutting and Waterloo Tunnel mouth entrance nearby.

The oldest railway tunnel in the world still in use.

Courtesy of Liverpool Echo.

We are looking through the tunnel, (opened in 1836) from Edge Hill station platform towards Lime Street station terminus.

The line on the extreme left in the cutting is the Down Fast line. On the extreme right hand side is the Up Slow line, which in turn leads to a bi-directional Up and Down Slow line through the platform, shown in the picture, the Up Fast line being to the left.

Aerial photograph of Edge Hill looking west, 1994.

Courtesy of J Gerrard.

Starting at the bottom of the picture tis Olive Mount Junction signal box, where the lines to the right enter the tunnel, curving to the right, to connect with the Bootle Branch at Edge Lane Junction, situated just to the right of the road bridge, centre right.

Where the lines come out of the tunnel, just above the roundabout, is the former site of Pighue Lane signal box. The second bridge from the bottom is the former Circular Line, which went underneath the Gridiron Sidings but, as can be seen, is blocked off. The large white building with the tower, right centre, is Littlewood's Pools headquarters, in front of which is Liverpool Corporation's bus depot (formerly used by the trams).

Following the railway from the bottom of the picture, going under the last bridge, the line curves to the right into Edge Hill station; it continues through the tunnels for just over a mile to the present terminus in Lime Street.

Instead of taking the curve, go straight ahead as far as the dark spot under Liverpool's fine Gothic Anglican Cathedral, which dominates the scene. These are the Crown Street Tunnels, built in 1830, at the site of the terminus on the original Liverpool & Manchester Railway.

← Edge Lane Junction

↑ Olive Mount Junction Signal Box

Aerial photograph of Edge Hill looking east, 1994.

Courtesy of Joe Gerrard.

Starting at the bottom of the picture we can see Picton Road passing over the railway. To the left is the site of the former Exhibition and Park Sidings, stretching up to the new buildings in the centre. The gravitation Gridiron Sidings stretched from the little white building to the left of the road, up to the fifth bridge over the railway, looking from this vantage point. The small white building (centre right) adjacent to the road bridge is Edge Hill power signal box, with the Downhill Carriage Sidings above, curving to the right to Wavertree Junction. East of this curve is the location of the former Edge Hill Locomotive Sheds. Following from Wavertree Junction, on the right, the former Circular Line can easily be traced to the second bridge (passing over the main lines) which at one time continued under the Gridiron (now blocked off) curving towards the new buildings in the centre.

Until 1870, all trains to and from Lime Street were worked by rope using stationary engines housed on Edge Hill station platform, with shunting at the terminal station being carried out by horses up to this time. The engine house still exists today, and in 1959 the pulley wheel at the Lime Street end was discovered during modernisation work.

In 1885, widening of the large sandstone cutting was completed, enabling the tracks to be quadrupled. This 1½- mile long stretch of railway contains no fewer than seven tunnels on a 1 in 93 gradient. Opposite the former goods warehouse in Tunnel Road a row of bricks at ground level marks the location of Edge Hill No 2 signal box, demolished 26 years ago. The signalmen who worked there then would never have foreseen the destruction of their pride and joy.

This signal box along with Nos. 3, 5, 12, Wavertree Junction and Mossley Hill were replaced, as mentioned earlier, by the new power operated signal box in 1961.

The Author on the panel in Edge Hill power signal box, 1986.

Courtesy of Dave Hughes.

Edge Hill power signal box stands adjacent to Picton Road bridge, on its south-east side. It is quite close to the water tower used by steam locomotives years ago, but rusting now and awaiting its fate. No 12 signal box abutted this tower until its closure. A large open tract of land in front of the signal box is all that is left of the Gridiron Sidings. Edge Hill No 13, where Alf taught me the ropes, is no more, but the Automatic Telephone Company, renamed, still produces telecommunication equipment and stands sentinel over the empty waste. No more the aroma from Crawford's biscuit works: it is in the process of being demolished. Exhibition and Park Sidings have been lifted, leaving the offices adjacent to Picton Road bridge isolated, in stark contrast to the halcyon days.

It was here, 37 years ago, that I began my faithful connection with the railways.

So many people passed through these portals to begin a lifetime's service, witnessing the continuous activity associated with a large marshalling yard. Alas, only memories remain now, but fortunately I can record some of them for posterity. Reggie's signal box at Pighue Lane Junction has gone; no trace of the 'classroom' where I spent many happy hours during my signalman's training.

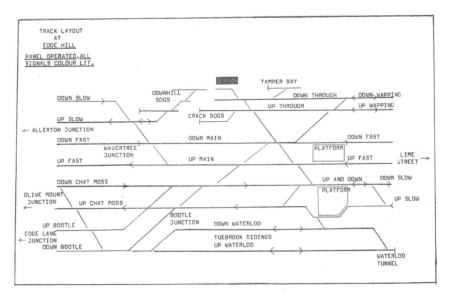

Edge Hill power signal box.

Upward of 3,000 freight wagons per day were dealt with in the yards in the Edge Hill area prior to the Railway Board's policy to dispense with single wagon loads, serving small private sidings, and to concentrate on bulk trains and containerisation. In addition, the introduction of diesel and electric traction to replace steam power, and the implementation of smokeless zones, coupled with the closure of many collieries, vastly reduced the amount of coal used and transported by rail. This, and rationalisation of the Merchant Shipping Fleet, and the closure of many Liverpool waterfront docks, sadly brought about the closure of the Gridiron Marshalling Yards and associated sidings. Beyond the main lines, a pile of bricks is all that remains of No 16 signal box; likewise No 3, a few hundred yards further to the east. The Crack sidings, formerly the Up and Down Wapping Goods lines, are now used to stable coaching stock, relieving congestion in Downhill Carriage Sidings. Stop blocks have been installed opposite the site of Edge Hill No 4 signal box, and the bridge carrying the lines to Olive Mount Junction and the Auxiliary line to the top Gridiron Sidings has been removed. Edge Hill Locomotive Shed, once covered by a permanent smoky haze and home to many famous engines and hundreds of men, will never again resound to the whistles and hisses associated with it for so long.

On the Up Slow line in Lime Street cutting.

Courtesy of Mick Langton.

247

On the Down Fast line at Edge Hill station. Courtesy of Mick Langton.

The **Circular** line and No 11 signal box are closed, the latter receiving an ignominious end at the hand of vandals who burned it down. The **'Roaring Rail'** on the original Liverpool to Manchester railway, near Olive Mount Cutting, is heard no more because the two lines were severed at Edge Hill No 3 signal box junction on the Wavertree curve, then stop-blocked to form private sidings, the connections of which are controlled by Olive Mount Junction signal box. These sidings are owned by the Liverpool Fuel Company, their premises being located on the site of the old locomotive shed which has, itself, now been closed. Wavertree Junction signal box arose from the ashes in 1948 to last another 13 years before final abolition.

The end of Edge Hill No 11 signal box.

Courtesy of 8D Association.

It had once been my ambition to work this, Edge Hill power signal box, but circumstances in 1962 and subsequent promotion in the Wigan area forestalled the idea. However, it now comes to be, quite by chance.

The original panel, built by Westinghouse and Company, was the forerunner of those in many multi-manned power signal boxes in Britain, but the train describer equipment left much to be desired and has been updated. To enable this to be modernised, a large separate panel is mounted on top of the original, serving solely for train descriptions throughout the area. Plans are now afoot to install a completely new panel because this one is life-expired.

The points from here are of the electro-pneumatic type, the compressor being located in a room underneath the operating floor. The synthetic material used for the connecting pipes is susceptible to puncture at places where it is exposed, and in this event, which is quite frequent, a loud hiss directs one to the source, where a piece of 'Sellotape' works wonders!

In Lime Street station. Photo by Terry Callaghan.

On Up Fast line in Edge Hill station. Photo by Terry Callaghan.

I am on the afternoon turn, and at 16.00hrs snow begins to fall heavily, soon overwhelming the electric point heaters. By 18.00hrs it is six inches deep, and slowly the railway grinds to a halt. Permanent Way staff are unable to keep the points clear for more than five minutes. Traffic builds up, with trains standing at successive signals for miles, but little can be done. At 21.00hrs I get relieved, but cannot leave my mate in this mess. I proceed to Wavertree Junction, with points clips and all the paraphernalia that may be of some use. The snow here is at least 9in deep because of its exposed position.

'Hello, Tony!' I hear, from a passenger sticking his head out of the Down London express. It is Jan Glasscock, the Area Manager, returning from one of his frequent jaunts.

'What are you doing up here?' he asks. *'Do you require any help?'*

'No, you're all right, boss. Drop off at the power box and give George a hand.'

He obeys my instructions. I know he can be of great assistance to my mate because of his intimate knowledge of the panel.

I stay at Wavertree Junction for several hours, clipping points and hand-signalling trains, but the Edge Hill station area becomes blocked, so I go there to evacuate passengers from a stranded train. At about 04.00hrs Eric Steward, the Area Operations Manager, arranges for a most welcome breakfast in the Downhill Sidings canteen.

Then it is back to the 'white-out'.

Just before daybreak the snow stops falling and, systematically, the points are cleared in time for the early morning workers' trains. After 22 hours at work I make my way home and fall into a deep sleep, well satisfied with my contribution.

Later, I receive the following letter:-

PC   ⇌ British Rail

British Rail (London Midland)
Rail House
Lord Nelson Street
Liverpool L1 1JF
Telephone 051-709 8292 Ext. 2800

Area Manager,
Liverpool.

Mr. A. Cook,
Signalman,
Edge Hill.

y/r
o/r   Date   13 January, 1986

Dear Tony,

BAD WEATHER – TUESDAY 7TH JANUARY AND
WEDNESDAY 8TH JANUARY

I would like to formally thank you for your
help in keeping the railway running during the
above. These circumstances tend to show up
the real 'railwaymen' and there is no doubt
you are in this category. I know you worked
exceptionally long hours, but had you have not
been prepared to stay and help, I have no doubt
there would have been delays of far greater
magnitude than there were.

Once again thank you very much.

Yours sincerely,

J. Glasscock.
Area Manager.

BR 14300/82

To be recognised as a 'railwayman' is an honour for me.

250

Three weeks later a woman is murdered, and her body is found buried in the railway embankment near Wavertree Junction. Again, snow begins to fall heavily, and the points in this area soon get blocked up. I ask a young platelayer to accompany me, in an effort to keep them clean. We approach the site of the tragic discovery and I point it out, saying:

'If you see a lady in white come from behind that bush, just ignore her!'

Arriving at the points, only a few minutes later, I find that I am completely alone.

My erstwhile assistant has vanished!

Looking towards Downhill Sidings during the middle of the night I observe an electric locomotive approaching the signal leading to the main line; not an unusual occurrence in itself, but this one is not going to stop! It passes the signal at danger, continuing on, passing the next one also. I set the points with the IPSs so as not to cause damage, but it comes to a stand right outside the signal box. I open the window and shout:

'And where the blinkin' heck do you think you are going?' or words to that effect.

I look down on the engine, waiting for the driver's head to pop out to enable me to give him another mouthful. An eerie feeling creeps over me as I realise that the engine is silent and the driver's compartment is empty!

It is New Year's Day 1986, and an engine *en route* from Downhill Sidings to Lime Street station becomes derailed outside the signal box. Severe damage is caused to the permanent way, making it necessary to call staff who are resting after the festivities. They arrive, not too happy, and bleary-eyed, spoiling for me what should have been a nice quiet day.

British Rail technicians from Crewe are wiring up the new panel in the console room, and it has been suggested that they erect a screen to avoid distracting us from our duties, but the signalmen feel it would be beneficial to witness the operation. Watching the installation of intricate electrical components and asking questions as to their functions, prove to be invaluable to us, giving an insight into the equipment we will be using. The panel, based on the NX principle, includes equipment never before incorporated into power-operated signalling.

ERSE (Electronic Route Selection Equipment).

In normal working conditions, as described earlier, NX panels are worked by means of Entrance and Exit buttons. If a malfunction occurs on the panel control, it is possible to override this by the operation of a by-pass button. In these conditions, only the entrance buttons are used and route-setting is governed by the lie of the electrically operated points.

At the moment these are being changed from electro-pneumatic to electro-hydraulic clamps locks.

Vast advances have been achieved in signalling technology since the first train passed this point over 150 years ago, but many accidents have occurred owing to the human element. New equipment, whether, mechanical or electrical, and no matter how sophisticated, will never eradicate this entirely, and a great deal of responsibility still rests with the signalman. Such is the case, working in by-pass, as total concentration is necessary on the part of the signalman during this period because of the higher degree of human involvement.

The Area Manager enjoys coming to the signal box to have a dabble on the panel, and indulge in the supping of my coffee. Whilst he is quite good operating the panel, he does have the tendency to clear the signals a little early, which is not really advisable in this signal box because the express passenger trains soon appear on the diagram once the description is received. As mentioned earlier, the Traffic Control monitors the running of the expresses, and any delay incurred can be traced. One day he clears the signals for a locomotive from the slow line at Wavertree Junction **(as usual)** when 'burp' - an express train is approaching. We both watch the progress, and subsequent stopping, of the train, and it gives me much pleasure to say to him:

'When I receive the report, I will tell the truth (as I always do?) and name the person responsible!' adding:

'Every man to his own!' Needless to say, there was no further communication from higher authority! **I wonder why?**

Original signal box at Liverpool Lime Street station.

Photo by D Ibbotson.

New signal box at Liverpool Lime Street station.

Photo by Ken Lowe.

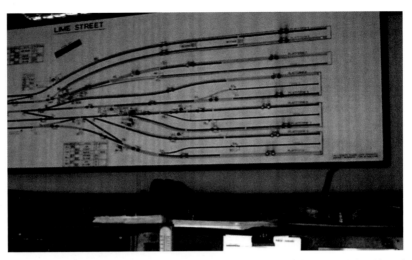

Diagram in Lime Street Station signal box. Courtesy of James MacKenzie.

Interior of Lime Street Station signal box.

Courtesy of James MacKenzie.

Miniature leverframe in Lime Street Station signal box.

Courtesy of James MacKenzie.

Now everyone has heard about the 'Great Train Robbery' of 1963 because it is so well documented, but not so the one that took place in 1986 at Edge Hill. In both, the persons involved had an intimate knowledge of railway operations.

To describe the events that took place here, it will be necessary to explain the method adopted by the gang to perpetrate their crime. On all trains devices are found known as 'Track Circuit Clips'. In the event of an accident or other event that necessitates the train crew stopping trains on an adjoining line, they can use these clips for the purpose. Two clips are joined together by a 5ft length of wire, and when placed on a track circuited running line the signal in rear is held or replaced to danger, a visual indication being displayed in the signal box.

Track Circuit Clips.

The mail train leaves Lime Street station on time, and my mate George clears the signals for it. He then observes the track circuit ahead of the signal in Edge Hill station platform becomes occupied, replacing the signal to danger. The normal procedure when a track circuit shows 'occupied' without the presence of a train is for the signalman to authorise the driver to pass the signal at danger, proceed with caution and keep a sharp look out. Unknown to the signalman, when the train comes to a stand at the signal, a gang overpowers the guard and begin to ransack the mail. In the meantime, the driver is instructed to pass the signal in accordance with the regulations and proceeds, still with the gang on board; **not part of the original plan.** In the countryside approaching Crewe the communication cord is pulled and, leaving the guard tied up, the gang alights. Somehow, the guard manages to free himself and raises the alarm. The robbery is now doomed to failure, as the gang is apprehended by the police while attempting to hitch-hike back to Liverpool, loaded up with the loot! (They are later to get their just reward.)

All long-service signalmen are familiar with the Permanent Way Ganger walking his length, a large hammer balancing on his shoulder, stopping now and again to bash a dislodged key home. He would enter the signal box, probably share a can of tea and discuss topical events, before continuing on his leisurely trek, returning to take charge of the men in his gang already at work on the track, using primitive implements such as hammers, shovels, sighting boards (or two stones) and a small can, and the track was always neat and tidy. **(Remember?)** Today things have changed, haven't they? The mechanical revolution is upon us. We have:

Tamping Machines, Grinding Machines, Packing Machines, Recording Machines, Ballast-Cleaning Machines, Lining Machines, Rail-Laying Machines, Ultra-Sonic Detecting Machines, Sandite Machines, and our newest acquisition a **Dynamic Stabilising Machine,** and the:

'RAILWAYS ARE IN A MESS!'

In operation some of these machines are comparatively quiet, but others sound like blasted machine guns going off, and almost invariably choose to fail right outside of the signal box.

So different to the tranquil days of the 'Brawn and flat-capped Brigade' that we remember with affection.

Some bright spark, (Mr S) at one time blamed delays on trains, because there were too many leaves on the line. Well! In my time there were too many trains to deal with. So many that the leaves didn't have time to settle! (Take note DB)

Vandals are the scourge of the railways at this present time, causing untold destruction and inconvenience. Twenty years ago vandalism was uncommon, but now it is rife. Little do these people realise the danger in which they are placing the travelling public and, indeed, themselves. A particular incident occurred involving one of the machines mentioned above.

Consolidating the track with Tamping Machines takes place mostly during the night and early morning, much to the annoyance of residents who live adjacent to the railway, because of the excessive noise, to say the least. A machine occupying the line directly beneath **Penny Lane (made famous by the Beatles)** overbridge breaks down. The time is 03.00hrs, and three mindless youths dislodge a heavy coping stone, capping the bridge. It crashes down onto the machine, immobilising it and causing damage estimated to run into several hundreds of pounds. The operator is only a few inches from being killed by the senseless action of these hooligans, who are never caught.

Empty coaching stock runs frequently from Downhill Sidings to Lime Street station until 09.00hrs. Electric locomotive No 86231 is hauling the stock for the West of England train, reporting No 5V55, due to leave at 08.55hrs. The coaches shudder to a dead stop outside the signal box and several track circuits become illuminated, totally unconnected with the move taking place. Picton Road bridge restricts visibility, but it is quite obvious that something is wrong, so I send the Emergency Alarm Signal to Lime Street signal box to prevent traffic from approaching. The Electrical Control Room Operator at Crewe makes telephone contact regarding breaker operation on the overhead line equipment in PL10 section, but I am unable to elucidate further information on the situation here. Shortly afterwards, the driver of the train confirms that the wires are down and his locomotive is lying on its side, blocking the Down and Up Fast lines.

Replacement of the double junction at Wavertree with a ladder crossing facilitates the introduction of Single Line Working which, incredibly, takes only five minutes, owing entirely to the relevant area being controlled solely by this signal box, and the immediate assistance of the Downhill Sidings Inspector. **The cause of this accident was a broken weld in the crossing leading out onto the main line.**

Accidents do happen, over which a human being has no control, but in other cases someone is to blame. The most carefully made plans can fail easily in one forgetful moment. In the major operations of placing new crossover roads in a ladder formation, the Overhead Line Equipment must be realigned, but to date this has never been done. It is decided by the powers that be, that isolations are not necessary and all electrically-hauled trains from Downhill Sidings will be assisted into Edge Hill station by a diesel engine in rear, with the electric engine on the front having the pantograph down. For days the system works without trouble, then someone drops a clanger.

The pantograph is left up and it tears down the wires at this busy junction, putting all lines out of action for several hours.

The first electrically-hauled passenger train passing through Lime Street cutting.

Courtesy of Ron Couchman.

A driver informs the signalman at Allerton Junction signal box of a suspected 'body' on the line at Wavertree Junction. A subsequent examination confirms this, but the 'body' is still alive, and the emergency services are sent for. In circumstances of this nature, instructions state that all locomotives and trains travelling over the line, prior to the incident, should be examined to ascertain which has been involved, but nothing is forthcoming in this regard.

Unfortunately, four days later the person dies, unidentified!

On to an amusing event.

I receive a telephone message to say that a passenger has erroneously boarded an empty stock train at Lime Street station, and has finished up in Downhill Carriage Sidings. Fortunately, I am shortly to be relieved, and as signalmen do not often get the chance to serve the public directly, I offer to take the person to Warrington in my car.

I belong to the plutocratic society now!

On the way we indulge in a friendly conversation, and I drop him off at his front door, only a mile from my own. Feeling pleased with my efforts, having had an appreciative passenger, I forget it; that is, until the following night, when at approximately the same time I receive an identical phone call, but I have no idea how he gets home as I decide that I am not operating a **'free taxi service'!**

It can be deduced from the text that quite a few signal boxes are homes to felines, but here the signalmen have close associations with a dog. Over eight years ago the shunters in Tuebrook Sidings adopted a black puppy which had strayed onto the line. In a moment of divine inspiration, someone christened him **'Blackie'!** Over the years he 'dogged' the shunting staff everywhere, becoming well known and part of the scene at Edge Hill. In 1984/85 the European Commission funds the remodelling of Edge Hill and Wavertree Junction, and relaying operations take place every weekend for months. This signal box becomes a focal point, with every Tom, Dick and Harry invading our privacy. Blackie, not to be outdone, joins them, not refusing any morsels offered to him. When all the staff finally leave for home on Sunday evenings, he is quite content, curling up in front of the panel. Today, Blackie is accepted as part of the furniture in the signal box, returning every Saturday night when the activity commences. His popularity can be judged from the occasion when the Area Operations Manager visits the signal box, and Blackie is missing. On entering, he first enquires about him, saying, 'I've brought him some biscuits'. After an hour or so, drinking my coffee, and smoking my cigars, he turns to me and says:

'Seeing Blackie isn't here, you might as well have the biscuits,'

'Oh! Thank you, very much!' I reply sarcastically.

Several motor cars have been found dumped, after being stolen, on the site of the old warehouse sidings beneath Picton Road bridge, but the discovery of a safe leads to intensive police activities. First, the British Transport Police are involved, and they establish that it belongs to a large bookmaker's company and it warrants civil police action. I am informed that the safe is intact and that 10% of the contents would be handed over as a reward, as it was I who discovered it first. Police vehicles move to and from the scene for several hours, while I calculate 10% of this and 10% of that, though not going beyond £50,000!

My appetite whetted, I proceed to the site of the crime, only to find the back of the safe is ripped open like a sardine can! 10% of what?

It is a bitter winter's night - enough to freeze them off a brass monkey! The Signal and Telegraph Department's two technicians and I sign on for a night's duty at 22.00hrs. The technicians are on duty for emergency purpose only, covering Lime Street, Allerton Junction, and this signal box for any electrical malfunction of the equipment. They are domiciled in an adjacent room (equipped with suitable beds!) to the operating floor. Roy, the youngest of them, always comes in, has a cup of tea, and shares the happenings of the day, and being an avid supporter of Liverpool Football Club this is often the subject of discussion when he reports for duty. At midnight he bids me goodnight, vanishing into his cubby hole! At 02.00hrs it begins to get very cold in the operating room, so much so that I have to don extra clothing in an effort to keep warm; but this is useless, as it gets colder, and colder, and colder. I now know what Scott of the Antarctic had to put up with on his expedition to the South Pole. Icicles begin to form on the inside of the windows, and I am unable to see out of them. I suppose I could wake up my friends in the next room for them to investigate, but, decide not to spoil their dreams! At 06.00hrs Roy comes in, bleary-eyed, as red as a beetroot, asking why I am wearing my overcoat. I explain, and he then tells me he had turned off the valve on the central heating pipe leading into the operating floor when he went to bed!

I won't relate what I said, but you can imagine!

Wembley, the home of English football, is always the aim of teams vying for the FA Cup. Two great teams, Liverpool and Everton, have qualified to play in this year's final. The exodus begins on a Saturday morning using all modes of transport. Twenty-two trains leave Lime Street in a blaze of Red and Blue. Segregation is non-existent among the supporters. The actual result is unimportant, but it is dubbed the **'Friendly Final'**. However, coming back to Liverpool, the story is different. In all my signalling experience I have never witnessed scenes of such utter chaos.

The first two 'footballers' (as their trains are commonly known) arrive as I come on duty at 21.00hrs, and are disposed of at Lime Street without any problems, but one must bear in mind that the normal passenger train service must be given preference over these specials; and as there are only nine platforms at the terminal station, trains begin to queue, one after the other, between Edge Hill and Lime Street, awaiting acceptance. Frustrated supporters alight in the tunnels, walking the short distance into Lime Street station, but their action causes a cessation of traffic on all the other lines, thereby stopping everything. Groups of banner-bearing fans jump off a train near the signal box, marching over the main line, chanting, to the road opposite. The same is happening at Wavertree Junction, Sefton Park and Mossley Hill, and little can be done to stem the jubilant throng intent on getting a last pint before the pubs close. Unfortunately, many are too late as it is now 3am before the last train is dealt with at Liverpool, eight hours after leaving London.

Track Circuit Block Regulations apply in all modern panel-operated signal boxes, but an event on Sunday 25th January 1987 alters this conception. The 'fringe' signal boxes, working to Edge Hill are those at Lime Street station, Allerton Junction, Olive Mount Junction and Edge Lane Junction. On this date Edge Lane Junction signal box is reduced to ashes by vandals, putting two signalmen out of a job, and emergency signalling has to be introduced.

Between Edge Lane and Bootle Junction signal boxes, Absolute Block Regulations operate, and we, the signalmen, are approached by management with a view to working this system in the future on this section of line.

Following our agreement, a block instrument is installed, and to date, both Track Circuit Block and Absolute Block Regulations operate in this signal box, a very unusual situation indeed.

The line between Olive Mount and Edge Lane Junction signal boxes is now closed and the points at Olive Mount leading from the Down Chat Moss line have been recovered and replaced by plain line. The facing points at Edge Lane Junction, leading to Olive Mount, are now clipped out of use, but as they are still connected to the defunct signal box frame (still standing) it is found necessary to provide an indication in this signal box for fear the points in question are tampered with. This is achieved by wiring up the track circuit indication to flash intermittently, again, something new in signalling practices. The small amount of traffic timed to run on this portion of line is diverted into the Gullet Sidings, then redirected via Picko Tunnel.

Over the years special trains running to Aintree for the Grand National, have been reduced in their numbers, to one. This particular train is undoubtedly made famous by its inclusion in the title of a book by Agatha Christie; I refer, of course, to **'The Orient Express'.** This beautifully kept train, each coach with its own name (girls' Christian names) arrives at Edge Hill station, where an engine is waiting to attach onto the rear to enable it to reverse then travel down the Bootle Branch.

Unfortunately, this move will never occur again, for two reasons.

First, vandals throwing stones broke two windows in a coach carrying the **'well-to-do'** on a section of track that has received the infamous title **'Bomb Alley'**; and secondly, the widespread problem of permanent way defects through lack of maintenance and financial economies. The result: no more passenger trains to Aintree to see the horses, instead:

'THE RAILWAYS ARE GOING TO THE DOGS!'

Headboard of the 'Orient Express'. Photo by Author.

But, that was not always the case. Years ago, a continuous procession of trains headed their way to Aintree, where a large group of sidings was sited. The first impression one gets when looking at the second picture on the next page is that the signalman working in that box has a cushy job. (I wish I had had the opportunity to work there!) Even Aintree Locomotive Sheds to the left are devoid of engines, taking into account the activity that abounds, what with the small number of wagons in the sidings.

The 'well-to-do'. Photo by Author.

Aintree Sorting Sidings and Engine Sheds. Photo by Ron Couchman.

A few more days and the sidings are cleared in readiness for the influx of traffic bringing passengers aboard the trains, who have loads of money which will be gleaned from them by the avaricious bookies, rubbing their hands. While the locomotives are standing idle, steaming away, the railway comes to a halt. The sidings staff, not to be outdone, disappear and go to the embankment alongside to enjoy a free view of the spectacle. Meanwhile, the signalman, in their absence takes advantage of the situation by pushing a platelayers' trolley along an adjacent line, stopping at an engine to load up a **little** Yorkshire coal 'for use in the signal box stove' then get his head down **(I repeat, signalmen are a versatile breed)** until it is time to release the trains to travel to Aintree station, to pick the passengers, the majority with lighter pockets!

All pictures taken in the Aintree area are courtesy of Ron Couchman.

Aintree Sorting Sidings on 'Grand National' day.

'Double-Headed.'

'Not forgetting the workers.'

Aintree Sorting Sidings: No 2 to the left, No 1 to the right.

Aintree Sorting Sidings West signal box.

Signalman Ted Parker in the above box.

Returning to a lighter side of signal box work, I wish to relate a particularly amusing story:

Any railway signalman will confirm that it is possible to work in a signal box and never meet, in person, the signalman in the adjacent one, although they may speak to each other over the telephone for years. I have worked with Alan, a signalman in Allerton Junction signal box for 18 months, but have never had the pleasure of meeting him. So, to put the matter right, I decide to visit him incognito on my next rest day off - unknown to him, that is! Donning a high visibility jacket over my uniform, with the regulation red pen protruding from my pocket to give that official look, I enter his domain.

Allerton Junction signal box. Courtesy of Andrew Gardiner.

'Good morning, signalman,' I say, with a faint smile on my face.

'Good morning to you, Sir,' he replies.

I really must look the part!

I spend a little time looking at the signal box diagram - all bosses do this on their first visit to a signal box - then move over to view the familiar landscape.

'And who might you be?' he enquires, squinting as if thinking, 'I've not seen this gaffer before.'

'I am the new Inspector from the depot,' pointing to the large building behind the signal box.

'Oh! You're the chap that's got Bill Jones's job, are you?'

'Spot on, that's me.'

The scene has now been set for my performance; but will it be successful?

'I am not very conversant with this area, having only being transferred from Buxton yesterday.' I tell him, and continue:

'Of course, you can tell by my lingo that I am a Scouser, but I've only worked on the 'Lanky' at Kirkdale.' He nods.

'Is this a very busy signal box?' I ask. **(As if I am interested?)**

He operates several levers and is kept reasonably occupied for a few minutes, and then says:

'Very much so,' going into details, purely to impress me. **(I've never heard such a load of tripe!)**

'I'd better put my name in the Train Register.' I say, taking the pen from my pocket.

He looks over my shoulder as I write, '**J Soap. Inspector**' and the time '**10.15hrs**'.

Without letting my eyes wander from the page, I say to him:

'I know what you are thinking, but my name is not Joe Soap, it is pronounced, So-ap!'

'Joseph So-ap, but you can call me Joe.'

'Do you fancy a cup of tea, Joe?' asks Alan, filling the kettle up.

'I prefer coffee if you have any - er, what did you say your name was?'

'Alan.'

While I am partaking in this welcome refreshment I glance over towards south Liverpool's football ground opposite (where I have been to watch a few matches) purely to withhold a natural urge to burst out laughing, but it would be a shame to spoil everything after getting this far!

I pretend to examine all the instruments in the signal box, until I come to the one connected only to my own.

'I've never seen an instrument like this before.'

'Well Joe, they have only recently been introduced into signal boxes, and are Emergency Alarms. We have no bells now, like in the old days.'

(The young whipper-snapper; he's still wearing nappies!) *'This one is to Edge Hill power signal box.'*

'If something goes wrong with a train or on the track, I press this button and my mate 'Cookie' will stop all trains coming in this direction.'

'Very interesting. Very interesting.' I say, adding, *'I'd like to meet this "Cookie" sometime and visit a power signal box.'*

'He's rest day today, but he will be on tomorrow, I'll mention it to him, and tell him to expect you.'

'That's great Alan; I will endeavour to be there early tomorrow morning. Thanks very much!'

Traffic is building up, and Alan is running up and down the frame, pulling and replacing levers.

'Do you think I could pull a lever over?' I ask.

'Yes! Pull No 46.' explaining how to get it fully over, with the least possible exertion.

'I wouldn't be able to cope with this,' I mutter, *'or, in fact, make a signalman.'* as I pretend to fumble the exercise.

He stands proud as a peacock, with rippling muscles, the latter obtained by using the exercise equipment placed on the locker near the gas fire.

'That's Garston Junction signal box over there,' he says, pointing, *'and the "White House" in front.'* (He is referring to the administration block built on the site of the old Speke, commonly called Garston, Locomotive Sheds. I've been to both many times.)

I observe a dropper wire has become detached from the contact wire on the Overhead Equipment outside of the signal box, and advise him to report the matter to the Electrical Control at Crewe.

He telephones immediately, informing them that 'Inspector So-ap' had brought it to his attention.

It is now time for me to leave.

Next day the Signalmen's Inspector visits his signal box and enquires who 'Inspector So-ap' is, when he sees the signature in the Train Register.

Later, in conversation with Alan, I let the 'Moggie' *(cat, not mouse!)* out of the bag and after a sexual expletive, my Mother and Father's marital status is questionable; that is as far as he is concerned.

The identity of our mythical inspector soon becomes common knowledge in the area, and forever a source of embarrassment to my friend and colleague, who gave a lot of people something to laugh about. **(Thanks Al, for the pleasure.)**

Lever frame in Allerton Junction signal box. Courtesy of Andrew Gardiner.

Garston Junction signal box. Courtesy of Ray Burgess.

264

Garston Church Road signal box. Courtesy of Ray Burgess.

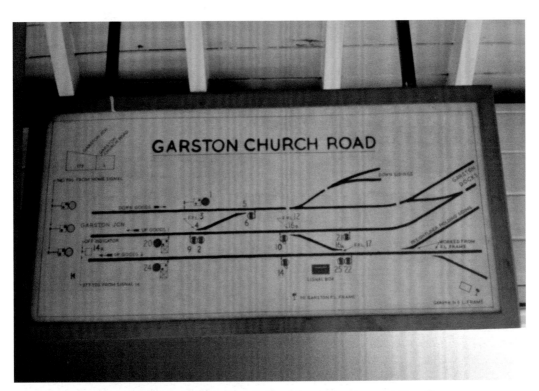

Diagram in Garston Church Road signal box. Courtesy of Ray Burgess.

I see a pinpoint of light in the distance, marking the end of Victoria Tunnel, my intended destination. On my left, nothing remains of Waterloo Tunnel Mouth signal box that backed onto the Up Slow line from Lime Street station. It is here I start my walk under the City of Liverpool.

One line enters the tunnel, but travels only about ½-mile, it being used as a shunting neck for trains working in Tuebrook Sidings, when the beam of my torch falls on a contraption, standing against the black, grimy wall; something I have never seen before. After closer examination I assume it to be a **Treadle Gong**.

A 3ft-high square iron plate is mounted onto the tunnel wall, and a striker, the size of a small sledge hammer, is connected by means of rods and weight bars to a treadle, fastened on the inside of the nearest rail.

The eerie silence is shattered by a resounding gong that echoes within the overpowering darkness, as bits of corroded metal fall onto the dampened ground, smoothed by the constant seepage of water through the porous sandstone. After 16 years of disuse it still actually works, but never again will it ring as a train approaches the exit of the tunnel, as in days gone by.

A few years ago a coal train ran away from the Gridiron Sidings and careered into the tunnel, demolishing the newly erected stop block. The chassis of the brake van, upside down, bits of wood and twisted metal piled high, litter the area where it finally came to rest, deep under Wavertree Road. In the quietness, drops of water falling from the arch form small shimmering pools that glint in the torch light. I look in each direction and the white semi-circles appear to be of the same size, and up above, I estimate, stands the University of Liverpool at the top of Brownlow Hill. Continuing on down the 1 in 60 gradient, I hear the sound of running water, its source unknown.

The thought passes through my mind that I should turn back.

Courageously, I carry on, reaching an underground spring, mushrooming several inches from the ground in the centre of the tunnel, its water (ultra-clear) running in rivulets, delta fashion, towards the side walls. A faint rumbling causes me to stop and listen: a train is approaching though, thankfully, not in this tunnel which is devoid of sleepers and rails! I presume my geographical location to be in the region of St George's Plateau in Lime Street, and that the train is running in the single-bore tunnel between Moorfields and Lime Street stations. After dodging the miniature water flows for a few hundred yards, they all converge and disappear into a man-made trench built during the construction of the tunnel, presumably to contain the hawsers that hauled traffic up to Edge Hill prior to 1895. A scurrying rat alarms me as I near the end of my quest. My eyes take several minutes to adjust to the bright daylight in the cutting, no more than 200yd long and filled to a depth of at least 6ft with piles of junk thrown over the walls, high above. Clambering over beds, settees and rotting mattresses, I arrive at the entrance to Waterloo Tunnel, rising sharply upwards for a distance of approximately ¼- mile.

So sharp is this gradient that the sleeper ends were bedded in concrete for its full length on both sides of the tunnel.

These lines of concrete, with square indentations, are all that remain to remind one of the tunnel's original use. In daylight once more, a small grass cutting leads to an overbridge that carries the Link line from the north before it plunges underground approaching Moorfields station, a few hundred yards away. On this bridge, in stucco, is a mythical Liver Bird, the symbol of Liverpool, beneath which many millions of passengers have passed before catching sight of the port's famous waterfront and the ships that would transport them to far-off places. I ponder the reason for this particular, insignificant bridge being so adorned with the emblem later acquired by Liverpool Football Club, which more recently adopted an anthem that epitomises the general attitude of people here, and would become synonymous with this great city, the world over:

'YOU'LL NEVER WALK ALONE'.

Did this bird, now perching, forlorn on this bridge, cast a companionable spell over all those who passed beneath? **I like to think so.**

At times traffic tends to build up at this very busy junction, and it is necessary for a signalman to assess the situation ten-or-more minutes hence. I found, not to the liking of some of the upper management, that keeping trains on restrictive signal aspects is definitely to be preferred over setting routes with green signals, knowing the possibility of two or more trains could be stopped awaiting its passage. Working to the above criterion, I observe a train approaching on the Up Fast line from Lime Street station and decide to give preference to a local train from Wigan to cross over in front of it from the Down Chat Moss to the Down Fast line.

Just managed to clear the signals without stopping the express!

Decisions such as this take place many times during a turn of duty. Only a few minutes later the Area Operations Controller wants to know the reason for the delay.

The normal reply is as simple as '**congestion**', and this is usually accepted without question. However, shortly after, the Regional Controller at Crewe makes an identical enquiry. My immediate reaction is one of disbelief for such a fuss to be made of an express being delayed one minute; that is until I am informed the new Area Manager is travelling on it! I explain the reasons, then forget about it. Three days later I receive a letter requesting a written report. What a joke, I think, replying in a manner suitable for such a trivial occurrence:

'Sir,

As a result of severe congestion at Edge Hill on the said date, the above-mentioned train was delayed by 1 minute.

I acknowledge that one is always wiser after the event, but in this instance, I must inform you, I would have made the same decision again.' (I continue, still treating the matter as a huge joke.)

'May I remind you the day in question was Friday the 13th, and anyone travelling through Edge Hill on that date must take "pot luck".

Yours respectfully,

A J Cook. Signalman. Edge Hill PSB.'

I am soon to find out our new Area Manager has no sense of humour, for I am formerly charged with delaying the train unnecessarily, and subsequently receive a severe reprimand, this to be entered on my service record.

What a complete waste of ink!

I consider the likes of the above as very petty, because at times signalmen are often called upon to make split-second decisions, knowing the responsibility is fully on their shoulders. May I refer back to the basic signalling principles under the Absolute Block Regulations:

A signalman must always observe a tail lamp on every train: this is an indication that the train is complete.

All trains running on British Railways today are fitted with continuous brakes, operated either by vacuum or air. If a train were to break into two or more portions, the severing of the brake pipes would activate the brakes, bringing all portions to a stand immediately; unlike the old days of loose-coupled trains when, in similar circumstances the rear portions of the train were at the mercy of the gradient, causing in some circumstances, untold damage, as the wagons careered out of control. Bearing this in mind, I observe a fully-fitted Freightliner train passing the signal box, minus its tail lamp. This is not unusual here, because, tail lamps are frequently stolen from trains travelling at slow speed in this area; whether they have monetary value, I do not know.

The question arises, if the train had broken in two, it would have stopped with the brake application mentioned. So it would be safe to assume that the train is complete in these circumstances, but the regulations state that the train must be stopped and examined.

I contact the Gullet Sidings charge man and request him to examine the train, and you can imagine my surprise when I am informed the engine is attached to only half of its vehicles. This impossible situation warrants thorough investigation, so the locomotive is detached and sent along the adjoining line to examine the line as far as the next signal box.

Two miles from Edge Hill, the engine crew find the missing wagons at a stand.

Arrangements are made to facilitate the removal of the vehicles, and it is only then that the circumstances which led to this unbelievable incident are learned.

Apparently, the driver observed an obstruction in the form of a sleeper placed across the track in front of his train. Stopping, he alights from his locomotive to remove it. Unbeknown to him, a gang has detached the rear vehicles, reconnecting the brake pipes on the front portion. The driver releases the brakes, and receiving the correct indications in his cab, continues on his journey as normal, not suspecting anything is amiss. The unexpected can happen, as in this instance, which in turn could lead to a very serious accident.

There is certainly a moral here for all signalmen:

'DO NOT TAKE ANY CHANCES'.

The environment in signal boxes has vastly improved from oil lamps, coal fires and the regulation lino. The older type manual boxes have now been fitted with false ceilings to conserve energy. **(This would not have been welcomed by Harry at Woodside Sidings. Where would he have dried his tobacco?)** Only the other week, management agreed to our application to have the floor carpeted, and gave us the option of colours, the final colour being a deep maroon. This is followed by a microwave oven, but the application for a reclining chair fell on stony ground. We didn't even get a reply.

The installation of the new panel has highlighted problems with the 25-year-old Train Describers which are life-expired. It is not possible to couple the two up. So it is decided to replace them with Visual Display Units (VDUs) and keyboards. Two 11in screens cover the area from Lime Street to Allerton and Olive Mount signal boxes. A 5ft x 4ft x 4ft cabinet holding the electrical components for the VDUs stands beside the panel at least 9ft from the signalman's desk. The proposal is to place the screens on top of this cabinet, but the descriptions are only ½in long x ¼in wide: far too small to see, unless the viewer is 12in away.

The signalman would have to walk to the cabinet every time a description is received.

Certainly, most unsatisfactory for the efficient running of this signal box.

An application is sent to management requesting that the VDUs and keyboards be placed on the desk for easy operation, but is turned down for the following reasons:

COST

1 **(Huh!)** The whole system is costing approximately £80,000,

   and

2 The advanced stage of the installation, which cannot now be altered.

We'll see about that!

I approach the Chief Installer asking him is it possible to place the screens and keyboards on the desk, and the cost involved.

He replies, *'The cost of two plugs, say a couple of quid, but there will be a problem with the solid concrete floor, i.e. no channel to run the wires.'*

I notice a Signal and Telegraph engineer outside the signal box cutting some steel, using a hand held circular saw.

'I'll soon fix that up.' I reply.

Ten minutes later the signal box is filled with clouds of dust, as the circular saw easily penetrates the concrete. A hammer and chisel completes the operation. The wires are run from behind the panel to the desk, and covered in. Out comes the **'Hoover',** down the carpet, and the VDUs are sitting in their permanent position on the desk. Soon after, a member of the management's team enters and makes a favourable comment about the set up!

Signalman Dave Hughes and box lad (?) in Edge Hill power signal box.

(Note the position of VDUs on the desk.)

Putting VDUs in signal boxes baffles me, because for over one hundred years Block Instruments, Single Stroke Bells and other ancient equipment has operated efficiently, with the minimum of maintenance. I cannot accept that VDUs would last anywhere near one hundred years; in fact, those installed in this signal box are a pain in the ****** neck! Being on continuously, the heat is affecting the works. They switch off automatically, setting off a fault alarm which is loud enough to protect the Bank of England. This is not all: in the process, all trains are lost, and we must ascertain by telephone where they are located. Until the system cools down and switches on again, all trains must be signalled using the telephone. In addition, other faults occur, where it is necessary for technicians to be called out to rectify them. This necessitates bringing on duty a Relief Signalman to assist us.

So much for modern technology. (Pigeons would make a better job of it!)

Management has decided to replace the Traffic Regulators working here, with box lads. This means all the responsibility for running the box is placed entirely into the hands of the signalman. Come early Monday morning I hear the sound of jingling chains turning, I see a sight that defies description - however I shall try.

I see a figure in a black leather coat with hundreds of tassels, festooned with garlands of silver chains, stars, and crescent shaped moons placed at random covering a tee shirt advertising the cattle disease **'ANTHRAX'.** This, in turn, is tucked into a pair of jeans coloured in various shades of blue, with bleached white patches in an abstract design contrasting with the highly polished cowboy boots! Topping all this regalia, with unkempt hair protruding from under a jet black helmet emblazoned with a hideous red dragon, is none other than our new box lad Robbie, looking very much like a visitor from another planet.

He has graduated from the management's Youth Training Scheme **(I wonder where they pick them from?)** but he quickly settles down to the duties designated to him. It soon becomes apparent that here we have an extraordinary lad, not only in his mode of dress, but in his adaptation to signal box work, continually asking questions on signalling practice and principles. So much so, I offer to tutor him in Rules and Regulations, but only as long as he remains interested in the subject. It doesn't take him long to memorise the Bell Codes. After a further two weeks he masters all the Absolute Block Regulations at the age of sixteen, which is extremely commendable.

When any of the bosses visit the signal box I ask them to fire questions at him. Rarely does he fail to answer them correctly.

You can imagine my disgust when I am detailed to report to Lime Street for my biennial Rules examination. I ring the Area Operations Manager complaining strongly about it, but in the usual diplomatic manner expected from the management, he says:

'Come down to the office, you know more than the inspector that is taking you anyway.'

I capitulate, knowing I'm going to have a day off work!

Entering the office I notice this young **'whipper-snapper'** of an inspector has all the Rules and Regulation Books on the table in front of him. I likewise place mine in a convenient position.

'Why have you put your books on the table?' adding, *'You are not allowed to do that.'* Pointing to his, I say, *'Yours are there, mine here. You open yours, I open mine.'*

Without more ado he begins to fire questions at me without reference to any book, and I know this chap knows his stuff. Mind you, knowing the rules does not necessarily mean one would make a good signalman. At times, we clash and have different viewpoints. Only then are the books opened, and the issue thrashed out, but, in one instance he questions my answer, saying:

'That is not in the rule book.'

'I know quite well it is not in the rule book, but that's the way I do it. If you can think of a better way, please let me know!' After four gruelling hours, probably the hardest I have had to endure throughout my railway career, he says, *'I am satisfied with your knowledge of the Rules and Regulations.'* I snap back by saying, *'But you have missed something out.'*

'Have I? Such as?' he asks.

'You didn't ask me who printed this book,' holding it in front of his eyes. *'Do you happen to know?'*

'I haven't a clue.' he replies.

'Well, Bemrose Ltd, printed this one, and McCorquodale's this.' I say, adding:

'I know the Rules and Regulations books from the beginning to end, which is a lot more than you do!'

The next day a very officious gentleman enters the signal box greeting both me and the box lad.

'Good morning, gentlemen,' he says. He introduces himself. My name is **(you know who, as I do.)** He recognises me as being his tutor on the rules and regulations at Warrington a few years before. I enquire of him, *'And what are you doing now?'*

'Oh,' he said, continuing, *'I am on the Railway Board in London.'*

All this in such a short space of time.

270

'*Do you know,*' he says to me, '*I remember the last thing you said to me when I finished learning the rules with you at Warrington.*'

'*Oh! Yes, and what was that?*' I enquire.

'*You said to me, as long as I work on the railways,*' adding. '*You will never be a railwayman, or know as much as me.*'

Railwaymen don't push pens!

'*Yes, I remember saying that,*' adding, '*and I reiterate that very statement today.*'

Robbie bursts out laughing, as this 'fella' leaves the signal box, his ego obviously deflated, but, he deserved the treatment. **Trying to convince me he knows it all!**

I often wonder if he ever recalls being taken down a rung by a humble signalman?

Signal boxes, by their very nature, are placed at strategic locations, and from the confines therein it is possible to see not only the area of control but a great deal further. It is 06.30hrs, and Robbie and I have just booked on duty. Shortly after, I notice a chap walking along a public road opposite the signal box.

'*Robbie, come here a minute. Do you recognise that man over there?*'

'*Nup! Never seen im before in me life.*'

'*Well, he is a train robber.*'

'*Howd'ya know dat den?*' he says disbelievingly, in a strong Scouse accent. '*Dat's impossuble.*'

'*Now let's see.*' I say, fingering through a copy of the timetable.

'*Yes, we have a mail train leaving Lime Street at 07.10hrs and that bloke's after catching it.*'

'*Gerraway, you cudn't know dat.*'

'*Look there,*' I say, pointing. '*He has met up with two of his compatriots.*'

'*Aw! gorray der not doin' an 'arm.*'

The route to be taken by the train has a speed restriction of 5 mph, so it is easy for anyone to jump on board, if they so desire. The British Transport Police are informed of our observations, and request us to hold the train back until they can position themselves. The train is thus stopped at the signal box with a red flag, and the driver told to await further instructions.

Cackling from walkie-talkies indicates that the 'bobbies' have reached their appointed places.

'*Driver, proceed as normal.*' I tell him, also the reason why his train was stopped.

'*Okay bobbie!*' he shouts.

Slowly the train pulls away. The three men now begin to cross over the four main lines and board the slow moving train, but their journey is probably the shortest they'll ever make, for they are immediately arrested and taken into custody.

'*How did'ya no day wer train robbers?*' enquires Robbie.

'*Oh! I found that was easy, because that road leads to office blocks, and people working there have 'bobbies' jobs, and only start work at 9 o'clock. So it looked mighty suspicious to me, seeing a bloke in jeans at that time of the morning.*' I answer.

'*I think you'd make a gud poleeceman.*' says Robbie.

'*No! I do not think so. Do you not think I make a better signalman?*'

Frowning, he says, '*Yup*', hesitates a little, '*Yer not sur bad, but, not as gud as Little Bob!*'

'**Hmm,**' I asked for that, didn't I?

We burst out laughing in unison!

My ego is further deflated when Robbie informs me '**ANTHRAX**' is not a cattle disease at all, but a pop group.

Never heard of it.

The music they play is decidedly different from that of my teenage years when the **Andrews Sisters** and **Inkspots** were all the rage. For the rest of the morning, Robbie rings his mates stationed from Land's End to John O'Groats, to tell them, '*We cort der mail train robbers.*'

Robbie is a keen motor-bike fan, and his knowledge on the subject is good. Up-to-date literature on machines in the 600 and 750cc classes is scattered around the signal box. I tell him my son has won many awards racing 'Yamaha' 250cc LCs and TZs at Oulton Park, Aintree, Cadwell Park and many other circuits in Britain. At least we have a mutual interest and something to talk about, apart from the rules and reg's. Looking at his motor-bike jacket, I think. '**Yes, you ride a 'Kawasaki' 750cc machine!**'

'*What kind of bike do you ride, Robbie?*' I ask.

Proud as a peacock, he replies, '*A Honda 90!*'

I smile, but say nothing!

'*Signalman, there is no light in L/E 44, which appears to have a black plastic bag over the signal aspect.*' reports the driver of a mail train, from the signal less than 100yd from the signal box.

'*Proceed to Lime Street as quickly as possible, driver.*' my mate Little Bob replies.

(Robbie's mate as well?) I understand!

Only on its arrival at the station does it become known that a sinister plot to rob the train has been foiled. Little Bob is justly rewarded with £25 for his actions.

Two weeks later, on the night turn, I observe the same train on the track diagram passing through Mossley Hill station at normal speed, with all signals in the 'Off 'position. L/E 11 signal protects Wavertree Junction 1½ miles in advance of the above station, and the train appears to have slowed considerably.

The SPT (Signal Post Telephone) rings from this signal.

'*Standing at L/E 11, bobbie.*' says the driver.

'*The signal is "Off" for you, driver.*' I reply.

'*Oh, no its not. It is showing a full Red!*'

'*Hey! Wait a minute; a gang is boarding the train. I am getting aboard my loco and not moving until I get assistance.*' he says, hanging up abruptly. The police are summoned and soon reach the scene, but by this time the robbers have disappeared with the loot. The same method has been adopted, using a black plastic bag but, in addition, a crude, very well constructed signal made with simple kitchen equipment is sited adjacent to the blacked-out one.

A similar method was used during the 'Great Train Robbery' of the early 1960s.

We, the signalmen, are approached by management and asked to co-operate with the Transport Police, allowing them access to the signal box at any time. Even though signal boxes should be kept private, we agree.

Every night two policemen are domiciled in the box, armed with Walkie-Talkies, night binoculars - and their sarnies!

For the purpose of seeing out of the signal box at night, it is far better to have the main lights off. The route lights on the panel give satisfactory illumination around the desk area, but the rest is in darkness; this puts the policemen, who are lying down surveying the scene, in peril of being kicked or trodden on by us. However, my other mate on the opposite turn likes the lights on, which proves to be a mistake because the mail train is robbed again at L/E 44, right under the noses of the observant occupants in the signal box!

This highly professional gang is resorting to all kinds of tactics, thus being one step ahead of the embarrassed police force. Sarcastic slogans are appearing on walls around the area, poking fun at their inability to catch them. Cans of paint, brushes and other paraphernalia in plastic bags, are stacked in the corner of the signal box: for future evidence?

I look at the bags and wonder whether they have been loaned to us by the robbers!

So serious is this state of affairs that extra police are drafted in from Newcastle, London and many other places in an effort to catch the gang. The exact number is not disclosed to us, for obvious reasons, but there are a lot, judging that each section is given a call sign, e.g. **'Able One'** to **'Zebra One'**.

The serenity of the night is shattered by a high-pitched female voice.

'Control to Charlie One. Are you receiving me? Over!'

'Charlie One to Control. Receiving you loud and clear. Over!'

(The signal box is the control centre for the whole operation.)

'Control to Queen One. Are you receiving me? Over!'

'Queen One to Control. Receiving you loud and clear. Over!'

'Control to Queen One. The mail train has left Crewe on time. Over!'

'Roger and out!'

Night in, night out, it continues, unabated, with monotonous regularity.

'Control to Baker One. Can you see the two persons near Littlewood's car park? Over!'

This is it, I think!

'Baker One to Control, I have them in view. Over!'

'Control to Baker One. They appear to be "screwing" the white van!'

'Baker one to Control. Yes, they have screwed the van, and stolen the radio. Over!'

Subsequently, these two are arrested, but our gang is still at large.

'There! There!' I shout, pointing, tripping over the policewoman, lying on the floor and peering out of the window.

'There.' I repeat.

'One of the gang, silhouetted against the floodlights in Downhill Sidings.'

'Go and get him.' I say excitedly. **(Pound notes are dancing before my eyes.)**

'Sorry, cannot do that. All he is doing is trespassing.' says the lady in charge.

So the golden opportunity has been lost, I think.

'Tonight, we are keeping radio silence.' I am told by the now well established control officer.

'Hurray!' I exclaim.

'No more, Able, Baker, Charlie and Doggin' to contend with,' I say.

Come three o'clock in the morning, the police collect all the plastic bags and prepare to leave the signal box. *'You're going home early, aren't you?'* I ask.

'Yes, we've finished our business.' comes the reply.

I think what a total waste of time and money this has been. Breathing a sigh of relief, I report for duty the following night knowing, for the first time in months, it would be spent without intrusion on my privacy.

(The phone rings.) It is my mate Alan in Allerton Junction Signal Box.

'Hi, Tone! Heard the news?'

'Heard about what?' I reply.

'They caught the train robbers at Wavertree Junction last night!'

'Well, by the heck. No one told me!'

I sit down in total disbelief.

Oh! Well, the job has been completed successfully. Just a question now of collecting the substantial reward?

Prior to Robbie reaching his 18th birthday he leaves Edge Hill to attend a course at the Manchester School of Signalling. It is no surprise to me that he passes with flying colours and top of the class. He gains promotion in a very short time, and is at present working in one of the manual signal boxes in the Liverpool area. I have the pleasure of working in the signal box next to him on level terms. **(One signalman to another!)**

You will recall earlier that I wrote about Roy, the young Signal and Telegraph Technician, and how through his actions switching off the radiators, I nearly froze. As I said he is an avid supporter of Liverpool Football Club, going to most matches as shift work permits. So proud is he, waving the ticket to me for the big match tomorrow at Hillsborough, Sheffield.

Roy didn't come home, but his name lives forever, along with many more, on the memorial with its eternal flame outside his beloved club at **Anfield!**

The Regional Traffic Inspector advises me that major re-laying is taking place between Lime Street station and Edge Hill on the Up Slow line, and would I be prepared to act as Operating Department Supervisor (ODS)? I willingly accept for it gets me out into the fresh air. An ODS is responsible for overseeing all traffic movements to and from the site of work, liaising with the Inspectors from other departments who are also engaged in the project. Come Sunday morning, suitably attired with wet weather clothing, 'wellies', and hard helmet **(the latter as defence against missiles liable to be thrown from the top of the 70ft-deep cutting)** I make my way to Edge Hill station.

From a position at the end of the bi-directional Up and Down Slow line platform it is possible to see Lime Street station 1½ miles away. In this short distance there are as many tunnels as in the 400 miles between London (Euston) and Glasgow, although not all span the four lines; some have only two lines passing through, and one is of a single-bore construction. After leaving the station ramp, then passing under Tunnel Road bridge, I am immediately enveloped by a vast, deep cutting, the original sandstone now blackened with age. Bright green lichen spreads copiously, seeking sustenance from the porous stone. High up, above the electrification equipment, trees and grass cling perilously to small ledges, bringing a little colour into this bleak environment, the bleakness more pronounced in winter when huge icicles hang from the tunnels and cling to the cutting walls. At times the trees grow too big, causing them to be in danger of becoming detached from their rootholds and fall onto trains passing beneath. The Overhead

Line Equipment baulks access to them from the railway, so abseilers are engaged to remove them, much to the amusement of the local kids, as they disappear over the parapet. In addition to removing the trees, a thorough examination is made of the sandstone walls for signs of weathering or other damage.

Lucky for me, it is a nice spring morning as I trudge through bridges and tunnels to the site of work. During the night a ½-mile length of track has been lifted and all the ballast removed, leaving the original, smooth, sandstone bedrock exposed. I examine the cutting wall and can see the scratches made by the navvies' tools, also the brickwork filling geological faults and joints at the time of construction. A bed of hard-core ballast is laid, on top of which is placed the new track, ready-made in 60ft lengths at Castleton. Obtaining the correct levels is achieved by means of laser beams, somewhat different to the old days when 'T' boards in the hands of the ganger were the norm.

Gone, also, are the days when huge gangs of 50-or-more men toiled manually on re-laying, they being replaced by machine operators. The only problem encountered during the day involved a contractor's mechanical shovel causing damage to the Overhead Line Equipment. This is reported, and before the line is given back up to traffic, rectified by the fault team from Wigan.

My services are further called upon to act as 'Pilotman' on the Bootle Branch, owing to equipment failure. The duties entail travelling with each train either to Seaforth Freightliner Terminal or Liverpool Docks from Bootle Junction signal box on the former Lancashire & Yorkshire Railway. Again, I am requested to be the ODS on a ballast train working on the Single line at Fazakerley, also on the ex-L&Y Railway.

After reaching the top of the tree in the signalling grade, it is a natural progression to transfer to the dizzy heights of a District Signalman's Inspector, but I never had any such aspirations, even though many of my colleagues from earlier years took this step. Recently, the management approached me with a view to filling a vacancy in this grade owing to annual leave; I willingly accepted, if only to experience this facet of railway work.

Reporting to the office at Lime Street **(in my bowler hat and pin-stripes?)** I start to clear up the untidy desk, littered with all kinds of correspondence and rubbish; that is, until my counterpart asks me not to, saying :

'Don't clear the desk, or the gaffer will think we have nothing to do!'

As a result it stays in a mess!

Signalmen in one way or another are plagued with red tape, receiving 'please explain' letters for the most trivial things. Over the years I tended to ignore many, but some persistent 'pen-pushers' would send follow-ups. I would reply, **'I have nothing to add to my previous report.'** I can see now the waste of time it would be to plough through the mountains of rubbish, also the reasons I never heard any more!

'Tony, on the way home will you call into Ditton No 1 signal box? Collect the train register book, and bring it in tomorrow.' requests the Chief Area Movements Inspector.

Off I go to the signal box in which I have not set foot since 1962, the year I was made redundant. The change here is remarkable, a substantial majority of the levers now unused and painted white because of rationalisation. Trees grow along the whole route once occupied by the' Sacred Lines' and the connections into Messrs Evans' timber yard. The Prop Yard ceased to be used for pit-props years ago, the land it occupied passing over to the Sleeper Depot; but concrete sleepers have largely replaced the pickled, wooden variety, which accounts for the now very rusty rails. In front of the signal box, the crossing featured in the 1912 disaster has been removed, leaving the top junction to and from the old Slow lines still in existence. In addition, wagons dealt with at Ditton Junction have declined in number, as in most areas around the North-West. The yard, often filled to capacity in former days, now lies idle, apart from the occasional block train for the British Oxygen Company on the Hutchinson Estate.

The signalman informs me that an express train has failed in Runcorn station and an assisting locomotive is on its way from Garston. I board the engine on its arrival and travel along the Down Line in the Wrong direction to Runcorn. This gives me a chance to see from the Ditton Viaduct the rationalisation that has taken place in the Widnes area. West Deviation signal box still stands, but not the same one I worked in. This was replaced with a new box in 1967, on the Ditton Junction side of the old CLC line running from Moor Lane to the Hutchinson estate, this line having already closed on 6th December 1964. Jubilee Sidings is just derelict land, though Deviation Yard exists, the rails *in situ*, rusting under attacking vegetation, never again to be the hive of activity that it once was. On the right, a few lines on the giant Hutchinson Estate can be seen.

Approaching Britannia Bridge, I look for the lower quadrant semaphore signal on the left castellated tower, which I know was replaced years ago with a colour light; but, please forgive the nostalgia as I make this journey once more. Trundling over the viaduct, the busy road bridge on the left towers way over us and, beyond, the landing buttresses of the old transporter bridge are still to be seen.

The train is standing in the Up line platform, and our engine is attached to the front, the whole being despatched to London with the minimum of delay. While enjoying a cup of tea with the signalman, a message is received: **'Points trouble at Halton Junction'.** Cadging a lift on the next train heading in that direction, I drop off at the signal box and collect the crank handle.

A Crank Handle is specially designed to fit into points motors in order to operate them manually.

Trains are hand-signalled during the time of the failure until the fault is rectified by the Signal and Telegraph Department staff - armed with a hammer, spanner and a drop of oil, used in that order, which are all that is needed in most cases to get them working again. I head for home after reaching my car at Ditton Junction, again via a cadged lift, to arrive there at 9pm.

Before setting out next morning I receive a phone call instructing me to drop into Carterhouse Junction signal box to sign the Train Register.

As stated earlier when visiting a signal box, a Signalmen's Inspector must satisfy himself that the signalman is carrying out his duties correctly, in accordance with all rules and regulations. He must also check the signal box safety equipment, *i.e.* Detonators, Reminder Appliances, Single-Line Forms, Wrong-Line Order Working Forms and Isolation Forms (if appropriate for that signal box) and also be prepared to work the signal box if necessary.

Of course, there is always the possibility that a signalman could ask trick questions about the 'rules and regs', but they are probably identical to those that we 'sussed out' 30 or 40 years ago.

A detonator on the line.

Another phone call. *'Pop into Ditton No 2. The signalman has a letter for the boss.'*

Off I go, along the 'Stinky Mile' again, though not on a push-bike as in days long past, but in the comfort of a car. Opposite the signal box is sited a stop block, adjacent to the Down Slow line. It marks the location of the old Ditton No 2, and I am the only railwayman left to have actually worked in it as a signalman. In its hey-day, the signal box was the busiest in Class 2 category throughout the Liverpool Division, and many relief Signalmen kept away from the hard graft associated with it. Today, traffic is confined to main line running, the Fast and Slow and vice versa crossings having been recovered, along with numerous other sets of points, and their corresponding signals.

Partaking in a cup of tea, the signalman and I reminisce until a phone call is received, putting the dampers on the proceedings.

'Collect the Train Register from Hough Green signal box.'

Hough Green, only a couple of miles by road from Ditton, is on the former Cheshire Lines Railway.

This railway opened on 1st August 1873, the station here in May 1874. The signal box replaced an older one about 20 years ago and contains an LMS Standard Frame. Today it is only a Block Post signalling trains between Widnes East Junction and Halewood East signal boxes, but at one time it boasted a junction laid on 1st July 1879, forming a loop, via Moor Lane signal box, Widnes Central station and Tanhouse Lane station, linking up with the main line again at Widnes East Junction signal box. This loop line was jointly owned by the CLC and the Great Central and Midland Railway companies.

At the eastern end of the loop, a south-to-west spur linked up at Widnes West Junction, but, owing to trouble over the running rights between the above-mentioned companies, this spur closed on 29th February 1880. Passenger trains running via the loop were minimal, and their timings not suitable for railwaymen travelling to and from work on the normal shift patterns, with one exception. A Saturday-only train from Liverpool stopped at Widnes Central station at 12.45pm, giving ample time to relieve their mates before 1 o'clock anywhere in the Widnes area; that is, provided they had a bicycle.

Freight traffic serves the large Hutchinson Estate from sidings controlled by Moor Lane signal box, passing over the Low Level Line at West Deviation Junction a few hundred yards away. At Tanhouse Lane connections lead to the giant United Sulphuric Acid Company's sidings, who receive block trains of anhydrite from Long Meg via Halewood Sidings.

The entire Loop Line closed in December 1964, as already stated. This took place when the Chord Line was laid from Widnes No 1 signal box (on the former St Helens & Runcorn Gap Railway) to Tanhouse Lane, the trains travelling on a more direct route through Wigan and St Helens.

This visit to Hough Green signal box proved to be my first and last.

Hough Green Junction signal box. Courtesy of Mick Langton.

Similar to the fate of Halewood East Junction and Widnes East Junction signal boxes, this one succumbed to the ravages of fire at the hands of arsonists.

Finally, I arrive at the office in Liverpool at 2pm to find reams of paperwork conveniently placed on the desk in front of my chair. Right! I'll make a start. 1st letter TFA **(take further action)**. 2nd letter WPB **(waste paper basket)**. 3rd letter WPB, and so on, until the basket is full and I go looking for an empty one to continue my work. Looking around the office I see about 25 people sitting at desks, and all they seem to be doing is passing bits of paper to each other, occasionally, taking a piece to the filing cabinets at the far end.

'A bit of a dead end job, this is!' I think to myself, which is subsequently confirmed when I am handed a piece of paper informing me of a site meeting the following day at **Anfield Cemetery!** I have been selected to act as the Operating Department Representative. Arriving outside the gates, our party of eight is treated suspiciously, with solemn glances, by a group of bystanders with heads bowed, who obviously think we are mourners at a forthcoming funeral.

The entrance to the cemetery is a magnificent, exquisitely carved sandstone structure, built in the form of a small castle which supports the Bootle Branch Line passing over it. Liverpool Corporation hired contractors to repair and sandblast the graffiti-covered gateway. It is necessary for the workers to have access to railway property during this work, and a plan is formulated, with the agreement of all parties. I submit my report to management, who attempt to lure me from my signalling position, but I won't take the bait!

I want to remain one of the boys!

'Tony, will you make an out-of-hours visit to Olive Mount and Huyton Junction signal boxes tonight?' I am asked by my superior. Walking through the dark, dismal Olive Mount cutting so late at night makes my heart beat a little faster, especially when nearing the now unused tunnel **(the haunt of the top-hatted gentleman with the long frock coat!).**

After a quick check of the Train Register and an even quicker exit from the cutting, I proceed to Huyton Junction. Paul, the young signalman on duty, is one of the first box lads I had in Edge Hill power box, and I notice he has his rules and regulation books on the table (probably to impress me)!

'Have you heard about the new ruling?' he enquires.

'Which one is that Paul?' I reply.

'About the discrimination against women!' adding, *'British Rail has issued a directive that the word "Signalman" is discriminatory, and all references should be erased and substituted by "Signalperson".'* he tells me.

'I have started on mine,' he says, showing me his Block Book, 'Signalman' crossed out and 'Signalperson' written neatly above. I hold my breath because I have the urge to burst out laughing, but decide against it, saying:

'Thanks a lot Paul; when I return to the power box next week I'll start on mine!'

My job is done here at Edge Hill, as management have decided that my services are required at Warrington power signal box again, as a **'SIGNALMAN',** and this is where in September 1994, **'my journey on the railways'** finished.

A truly fascinating, and enjoyable, journey from beginning to end!

'Lion' in Lime Street station. Courtesy of Liverpool Echo.

In Lime Street cutting; single-bore tunnel is to the right.

Courtesy of Liverpool Echo.

CHAPTER FOURTEEN
LOOKING BACK

The old adage **'one must always look to the future'** is good advice, but occasionally it does no harm to look back and reminisce about the 'good ole' days, and these they truly were! I have seen many changes on the railways in the last half-century, with diesel and electric power taking over from steam; power operated signal boxes replacing those manually worked; Dr Beeching's proposals being brought to fruition, with the closure of the branch lines; and rationalisation programmes making many men redundant. In this time, also, the personnel structure has altered considerably, as in other nationalised industries, where the workforce now comprises more **'chiefs than Indians'** with the result that morale has declined.

As stated in the introduction, my family was bombed-out twice during the 'May Blitz' of 1941 whilst living on the Wirral, and it is recorded that we all perished. However, this was not the case and we moved to Liverpool where, in fact, an incendiary bomb hit this house but, thankfully, everyone survived. This house still stands today; in this eight-roomed house, seven, including the cellar, have fireplaces. The chimney pots are placed in the centre of the tiled, angled roof. The bomb actually went down one of these chimneys, finishing up in the cellar and setting fire to the house. At that time all houses were issued with implements to use if a situation of this nature occurred. My grandfather, with the aid of the scoop, picked up this flaming bomb and threw it into the road. The central walls of the house were built of wattle and plaster, the bomb actually going through one of these. Evidence to confirm this can still be seen in the form of the burn marks tracing the route the bomb took; that is, if you care to strip off the wallpaper.

Liverpool has always been the hub of transport technology, so allow me to give you a few facts about this. Large tram sheds were dotted all over the city, including ones at Edge Lane, Old Swan and **Penny Lane.** In early 1943 I attended Toxteth Technical Institute at the northern end of Aigburth Road, and opposite stood the Dingle tram sheds.

Dingle station on Liverpool Overhead Railway. Courtesy of D J Norton.

'DINGLE': now, that rings a bell for the citizens of this great city, because quite close to the tram shed is the **underground** section of the **OVERHEAD Railway!**

True! The Liverpool Overhead Railway started underground!

I can recall the many occasions going down in the lift to the station platform to join the electric train and travel along this fascinating railway, enjoying the sight of Liverpool's famous waterfront, with the ocean-going liners and cargo ships in the numerous docks along the route.

Underneath the Overhead Railway, the Liverpool Docks and Harbour Board ran its own steam railway, transporting wagons to the various docks of all sizes on the route. It was not uncommon to be travelling on a tram – 'bone-shaker', a *nom de plume* given by local people to those without a roof where the passengers are open to the elements if travelling on the upper deck, in rain, hail, or shine to Pier Head - for it to stop to allow the passage of the '**Dock Road Express**', with its whistle blasting out, signalling its approach as if to say, *'Get out of my way!'* and this without the use of traffic lights.

A case of, 'After you my friend, or should I go first?' Take your pick!

After travelling through the half-mile-long Dingle Tunnel, we reach daylight again, high above the Cheshire Lines Committee Railway at Brunswick; this will be dealt with later on in the book.

In Brunswick Liverpool Overhead Railway station. Courtesy of D.J Norton.

One would think that a purpose-built railway of this nature would be perfect in every sense, but I can assure you in this instance it is far from the truth. Sitting in the front of the train, viewing the line from the driver's vantage point, one can immediately see that it is not level; in fact it undulates like the waves in an ocean, up and down. Sea-sickness could be brought on by the unstable, oscillating coach. However, the scenery takes one's mind off the uncomfortable ride. During the war this railway took a terrible battering, and large parts of it were destroyed by bombs.

Liverpool's railways, on the whole, can boast many of the world's 'firsts'. The Overhead Railway can claim to be the first elevated railway in the world, being opened on 4th February 1893. It was also the first in the world to use Automatic Signalling and Colour Light signals, and the first to introduce elevators for the use of passengers.

Originally the plan was to use steam engines to haul the trains, with the structure being floored to catch any cinders that fell onto the track, but this idea was rejected and electric traction powered by 500v DC was introduced.

Running contiguous with the Overhead Railway throughout its entire length is the **Dock Road.** Ask anyone in Liverpool where the **Dock Road** is and they will tell you exactly where it is.

But they are definitely misleading you, because **Dock Road** is a small, insignificant road in Garston, south Liverpool. These days, with modern technology, if you are rich enough to own a **SatNav** put in Dock Road, Liverpool …. and you will finish up in Garston!

Not many of the people living in Liverpool know there is **no 'Dock Road'** running contiguous with the Overhead Railway.

No Dock Road?

Yes! No Dock Road!

Sefton Street, which is near Brunswick, followed by Bath Street, then Waterloo Road, and finally Regent Road form the '**Dock Road'**. But there is **no Dock Road. Correct!**

The people of Liverpool colloquially called the Overhead Railway the '**Docker's Umbrella**', because dock workers had to pass underneath it to reach their places of work, and it was always referred to by this name. I, myself, sheltered under it many times during rainy periods, listening to the trains passing high above. A private company owned and ran this railway, and as such was not nationalised in 1948. However, because the structure was in very poor condition and the directorship was unable to finance repairs, it went into liquidation. They did try hard to get financial backing from several sources, but were unsuccessful and finally closed the line on 30th December 1956. The following year it was dismantled, much to the dismay of the population, including myself. A truly sad loss.

On 24th July 2012 the tunnel at Dingle collapsed. The houses above were badly damaged and it was necessary to evacuate the occupants.

There is only one small stretch of the Dock Railway that survives and this is where the former LNWR passes over the '**Dock Road**', continuing to Canada Dock and the Freightliner terminal at Seaforth. In my capacity as the temporary Signalmen's Inspector at Lime Street station, during an electrical failure of the signalling equipment I was designated to be the Pilotman working the trains over this section of line. As I stated earlier, Liverpool can boast of many firsts, but here at Seaforth Freightliner Terminal it can boast a **last!**

Explanation:

When the railways were first opened in September 1830, policemen ('bobbies') were employed using red flags to signal trains. These became the modern day signalmen. In these days of advanced technology, one cannot comprehend that policemen are still being used to signal trains. Well, allow me to educate you! Come here, to this location, and you will see this method of signalling is still in use; this is hard to believe, but true!

~~~~~~~

Merseyside has always been associated with the sea, and in my early life these maritime connections were dominant. I recall on 7th July 1938 having a day off school and being marched down to Cammell Laird's shipyards to witness the launching of the RMS 'Mauretania'.

Recently, a fellow signalman of mine, Ray Burgess, informed me that his father was detailed to travel on the doomed HMS 'Thetis', mentioned in the introduction, but a quirk of fate took a hand, and he was transferred by the management of Cammell Laird's shipyards to embark on the sea trials of the 'Mauretania'; he was presented with the postcard below, on completion.

RMS 'Mauretania'. Courtesy of Ray Burgess.

Other famous ships associated with Liverpool include the 'Titanic' and 'Lusitania'.

A flotilla of war ships on the River Mersey. Ron Couchman.

Even the powerful force of the Royal Navy can overshadow the ever-present Mersey Ferry, plying its way from Pier Head to Seacombe.

Seacombe ferry landing stage can be seen under the ventilation shaft of the Mersey Road Tunnel in the centre of the picture. Courtesy of Liverpool Echo.

The **'Royal Iris 2'** and **'Royal Daffodil 2'** were regular Mersey ferry boats sailing between Liverpool, Birkenhead, Seacombe and New Brighton.

During the war, in addition to Liverpool and Birkenhead getting hammered with bombs, ships were not immune, and many were sunk in the River Mersey itself. One ship was bombed in the middle of the river, in a direct line between Pier Head and Seacombe **(see above picture)** and its masts protruded out of the water to some considerable height. It actually settled on top of the Mersey (Road) Tunnel beneath, the ferry boats from Liverpool sailing past it on the port side and, in the opposite direction, the starboard side. It was many years before this ship was removed; unlike other wrecks nearby, because of its proximity to the tunnel, explosives could not be used to shift it. It was eventually dismantled by divers. Meanwhile, the Mersey Railway between James Street, Liverpool, and Hamilton Square Station, Birkenhead, ran approximately from the bottom right of the picture underneath the left hand side of the pier.

I have devoted Chapter 16 of this volume to the memory of D J Norton, who spent a lot of his time recording features of the beloved 'DOCKERS UMBRELLA' that would have otherwise been lost. He did a grand job and, from now on, will never be forgotten. Thanks D J and Mark from me.

However, this aside, my aim was to write about the subject I know best:

SIGNALLING.

What of the signal boxes I have worked in, also those with which I became acquainted during my railway service? Sadly, the majority have been closed, some suffering an ignominious ending.

Trains still run with the same monotonous regularity on the Mersey Railway from New Brighton to Liverpool, little changed in the years since the '30s, but the line from Moat Lane Junction to Builth Road, on the former Cambrian Railway, connecting the valleys of the rivers Severn and Wye, was closed shortly before the 'Beeching Report' was published .

The imposing station buildings at Llanidloes are still standing, and from Gorn Hill, bare, bereft of its pine woods, I view the peaceful scene below, the faint, winding irregular outlines marking the path where the railway once ran.

Alas, little else remains.

Beginning at Edge Hill, Liverpool, where I started my long career, I shall endeavour to record when the signal boxes closed.

CLOSURE OF SIGNAL BOXES IN THE EDGE HILL AREA

Edge Hill No 1	**5th July 1947**
Edge Hill No 2	**27th August 1961**
Edge Hill No 3	**28th August 1961**
Edge Hill No 4	**13th April 1969**
Edge Hill No 5	**27/28th August 1961**
Edge Hill No 7	**1927**
Waterloo Tunnel Mouth	**1st September 1974**
Edge Hill No 12	**8th December 1957**
Edge Hill No 13	**25th April 1976**
Edge Hill No 16	**23rd May 1982**
Pighue Lane Junction	**15th February 1976**
Edge Lane Junction	**22nd February 1987**
Olive Mount Junction	**16th May 1988**
Broad Green Station	**13th December 1970**
Wavertree Junction	**27th August 1961**
Park Lane Goods	**1st November 1965**
Waterloo Goods	**6th September 1970**

That completes the demise of the signal boxes in the Edge Hill area. The only remaining signal boxes in operation at this time being:

Edge Hill power signal box, opened in 1961; and **Liverpool Lime Street Station.**

However, plans are afoot to build a new panel-operated signal box at Liverpool, which will cover the whole area above - or so they say.

Shipping serving the port of Liverpool has declined drastically over the past few years. As a result all railway connections were severed, except for those at Hornby and Alexandra Docks, and the container base at Seaforth in north Liverpool. The container base at Aintree closed in 1987, followed by the pre-fab depot at Fazakerley in early 1988, but this depot, although now closed, will forever live through the eyes of television. From its position on a high embankment one obtains a free grandstand view of the world-famous **'Grand National'** at Aintree racecourse, and clips of past races are screened regularly showing many railwaymen enjoying the spectacle. No doubt spectators will continue to use this vantage point, but trains and piles of sleepers can be seen only on film. The fate of the Bootle Branch seemed uncertain, because only one freightliner train ran in each direction on weekdays, with one or two wagons going to the grain silo; coupled with the fact that the facing points leading to this line from Olive Mount Junction were dispensed with, transferring the traffic to the Gullet Sidings, where trains had to run round causing a lot of delay. Thankfully, however, a single-line junction was reinstated on 6th March 2009, controlled from Edge Hill power box. On the site of the old Gridiron Sidings a new technology park is being constructed, bringing vital employment to the City of Liverpool. On the roadside wall of the Olive Mount Tunnel in Rathbone Road can be seen the words:

'WAVERTREE TECHNOLOGY PARK'.

But to me this area will always remain the **Gridiron.**

Time has never erased the memories that I now share with younger railwaymen who were never lucky enough to see the railways in their hey-day, as I did. Even today, signal boxes are being called '**Signalling Centres': unfortunately, not to my liking.**

Proceeding along the main line from Liverpool, we reach Mossley Hill station, where at one time the signal box was situated between the Up and Down Fast lines. Allerton Junction signal box is *in situ,* as is Speke Junction, but Garston Junction box, which controlled traffic to the engine sheds and to the docks, was destroyed in an arson attack. Church Road box, nearer to the docks is also now closed.

Woodside Sidings signal box (Harry's Domain) was quite close to the Ford's Motor Company, and this is still in production at Halewood. It transports components by rail to and from their other factories. The sidings at one time were controlled by Ditton No 2 signal box, but have now been transferred onto the panel in the new power box. The overall scene has not altered much, the 'Horse's Rest' still occupying its countryside setting, even though Liverpool Council built a large housing estate just over a mile away.

The old Ditton No 2 signal box, which stood between the Down Slow line and Ditton Goods Yard, was replaced with a new box, opened in November 1960, but this was superseded by the new power signal box, situated on the southern side of Ditton Yard - this also replacing Ditton No 1 signal box, built in 1956. The new power box, opened on 10th December 2000, is a brick-built structure of 'Railtrack' design, fitted with a Henry Williams Ltd 'Domino' NX Panel.

On Ditton Viaduct. Photo by Les Fifoot.

Ditton Junction power signal box.

Courtesy of James MacKenzie.

Interior of Ditton Junction power signal box.

Courtesy of James MacKenzie.

Panel in Ditton Junction power signal box.

Courtesy of James MacKenzie.

The 'Sacred Lines' (the Up and Down Fast lines) between Ditton No 1 and West Deviation signal boxes were closed and lifted many years ago, along with the connections to Messrs Evans' timber yard and associated sidings. The Prop Yard had, by this time, outlived its usefulness. This land is now being used by the Sleeper Depot where, owing to the introduction of pre-stressed concrete sleepers, the work has lessened appreciably. Continuing towards Widnes we arrive at the site of West Deviation Junction signal box, built in 1884, with a 50-lever LNWR Frame. This was replaced by a new box on 15th February 1967, with a BR LMR Type 14, 35-lever frame and, similar to others, ended up being wrecked by vandals; this after being operational for only 20 years. The line from Widnes No 7 signal box, along the former St Helens & Runcorn Gap Railway, was singled and severed north of Farnworth & Bold station, for the sole purpose of servicing Messrs Peter Spence's chemical works and the 'Everite' asbestos works opposite.

Today, in October 2014, looking down from Lunts Heath Road bridge, a modern road is seen going south into Widnes. (See pictures on page 290.)

Widnes No 2, Level Crossing signal box (Ann Street) was replaced with Automatic Half-Barriers, controlled from Widnes No 1 signal box (Vineyard) using Closed Circuit Television (CCTV). This box still controlled the lead to Tanhouse Lane on the old CLC, but the railway board had every intention of closing this line. To enable this to happen, it was necessary to lay a new connection from the existing line between Widnes No 7 and Carterhouse Junction signal boxes. Finally, the railway closed in 1982, and a new road from Widnes to Warrington follows the path of the original railway line between Ann Street and Vineyard signal boxes, before veering right onto what was formerly the waste land occupied by the gypsies. Returning to West Deviation Junction, the lines from here, via Waterloo Crossing, to Widnes No 4 were closed on 10th March 1969. The latter (Dock Junction) signal box survived until 18th April 1982. Associated Portland Cement Manufacturers' (Blue Circle) Sidings, controlled by CCTV installed in Vineyard signal box, closed when the Anhydrite trains ceased running from Long Meg, and this signal box eventually closed on 18th April 1982.

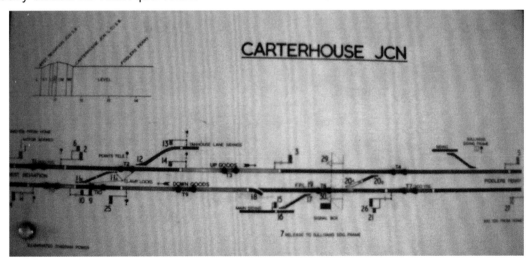

Carterhouse Junction: the new layout on the box diagram, described above.

Courtesy of Ray Burgess.

Carterhouse Junction signal box is the only remaining one operating in Widnes, controlling the small 'Tarmac' sidings and the connections to the ICI Pilkington Sullivan's works. The signalmen now working in this box are, in my opinion, somewhat cosseted because they are issued with oxygen masks, for fear of chemical leaks from the nearby plant.

In 'my day', I never heard of any signalman succumbing to chemical poisoning. It was a case of a good ole' sniff to clear the lungs out!

Eventually, it had to happen. This signal box was taken out of use, and finally dispensed with, on 4th April 2007, thereby completing the devastation of the railways in Widnes.

On the other side of the River Mersey, Runcorn Station signal box is still in existence, the station's platforms having been extended up to it to accommodate the longer trains, but the Warehouse Sidings have closed and are now a car park, and the layout opposite them is considerably reduced. Folly Lane signal box, the first of many in which I was passed competent to work, closed in 1960 and was replaced with a ground frame operated by shunting staff. The Up and Down lines from Runcorn have been singled, and trains still service Castner Kellner's chemical works, but the single line to Runcorn Docks and the electric works has been removed.

Likewise, Halton Junction signal box still stands, but in the centre of a large housing estate. (Hopefully, they have had a toilet installed in the box.) The Down Loop line has been recovered and the ground frame it controlled at Sutton Weaver disconnected.

CLOSURE OF SIGNAL BOXES IN THE WIDNES AREA

Mossley Hill	**6th March 1961**
Garston Junction (destroyed by fire)	**27th July 2003**
Church Road	**13th July 1993**
Woodside Sidings	**6th March 1961**
Ditton Junction No 2	**10th December 2000**
Ditton Junction No 1	**10th December 2000**
West Deviation Junction	**19th December 1988**

West Deviation Junction signal box. Courtesy of H.G.

Widnes No 7	**18th April 1982**
Widnes No 6	**10th March 1969**
Widnes No 4	**8th April 1982**
Widnes No 2	**3rd December 1973**
Widnes No 1	**18th April 1982**
Appleton Station	**11th December1966**
Farnworth & Bold Station	**4th November 1973**
Carterhouse Jn	**Out of use 3rd December 2006; demolished 14th April 2007**
British Alkali	**12th June 1955**
Folly Lane	**1960**
Sutton Weaver	**6th March 1961**

This picture taken in 1959 shows, left to right, the Runcorn transporter bridge, the new road bridge (under construction) and the railway bridge. Photo by Eddie Bellass

This picture, taken in 1988 from a similar position, shows the scene after

the carnage that took place of the railways at Dock Junction in Widnes.

Note Ditton Viaduct in the background. Courtesy of Ray Burgess.

I never thought that after leaving Widnes over 50 years ago in 1962, to go to work in Wigan, that I would get a book published about signal boxes which I treated as my second homes; but, unlike other people who robbed the public purse to pay for theirs, I was actually paid for going to mine!

Being a signalman in the early years was a lonely profession but, there again, one had plenty of time to reflect on many things, including solving the world's problems, without hindrance; except, perhaps, when traipsing into a field with a can to obtain water from a village pump in order to make a brew of tea, which, certainly, brought one back to reality.

Then and now at Farnworth & Bold. Both pictures were taken from Lunts Heath Road bridge.

Upper photo by J M Tolson, courtesy of Sankey Canal Restoration Society.

Lower photo by Paul Wright.

Appleton station after closure. Photo by John Wilson, courtesy of 8D Association.

Site of Widnes South station, with Carterhouse Junction Distant Signal.

Photo by John Wilson, courtesy of 8D Association.

Widnes South station in 1988, with the site of No 7 signal box on the right.

Courtesy of Ray Burgess.

Let us now proceed to:

THE WIGAN AND ST HELENS AREA

Commencing in the north, the Slow lines from Standish Junction to Balshaw Lane signal boxes closed in 1971, both Coppull and Balshaw Lane stations having closed earlier. A new junction was laid from the now Down Main Line onto the Slow Lines at Balshaw Lane, which is now controlled from Preston power signal box. Standish ceased to boast a junction when the Whelley Branch line closed as far as Platt Bridge Junction, thus severing the line from De Trafford Junction to Hindley No 2 on the former Lancashire & Yorkshire Railway, when Warrington power signal box opened in September 1972. At Platt Bridge Junction the single line to the CWS works was retained, though not through to Bamfurlong Junction. A ground frame was installed on the Up East Loop near the 'flying junction' and a single line, previously the Up Whelley line, was used to service the glass works, the guard of any train being responsible for turning the hand points at the old Platt Bridge Junction before reversing along towards the works. However, in the mid 1980s this traffic was discontinued.

It is a pleasure that I can relate (early 1990s) the resurrection of the line from Springs Branch via Platt Bridge, but only as far as Bickershaw opencast mine, and then only a single line worked under Token Regulations. Coal traffic continues to be transported from Bickershaw Colliery, even though the Albert Pit has ceased production, but the connection underground of this and Golborne Colliery assures the future of this line - but for how long?

This remains an enigma!

As a result of the above-mentioned linking of the two collieries, the one at Golborne has ceased to lift coal, its only function now being to transport the miners to and from the coal faces, with the obvious happening in regard to the railways.

The Chord line also presents a dismal picture, with the Shell Oil Company laying a pipeline from its refinery at Ellesmere Port direct to the depot at Haydock, thereby cancelling their contract with the Railway Board.

In addition, the Lowton Metal Sidings at Ashton-in-Makerfield are no longer used, but new sidings have been installed close to Edge Green bridge, justifying the connection with the main line.

It is a matter of conjecture as to how long it can be retained.

All the signal boxes covered by relief signalmen based at Wigan on the former LMS are now closed, with the work transferred to Warrington power signal box.

Balshaw Lane Station	**5th November 1972**
Darlington's Sidings	**20th September 1964**
Blainscough Sidings	**5th November 1972**
Coppull Hall Sidings	**17th November 1970**
Standish Junction	**15th January 1973**
Victoria Colliery	**20th September 1964**
Boars Head Junction	**1st October 1972**
Rylands Sidings	**1st October 1972**
Wigan No 2	**1st October 1972**
Wigan No 1	**1st October 1972**
Springs Branch No 2	**1st October 1972**
Springs Branch No 1	**1st October 1972**

Crompton's Sidings	20th February 1972
Bamfurlong Junction	1st October 1972
Cross Tetley's Sidings	6th May 1961
Bamfurlong Sorting Sidings	1st October 1972
Golborne No 1	1st October 1972
Golborne No 2	1959
Edge Green	6th February 1933
Long Lane	8th October 1945
Golborne Junction	17th September 1972
Whelley Junction	18th June 1967
Haigh Junction	18th June 1967
Roundhouse Sidings	1st October 1972
Lindsay Colliery	March 1957
Rose Bridge Junction	July 1938
De Trafford Junction	1st October 1972
Amberswood West Junction	19th May 1969
Amberswood East Junction	18th May 1969
Platt Bridge Junction	15th March 1973
Bickershaw Junction	24th August 1969
Fir Tree House Junction.	18th May 1969
Ince Moss Junction	1st October 1972
Garswood Hall (Siding 8th September 1968)	25th September 1972
Bryn Junction	April 1969
Bryn Hall	20th December 1956
Garswood Station	1st October 1972
Carr Mill Junction	24th September 1967
Gerrards Bridge Junction	16th February 1969
Pocket Nook Junction	1st October 1972
St Helens No 3 (Raven Street)	11th June 1972
Ravenhead Junction	11th July 1990
Broad Oak Junction	16th November 1969
Sutton Oak Junction	27th May 1989
Prescot Station	25th September 2012
Huyton Junction	1939

Huyton Quarry Station Downgraded to Shunting Frame	**25th November 1973**
Accidentally demolished by crane during engineering work	**9th November 1976**
Top of Whiston	**15th January 1961**
Whiston Bank	**c1914**
Rainhill Station	**26th March 2007**
Lea Green Sidings	**25th June 1967 17th**
St Helens Junction No 1	**September 1972 17th**
Bold Colliery Sidings	**September 1972**
Parr Moss	**July 1884**
Collins Green	**15th August 1965**
Earlestown No 5 Destroyed in arson attack by vandals	**17th September 1972**
Earlestown No 4	**17th September 1972**
Earlestown No 3	**17th February 1968**
Earlestown No 2	**17th September 1972**
Earlestown No 1	**17th September 1972**
Newton-le-Willows	**17th September 1972**
Lowton Junction	**17th September 1972**
Parkside No 2	**17th December 1961**
Parkside No 1	**17th September 1972**
Kenyon Junction	**17th September 1972**
Glazebury	**3rd October 1965**

St Helens No 2 (Shaw Street) meanwhile is still operational, but is soon to close along with Huyton Station box in late 2014/early 2015.

Not long to go for these two now, as the area formerly controlled by them will be the first piece of the network to go under the control of Network Rail's all new ROC (Regional Operations Centre) now being built and fitted out at Ashburys, east Manchester.

Wigan Wallgate is still in operation, though no longer has its 75-lever frame, which has been donated to the East Lancashire Railway Company who have used most of it in Bury South signal box. The area at Wallgate was re-signalled with LED (Light Emitting Diode) signals in 2004 and is fitted with a brand new TEW Systems Type SM 48 NX Panel.

Three pictures of Boars Head Junction: then and now.

CLOSURE OF SIGNAL BOXES IN THE WARRINGTON AREA

Vulcan Bank	**17th September 1972**
Winwick Quay Sidings	**17th September 1972**
Winwick Junction	**17th September 1972**
Dallam Branch Sidings	**17th September 1972**
Warrington No 5	**12th January 1969**
Warrington No 4	**22nd November 1970**
Warrington No 2	**17th September 1972**
Warrington No 1	**17th September 1972**
Walton Old Junction	**17th September 1972**
Walton New Junction	**2nd June 1968**
Acton Grange Junction	**17th September 1972**
Norton Level Crossing (downgraded to LC ground frame)	**3rd September 1972**
Norton Level Crossing (final closure)	**13th November 1983**
Daresbury	**3rd September 1972**
Preston Brook	**13th March 1961**
Birdswood	**13th March 1961**

FORMER LANCASHIRE & YORKSHIRE RAILWAY

There have been a few substantial alterations in the last 15 years, the railway being reduced in stature to one for local passenger traffic between Liverpool, Manchester, and Southport. Prescott Street depot has closed and one of the few private sidings, that at Gathurst is, I am told, to be closed in the near future.

Signal boxes remaining in the Wigan area include:

Rainford Junction

I note, in a recent picture, taken here, that the token is still handed to the driver using a stick. This 40 years after I introduced this energy-saving idea!

Parbold Station, and last, but not least,

Wigan Wallgate. All the rest have disappeared, with the exception of one:

Douglas Bank

This was burned down by arsonists, but, like the phoenix, arose from the ashes and was rebuilt in all its former glory. It is now situated in none other than the **Wigan Pier Museum**. If anyone does visit this signal box, I can advise you that it is not uphill to the block instruments, as it was in my day! However, I have been informed recently, that **this box has been removed from the museum.**

Douglas Bank signal box after arson attack. Courtesy of Lawrence Thorpe.

Lever frame in Douglas Bank signal box.

Before and after the fire.

CLOSURE OF SIGNAL BOXES ON THE FORMER L&Y RAILWAY

Crow Nest Junction	28th July 2013
Hindley No 1	26th January 1969
Hindley No 2	1st October 1972
Hindley No 3	5th November 1967
Ince Station	1st October 1972
Pemberton Junction	31st August 1969
Worsley Mesnes	27th July 1941
Westwood Park	5th November 1967
Winstanley Colliery	17th December 1967
Orrell East	17th December 1967
Orrell West	19th November 1972
Holland Moss	9th June 1966
Ditton Brook	10th March 1968

WARRINGTON CENTRAL

Old meets new here at Warrington Central station, with a large retail store being erected behind the signal box on the site of the former Cockhedge cotton mill, which was demolished in 1983. It brings a little colour to the dull landscape but, opposite and in complete contrast, the giant warehouse owned by the railway is falling further into decay. Plans are afoot to redevelop the site but, as yet, it appears to be only a dream. Nature is invading the area between the rusty rails, forming a picture of desolation. Widnes East Junction signal box, situated in the 'Green Belt', is surprisingly subjected to the attention of vandals and burnt down, with the result that two more railwaymen have lost their jobs. Temporary signalling methods are introduced until it is decided whether to rebuild it, but its importance is negligible in relation to the traffic flow, and the decision to install another Intermediate Block Section is taken, making a total of three consecutive sections worked under these conditions (probably the first ever on Britain's railways).

CLOSURE OF SIGNAL BOXES ON THE FORMER CLC RAILWAY

Liverpool Central	10th December 1972
St James	3rd September 1934
Brunswick North	12th December 1973
Brunswick South	20th September 1936
Otterspool	12th December 1973
Mersey Road	24th May 1933
Cressington	4th September 1977
Garston Station	23rd July 1967
Hunts Cross West	5th December 1982
Hunts Cross Station (or East)	15th February 1970
Halewood West	14th May 1967

CLOSURE OF SIGNAL BOXES ON THE FORMER CLC RAILWAY (CONTINUED)

Halewood West Junction	**21st October 1962**
Halewood East Junction (damaged by fire)	**26th October 1981**

Halewood East Junction signal box. Courtesy of Ray Burgess.

Halewood East Junction (Finally Closed)	**24th January 1982**
Springfield	**29th September 1929**
Hough Green	**18th December 1988**
Moor Lane	**6th December 1964**
Tanhouse Lane	**6th December 1964**
Widnes North (Farnworth Station in Signal Box Register)	**8th October 1967**
Widnes East (damaged by fire)	**5th April 1987**
Widnes East (finally closed)	**13th December 1987**
Sankey Station	**24th October 1965**
Burtonwood	**16th December 1973**
Sankey Junction	**3rd March 1969**
Bewsey	**11th November 1973**
Warrington Sidings	**11th November 1973**
Warrington Workshops	**11th November 1973**
Padgate Junction	**12th March 1969**
Padgate Station	**26th February 1967**

CLOSURE OF SIGNAL BOXES ON THE FORMER CLC RAILWAY (CONTINUED)

Risley West	**1st March 1970**
Risley East	**17th September 1962**
Risley Moss	**13th June 1964**
Dam Lane Junction	**25th November 1973**
Glazebrook West Junction	**3rd March 1969**

Allerton Junction, Hunts Cross power signal box, Warrington Central and Glazebrook East Junction boxes are all still open and operational at the time of writing.

CHAPTER FIFTEEN

WHAT IS THE FUTURE FOR SIGNAL BOXES?

It was only after realising that railways were of special interest to so many enthusiasts that I decided to have this book (in the loft for 20 years) published. I was unaware how much help and encouragement I would receive for it to come to fruition. Two people stood out of the many that offered their services, and for two entirely different reasons. Both have good knowledge of railways as a whole, one that I could never achieve; and strange as it may seem, one worked on the railways, the other did not. Throughout this book I have purposely used Christian names only, solely because it is more personal, and I see no reason why I should not continue to do this in this instance. Harry was a signalman like myself, but his interests far exceeded mine inasmuch as he kept up with the developments in the signalling grade, from which I detached myself 20 years ago, when I retired.

Allow me to quote Harry's words as he wrote them to me-

'The Power Signal Boxes (and many Mechanical Boxes) that closed have all been abolished, migrated, and had their areas of control consolidated and centralised in one location (in most cases Signalling Control Centres) which, in turn, themselves later on go into a Regional Operations Centre.

for example:

Coventry, Saltley, Walsall Power Signal Boxes have gone into the new West Midlands Regional Operating Centre (WMROC) that's been built just a stone's-throw from the old Saltley Power Signal Box. Cheadle Hulme, Sandbach, and Wilmslow Power Signal Boxes have gone on to 'Manchester South' Signalling Control Centre, whilst Ashburys, Guide Bridge Power Signal Boxes and Stalybridge Manual Box have gone into the 'Manchester East' Signalling Control Centre. Manchester East and Manchester South will no doubt end up as workstations in Manchester Regional Operating Centre. Most (if not all) of the boxes around here will go, and their areas of control will go on to workstations in Manchester Regional Operating Centre at Ashburys within the next few years. On average, around 60 signal boxes a year are now being abolished on the national network in the United Kingdom. The signal box as we know it will soon be a thing of the past, and only to be seen on preserved railways.'

Harry goes on:

'When I look back through the records it really does bring home the amount of boxes that have gone. At least we can say that we were part of it, eh? Looks like Warrington Power Signal Box will be the first of the 1970s West Coast Main Line Power Signal boxes to go in 2016/17 when the area controlled from Warrington is scheduled to go onto a 'workstation' in Manchester ROC at Ashburys. As I type, the new ROC building has already been built and the Signal and Telegraph department staff are currently fitting it out with the equipment that will eventually control the whole of the signalling throughout the North-West. The first stage of Manchester ROC goes live later this year with the areas controlled by Huyton and St Helens being the first to go in there. Basically, how they kill a signal box these days, more often than not, is not actually to re-signal an area as such, but to partially re-signal, consolidate existing areas, then migrate and re-control them from one location. The signal numbers will be kept in their present form in some cases, using the same equipment, signals, routes etc, just being controlled from one central location. So it will be more than likely that in the not too distant future we will find for example that all:

MP (Manchester Piccadilly), PN (Preston), WW (Wigan Wallgate), WN (Warrington) areas will be controlled from one place using heavily automated pre-programmed computer-controlled workstations in an office environment at Ashburys, Manchester.

I have seen some photographs of the new ROC. It is three storeys high and will have about 30 desks in it, each one having a keyboard and a touch-screen phone concentrator with around four monitors on it that act as 'workstation' in place of a panel.

Tomorrow's 'New Signal Box' will look like a call centre.

Even the Electrical Control Room at Crewe (ECR) is being consolidated in this building. In all, the Signalling, ECR, AOC, and Area Management etc, will all be under one roof and in one place.'

'All the eggs being in one basket.'

'NOT MY CUP OF TEA, GIVE ME A FRAME OR GOOD OLD NX PANEL ANY DAY.'

Harry goes on to say:

'Although I only caught the tail-end of British Rail, I am proud to say that I was a signalman. Personally, I don't favour the thought of working in one of the ROCs. I would feel 'divorced' from the infrastructure that I was operating. These days it is actually easier to get rid of Power Signal Boxes as all the infrastructure is already there. It has Track Circuit Block, power operated with indications etc, and all they really have to do is kill the panel by tweaking and marry them all up, then consolidate the areas of control. Not that difficult, when you think about it.'

This is an example of what has occurred. All the following signal boxes have closed:

London (Euston)

Bletchley

Wolverhampton

Norton Bridge

Saltley

Walsall

Rugby

Nuneaton

Coventry

Leicester

Sandbach

Wilmslow

Guide Bridge

Ashburys

Hooton

Paisley

Trent

The box lad John, who trained me in Edge Hill No 13 in 1947, retired as a signalman in Trent signal box.

'This is the end of an era, and can you believe that people are getting nostalgic about Power Signal Boxes now?'

'There are even plans to preserve the NX panel out of Swindon power signal box, which suffers the same fate as those above, later this year. Mechanical signal boxes can be a little harder to get rid of, as one must start with new signalling from scratch, but in many cases the re-signalling jobs are being done using modular signalling, where off-the-shelf parts are used, thus speeding up the abolition.'

Harry finishes by saying:

'Not a good time to be a Signalman.' *(How right he is!)*

Thank you so much, Harry, for this in-depth explanation of the future of railway signalling; and rest assured, we together have re-kindled our own interest in the subject and given others a chance to read about this wonderful occupation with which we are both proud to be associated.

Terry was keen to begin working on the railways years ago, but it never came to fruition. However, this did not deter him from showing an interest in them. I made contact with him for the first time less than a month ago. He has telephoned me on lots of occasions and sent regular e-mails about railways in general, and I have found his knowledge to be far superior to my own. It is through this interest in my project that he has, unwittingly, been successful in bringing me back into contact with many of my work colleagues with whom I had lost touch 20, 30 and even 40 years ago. For this I am truly grateful, and hope in the near future I will get to meet Terry and probably buy him a drink! *Tony*

Oh, by the way, I never got a reward for catching those train robbers at Edge Hill!

At Lea Green. Photo by Terry Callaghan.

At Parkside. Photo by Terry Callaghan.

CHAPTER SIXTEEN

THE LIVERPOOL OVERHEAD RAILWAY

This view is familiar to people the world over, but almost all are unaware that behind these three magnificent buildings once ran a unique railway line. This railway closed in 1956, but thankfully the late D J Norton, a prolific photographer, made an effort to record it for posterity. His son Mark, who was born after his dad died, has given me permission to use the photographs he took, and others in his collection. Whilst I, myself, did not work on this railway, I did travel over it on many occasions to view the ships (including the 'Empress of Canada' which caught fire in Gladstone Dock on 25th January 1953) in the numerous docks along its seven-mile route, and think it is worthy of a section in this work because of its historical interest. Now, I have already recorded a little about this railway in the book, so I shall concentrate on showing the pictures, helped along by some brief descriptions.

Map by Alan Young.

Dingle station looking south. Photo by D J Norton, courtesy of Mark Norton.

Cap badge of workers on the Overhead Railway.

The northern exit to the half-mile Dingle Tunnel.

The Liverpool Overhead Railway begins underground at Dingle station.

The train leaving the lattice work bridge, which joined onto the tunnel,
is travelling on the now-Overhead Railway. Brunswick Yard is underneath.

Northern entrance to Dingle (CLC) Tunnel.
Brunswick signal box to the right; Brunswick Locomotive Sheds to the left.

Custom House. Liverpool.

Custom House with station on the Overhead Railway in front.

Canning station on the Overhead Railway.

(Renamed after the Custom House was destroyed in bombing.)

Typical scene near the Pier Head, Liverpool.

Buses are on 'Dock Road', near the Liver Buildings, Liverpool.

Pier Head station on the Overhead Railway.

Castle Street, Liverpool. Town Hall at the top, left.

(The archway leads to the famous Goree Piazza.)

Scene at Huskisson Docks.

The 'Docker's Umbrella'.

Huskisson Dock station.

James Street, Liverpool.

It was from the building directly in front, owned by the White Star Shipping Line, that the sinking of the 'Titanic' was announced to the general public in Liverpool.

Seaforth Sands station.

Near James Street station, Liverpool.

The white building is the ventilator shaft for the Mersey (Road) Tunnel.

Bomb damage near Pier Head, Liverpool.

The cause of so much damage to the people and property on Merseyside during the 'May Blitz' 1941.

311

Looking towards the Liver Buildings at Pier Head.

Bomb damage on the Overhead Railway.

More bomb damage on the Overhead Railway.

Seaforth Sands station.

Seaforth & Litherland station.

Seaforth Sands station.

Liverpool Overhead Railway coach.

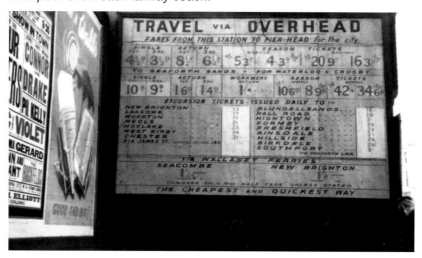

Prices for travelling on the Overhead Railway.

The 'Dock Road Express'.

Overhead Railway being dismantled at Pier Head, 1956.

The same viewpoint as previous picture after the demolition of the Overhead Railway.

The world's first Railway Colour Light Signal.

Notice the driver in standing position.

'Horses, and train on Overhead Railway.'

'The end is nigh.'

CHAPTER SEVENTEEN

THE DEEPING ST JAMES SIGNAL BOX SAGA

You will recall that I mentioned in the introduction that I was born in Stamford in Lincolnshire. Well, on 5th September 2014 the following article was published in the *Stamford Mercury*:

Deeping St James signal box. Courtesy of Karen Clare.

'SIGNAL BOX PLANS ARE NOT GOOD ENOUGH'

Campaigners fighting to save their signal box told Network Rail their response was 'not good enough.' More than 40 people packed into Deeping St James Scout Hut on Tuesday.

They were joined by a representative from Network Rail, the company which wants to demolish the signal box in Station Road, Deeping St James, to make way for new automated barriers. The work is part of a £280m modernisation of the Great Northern Great Eastern line between Doncaster and Peterborough. But people in Deeping St James believe the 19th century building is a historic landmark in the village, particularly as it is the only place where you can still see a sign with the village's original name, St James Deeping.

Communications officer for Network Rail Mark Walker told people at the meeting: 'Over the last couple of months, the Deeping St James community has been very active on the future of St James Deeping signal box and we understand your desire to protect part of the heritage of your community.'

'Since the campaign started a lot of people in our project team have been trying to devise some sort of solution to ensure that the signal box, or some elements of it, are transferred into your custody.' Although we will demolish the structure, we will be donating the bricks as a kind of kit for you to rebuild the signal box in a location of your choice.'

But Deeping St James parish councillor Judy Stevens, who chaired the meeting alongside county councillor Phil Dilks, said: 'I'm really glad that Network Rail has taken on the thoughts and concerns of the people of Deeping St James and I thank them very much for coming up with a plan which we all appreciate them doing.' 'But, it's not good enough and we've all made our position clear.' Deeping's MP John Hayes (Con) also attended the meeting and delivered a letter from the Minister of State for Transport, who promised to review Network Rail's plans to see if the signal box could be kept intact.

317

After the meeting Mr. Hayes said: 'The case I made to the minister was if this is happening in Deeping St James, it must be happening in other places as well.'

'I totally support this campaign and I don't want to see any historic structures destroyed, damaged and lost.' 'If we don't fight this, next time it will be something dearer that we'll lose.' 'You'll have my support and I'll take this to the very top.' Coun. Dilks (Lab) added: 'Network Rail have failed to make a sound engineering reason for demolishing a much-loved landmark.' 'I'm convinced that railway modernisation can be achieved without sweeping away our heritage.'

On the road outside Deeping St James signal box. Courtesy of Karen Clare.

My first impression of this article is the fact that not a mention was made of the signalmen who would be losing their jobs when the signal box was closed. When Warrington power signal box opened in September 1972, 13 signalmen (I being one of them) replaced 160 men who were made redundant, and over 40 signal boxes were demolished. There were no meetings held with the public to discuss the closure of any of these signal boxes.

The modernisation went ahead as planned. Okay, the redundant men were given a choice of vacancies in all departments of the railways, and none was actually put out of work. It was a big personal blow for most of them to be put in that situation, but it was a matter of accepting that progress must be made.

Original nameboard of Deeping St James Signal Box. Courtesy of Lynda and Stuart Hall.

Coming back to this article, the people of Deeping St James and the meeting they held, I can see how passionately they cherish their signal box, in contrast to the attitude of Network Rail's representative: **'We'll knock your signal box down, but we will give you the bricks.'**

'How very considerate they are.'

I would call it an insult of the highest order. The promises made to those of you at the meeting will never come to fruition, because I've experienced that when the hierarchy of the railways want something they get it, and that any opposition encountered, such as that at Deeping St James, will just fade away as time goes by. The truth is that Network Rail did not offer to rebuild your signal box, because it would have cost them too much money. That is what they will say and, sadly, you are going to finish up

WITH A PILE OF BRICKS!

Sincerely, I hope I am wrong!

Members of the Action Group. Courtesy of Karen Clare.

Plus some more! Courtesy of Karen Clare.

So many people from Stamford have been in touch with me, either by e-mail or telephone, voicing their woes over the future of this signal box at Deeping St James, and I could not stand aside without doing something about it.

I received the following letter from two residents at Deeping St James:

Dear Mr Cook,

Thank you for your letter which we read in this week's *Stamford Mercury* in support of our campaign to save the St James Deeping Signal Box. This morning we have had a meeting at the box, which was attended by John Hayes our MP, the local press and about 40 residents.

Our aim was, once again, to raise public awareness and large SOS letters (Save Our Signal box) have been covered in red ribbons and tied to the hedgerows as a visual protest asking Network Rail to listen to our objections and save our heritage. As well as members of our local community, a local school, who have been supporting our campaign, was also represented by the attendance of the Head Boy.

John Hayes has again had conversations with the Minister of Transport who is instructing Network Rail to look at alternatives; one being, as you suggested, moving the box as a whole to an adjacent piece of land.

This would be next to the old Stationmaster's house, which at the moment, although privately owned, stands empty.

If you feel that you could write to parliament expressing your views on this matter, it would be appreciated. We, like you, are aware that plutocratic bureaucrats are not interested in us, the general public, who have paid their wages and given them the comfortable lifestyle to which they have become accustomed.

It is time that big money and 'power' is not allowed to ride roughshod over the feelings of people and flatten our heritage. We are supposed to live in a democracy where people's views are valued and considered; this does not appear to be the case and before long, many of our historic sites will have been destroyed for 'modernisation'. History makes people what they are and it makes a community worth living in.

I repeat, thank you for your support. We would appreciate any advice that you can give us to move this campaign forward. Incidentally, the man at our public meeting representing Network Rail, along with several of his colleagues were giving us misinformation and fabricating facts.

Please continue in your endeavours to support us. Time is running out, as the line is due to be closed from 25th October to begin the butchering of our landscape.

Thanks again for your input to the *Stamford Mercury*.

Stuart and Lynda.

Final Appeal. Courtesy of Karen Clare.

Support our Signal Box campaign stall, with Marie Landen and Karen Clare.

Courtesy of Karen Clare.

To. Network Rail.

Re: The Demolition of Deeping St James Signal Box.

Sir,

I am a retired signalman (also having worked as the District Signalmen's Inspector at Liverpool Lime Street) of 50 years of railway service, working in no fewer than 80 different signal boxes, retiring eventually from the large Power Operated Signal Box at Warrington on the West Coast Main Line,

I have been following the campaign of the people of Deeping St James in their effort to keep hold of their heritage, and found your representative is telling these people a load of rubbish, by saying, 'We are going to demolish your signal box, but you can have the bricks.' I think that is very generous of him, acting on your behalf.

Today, I read in the *Rutland and Stamford Mercury*, I quote:

'You can have your signal box, without the levers.'

Would you please answer me the following questions?

'What good is a signal box without levers?' They are no good to you, and will only be dealt with as scrap iron!

'So how can you justify not letting these people have the whole signal box?'

I really do not think you could answer this truthfully.

I saw the implementation of the Electrification Schemes on both the Liverpool to Crewe, and the West Coast Main Line in the 1960s and '70s respectively, and British Rail never once came up with what is actually happening in Deeping St James. Hundreds of signal boxes have been demolished in the past 20 years, and in every case the railways have pacified the public by giving them what they want.

An example for your perusal:

Wigan is famous for its Pies, Rugby League Team and Pier, the latter of which was made famous by none other than George Formby, that great comedian.

Well, Douglas Bank Signal Box in Wigan was burnt down by vandals in 1985.

'Do you happen to know where it is now?'

'No, of course you don't.'

'Allow me to tell you.'

'It is in the Wigan Pier Museum, complete with levers, block instruments, and everything else you would expect to be in a signal box, even down to the familiar black kettle to boil the water for the signalman's brew.'

My advice to you is simple. Make sure that the people of Deeping St James keep their signal box.

Yours faithfully,

A J Cook. Retired Signalman.

The last train passing Deeping St James signal box.

Courtesy of Karen Clare.

From Network Rail.

Dear Mr Cook,

St James Deeping Signal Box

Thank you for your enquiry of the Network Rail National Helpline, regarding the St James Deeping signal box in Deeping St James, Lincolnshire. It has been passed to me as the issue to which you refer falls within the Great Northern Great Eastern (GNGE) modernisation project.

I would like to thank you for contacting us directly on this matter rather than relying on the media coverage for information, which has frequently been inaccurate and misleading on matters relating to the signal box.

To put the matter into broader context, you may be aware that as the national railway is modernised, all the old manual signal boxes will eventually become redundant. Recognising the heritage value of the historic signalling system, Network Rail approached English Heritage, Cadw, and Historic Scotland to undertake an extensive review of all signal boxes across the country.

As a result of this review, three listing bodies identified which boxes are of historical interest, and indicated to the Secretary of State which shall be listed. A total of 138 signal boxes are now listed in England alone. These boxes are now protected and the cost of maintaining them falls to Network Rail.

St James Deeping signal box was not one of those identified by English Heritage as suitable for listing. There is therefore no requirement for Network Rail to maintain the box once it is decommissioned, or to retain it on site. In addition, the footprint of the signal box impinges on the layout of the modernised level crossing, including the associated MCB-OD technology, meaning that it not only needed to be decommissioned during the GNGE project phase works in this area, but also removed from site in order to enable the level crossing upgrade to be completed within the phase 5 works period, without which the entire project would have failed to be delivered on time, or the crossing would have had to be taken out of the scope of the project and closed indefinitely.

In the summer of 2013 we were in contact with the Parish Council in Deeping St James to inform them of the GNGE modernisation programme, the upgrade of the level crossing, and our plans to demolish the signal box as part of that programme. At the time, the Parish Council requested only that we donate the signal box name sign to the community, given its historic significance, (in that the name sign erroneously carried the name St James Deeping) and we agreed to that request.

There was no subsequent contact from the Parish Council, the community, or anyone else on the subject until late June of this year when we were asked to meet Council representatives and member of the community on site. After the meeting, in early July, we were contacted again and asked if it would be possible to perhaps save the finials, fascia and any other decorative features, and having agreed to that, we were then subsequently asked to "save what we could" of the structure, within the limited time frame available within the works blockade.

This latter request was made to us on the basis that we could preserve as much of the original signal box as possible, the materials would then be handed over to the community to be used in a reconstruction of the signal box which would be undertaken by enthusiasts and volunteers as a community project, and that the Parish Council would identify a suitable location for this project.

In recognition of the fact that this demonstrated the strength of feeling in the community, we undertook, on our own initiative and to our own significant cost, to seek agreement from the train operators to extend the period of the blockage in order to provide additional time in which to increase the amount of original features and materials which we could save. In addition - and again beyond what was requested - we undertook to remove, sort, store and clean the materials, replace what cannot be saved with like-for-like materials, and deliver to the site designated by the Council all materials required for the reconstruction of an entire signal box.

Our undertaking to do this was presented to the Council and community in early September, and is what we proceeded to do when we dismantled the signal box on 22nd October. Contrary to any reports you may have seen which say otherwise, this does include the lever frame.

As indicated, Network Rail has no obligations at all to preserve non-heritage infrastructure, but with regard to St James Deeping signal box we have gone well beyond our normal commitments, and beyond what was requested. Further, this has been undertaken at a significant cost, both in terms of finances and resources.

I trust this information helps to clarify Network Rail's commitment to helping preserve the signal box for the community.

Yours sincerely,

Network Rail.

The Final night of Deeping St James signal box.

Courtesy of Karen Clare.

Signalman Sidney Clare at Deeping St James signal box.

Courtesy of Karen Clare.

Dear Sir,

Thank you so much for replying to my letter.

It is apparent to me that Network Rail/GNGE are committed to saving our signal boxes, once they understand the depth of feeling in the community. I was heartened to read that they have three Independent bodies to assess the signal boxes, and that 138 will automatically be saved.

For all other signal box saviours, I think you have made it quite clear that Network Rail, given the opportunity, would prefer to resolve the issues without press involvement, and that they are committed at times, and at some cost to themselves, to save our signal boxes, when an appropriate case is put forward. I am sure that corporate demands in this high tech savvy media world would prefer not to see the big man riding roughshod over the little man.

It would seem to me:

The power of the people, combined with the support of an interested retired signalman, along with GNGE, can really make a huge difference.

Early this year a relative of mine, who lives in Stamford, sent me a cutting from the *Rutland and Stamford Mercury* about Deeping St James signal box. I had completed the whole manuscript for the book, with a total of fifteen chapters, when this story popped up and I thought it warranted inclusion, primarily because of my interest in signal boxes and signalling in general.

Would you please tender my thanks to your team for saving Deeping St James Signal Box?

Thanking you,

sincerely,

Tony Cook. Retired Signalman.

The final destruction of Deeping St James signal box.

Courtesy of Karen Clare.

326

THE FINAL HUMILIATION AT DEEPING ST JAMES
COURTESY OF NETWORK RAIL

327

Letter received from Karen Clare, organiser of the Deeping St James Signal Box campaign.

Dear Tony,

Just to let you know Network Rail have agreed to hand over the entire box to us.

On the 22nd October 2014, at 21.00hrs, the last train was signalled at Deeping St James Signal Box, bringing to an end an era of great importance to residents in this locality.

A big majority of those witnessing this sad occasion gathered at the gates to see this train go by, with pumpkins expertly carved, lining the edge of the pavement opposite the signal box, lit, with the slogan:

'SAVE OUR SIGNAL BOX'.

Even Sidney Clare (my father-in-law) a signalman of long standing in the area, couldn't be persuaded to stay away, and actually went into the signal box on this very last day.

But, even he will tell you there are so many happy memories to look back on, and there must have been an awful lot of tea supped in that little, but unforgettable, signal box at Deeping St James Crossing, which will live on, hopefully, with the villagers taking over the guardianship.

Sincerely,

Karen.

This final letter received from Network Rail received on the 21st November 2014.

Dear Mr Cook,

Thank you for your letter in response to my reply on the matter of St James Deeping signal box in Deeping St James, Lincolnshire.

I was very interested to read your reply, and about your forthcoming book. You certainly do seem to have near unparalleled experience, having worked in over 80 signal boxes during your career as a signalman.

Your comments in relation to Network Rail's policy regarding historic infrastructure are well made. It is certainly the case that Network Rail cannot fund the preservation of every decommissioned signal box, but has nevertheless been proactive in this regard, and looked to external expertise to assist in the identification of signal boxes which should - and will - be retained for their historic/heritage value.

With regard to Deeping St James, this has certainly been a rather special case, with the requisite financial and resource commitment from Network Rail to preserve an unlisted structure going well beyond what is required or would normally be possible. As things stand, Network Rail is still in talks with the political representatives of the community with regard to the future reconstruction of the signal box on an appropriate site, and is hopeful that the matter will reach a positive conclusion.

I would like to thank you again for contacting us directly on this matter, and I wish you every success with your book.

Yours sincerely,

Network Rail.

So one would assume that this episode is now over. I can assure you **this is far from the truth**, for on 18th May 2015 I received the following communications from Karen Clare, and Stuart Hall, the Chairman of the St James Deeping Signal Box Group.

The first from Karen:-

Hi, Tony,

Find attached a picture taken on the 16th May 2015, showing the new automated gates installed by Network Rail. (They didn't last long!)

This picture will be placed at the end of the chapter, primarily for Network Rail management, and their staff to view.

The road and line were closed for two hours, waiting for railway engineers to travel from Lincoln to rectify the problem.

Richard is standing on the site of our signal box. This certainly would not have happened when our signal box was there, manned by a signalman.

Kind regards,

Karen.

Stuart wrote to the *Rutland and Stamford Mercury* thus:

On Saturday afternoon, at about 16.00hrs, one of the newly installed barrier gates at St James Deeping Level Crossing 'FELL OFF', blocking the road.

It was noticed by a goods train driver as he approached the crossing, who stopped his train to report the incident. This caused traffic chaos, and it was not until 18.00hrs that an engineering repair team arrived from Lincoln to fix the problem. Police also arrived to close the road, along with a Network Rail police lady in her van. This is not the first incident of failure at these gates; they have been stuck, in the upright position, with lights flashing, causing utter confusion amongst drivers in their cars and, in addition, they have also failed against traffic, blocking the road on their own, without being operated as they should be, by an approaching train.

As part of the campaign group 'Save our Signal Box', we are left with the question in our minds - was it not a better system when the box, manned with a signalman was in place, overseeing the operation as a whole? I, living near this crossing, feel less confident using it than I did beforehand.

The campaign to rebuild the signal box is continuing to make good progress, with some funding in place, and a rebuilding site under negotiation. To further the cause, the group is promoting the campaign by selling T-shirts, bricks and wristbands to raise funds.

A book is also available 'Journey of a Railway Signalman', which features the story of the St James Deeping box in its final chapter.

If you would like to help us raise funds to rebuild this 150-year-old heritage box, you can contact us on our e-mail address: saveoursignalbox@gmail.com

Kind regards

Stuart Hall, Chairman, St James Deeping Signal Box Group.

(The above incident could have led to a very serious accident involving both railway and road, perpetrated by the inefficiency on the part of the installers and management working for Network Rail.)

'Judge for yourself.' Courtesy of Karen Clare.

'At the going down of the sun.'

STOP PRESS.

Hello Tony,

With apologies for the delay, I am able to update you with positive news; although things are moving slowly, they are encouraging. Firstly, the purchase of the land has been agreed upon, the funding for it achieved from a local charity. The land is adjacent to the old Stationmaster's house, so the box will stand proudly near its original siting.

Secondly, Stamford College are on-board with the rebuild as a community project for their construction students and hope to include as many trades as possible: carpenters, bricklayers, and electricians. This rebuild is also being supported by some local companies, most notably, Manor Roofing who have volunteered to re-slate the roof for us when that stage is reached. We are now in the process of applying for planning permission for the rebuild and the wheels are in motion here. All the components for the box are now in our possession and being safely stored in a couple of containers kindly loaned by Deeping Direct Deliveries. One of the original signboards has now been renovated but I think will be kept inside the box for safe-keeping after the rebuild. Fundraising is continuing well, with the sale of brick sponsorship, Tee Shirts and of course your books. We are also well supported by the *Railway Heritage* magazine, which is following our progress. We are also prominent at local events and the interest and support has been most encouraging. The deconstruction of the box has resulted in the construction of group of people who are determined that the St James Deeping Signal Box will stand proudly again as the gateway to our village.

Sadly, on a more personal note – the Clare family have just lost their Dad and Grandad, who as you remember once worked as a signalman at the box. This has left Grandson John even more determined to see the box rebuilt.

We would like to thank you once more for the support you have given us and look forward to reading the next chapter in your book about our campaign.

Our best wishes to you.

Stuart Hall, Chairman, St James Deeping Signal Box Group.

~~~~~~~~~~

Sadly, signal boxes, signalmen and signalwomen, along with semaphore signals will just vanish in Britain after nearly 200 years of operation, and be replaced by 14 monstrous workstations, built in office blocks throughout the country.

Meanwhile, thankfully, through the dedication of the St James Deeping Signal Box Group, the signal box there will rise again, like the Phoenix and, God willing, I shall travel down to Lincolnshire to witness the grand reopening.

To conclude, and by way of a change from these morbid revelations, is the fact that signalmen, on the whole, have not really lost their sense of humour. It will be recalled in the 1950s, the introduction of the DMU fleet corresponded with the Russians launching their 'Sputnik', and railwaymen were quick to give this name to the trains. Today, there are 'Jaffa Cakes', 'Blue Riband' and 'Coffee Creams' running on our railways, in the shape of the new '142' diesel trains, notoriously unreliable (*they take the biscuit!*) and resembling boxes running on rails.

'What a versatile breed we are!'

But, isn't this where I came in?

PS Still not received an invitation from the home of the Corgis. (Oh! I wish they would stop dragging their feet. I could do with a day out!)

THE SIGNALMEN TRILOGY

'THREE RAILWAY SIGNALMEN AT WIGAN BECOME AUTHORS.'

All began their railway service as 16-year-old signal box lads.

The author of this book (Tony Cook) began working in Edge Hill No 13 signal box in 1947. Later, in 1962 he was made redundant from Ditton Junction No 1 box at Widnes and transferred to Wigan No 2 box on the West Coast Main Line.

In 1970 Dave Borshik and Gordon Ferris worked with Tony as his box lads, before eventually graduating as signalmen in their own right.

Tony gained promotion to a Special Class Relief Signalman at Wigan North Western station, and on a few occasions worked in Bamfurlong Junction signal box, located next to Golborne Station box in which Dave had become a regular signalman. Strangely enough, Gordon was a regular signalman in the next box south, that at Golborne Junction.

In September 1972 Warrington power signal box opened. Tony was fortunate to be selected as one of the original 13 signalmen to operate it.

Dave and Gordon, along with 160 other signalmen, were made redundant, both of them being transferred to signal boxes in the London area.

All contact was lost until last year, 2014.

Quite by chance, a colleague of Tony's made contact telling him he had seen a photograph on the 'Wigan World' website of him reporting for duty in Wigan No 2 way back in 1962.

It was at this time that Tony was amazed to learn that Dave had also written a book, **'OUT OF CONTROL'**, about his railway career from 1970 to 1995, before leaving the industry to follow other interests. Furthermore, and surprisingly, Gordon had also written a book, **'A RAILWAY LIFETIME'**. This traces his phenomenal rise from a signal box lad at Wigan to being a member on the Railway Board in London. Notwithstanding, Dave turned out to be a prolific author and wrote three further books, though two of these were not related to railways.

The first **'TO RUSSIA WITH LOVE'** is an unbelievable account of his ancestry in the Ukraine and Russia, during and after the Second World War. Dave's father was forced to join the German army, but was captured by the British and made a prisoner of war, then sent to England. Meanwhile his Uncle Peter fought on the Russian side and survived the war. It is a truly moving story and well worth reading.

The second of his books **'IT COULD BE YOU'** is a personal story of a very rare illness that befell him, which left him completely paralysed for months in intensive care at a hospital. Fortunately, he triumphed over this debilitating adversity with dignity, and with assistance from the hospital staff.

Later he re-joined the railway and was able to resume his career as a signalman in New Mills South Junction Signal Box in Derbyshire. It was in this box he decided to bring his story up to date and wrote his final book **'BACK IN CONTROL'**.

Prospective customers contact:

David Borshik   dborshik@hotmail.co.uk

Gordon Ferris   Imogen66708@gmail.com

Disclaimer.

The information contained in this work is correct to the best of my knowledge, and I apologise if any mistakes, spelling, grammatical or otherwise, are found.

It should be noted that the majority of the photographs in this book have been taken by working railwaymen and railway enthusiasts, bringing together a complete record of how the railways were seen well over 50 years ago. T.C.

John Brownlow, Area Manager Preston,

presenting the Author with his Retirement Certificate,

accompanied by his wife, Elizabeth.

Finally:

Cheers from three Wigan signalmen (retired) 2014.

(In the North Euston Hotel, Fleetwood.)

Cyril Peers. Author. Horace Davies.

From the Author.

I am grateful to many people for assistance tendered to me during the writing of this book, especially to:

Eric Steward, Peter Jump, **Malcolm Laidlaw**, Colin Green, **Brian Lunt,** Peter Hampson**,**

Cyril Peers, Lawrence Thorpe, **Ray Dutton**, Roy Gough**, Eric Coffey,**

Adrian Vaughan, **Brian Tighe**, Tony Callaghan, **Roy Wills**, Martin Bott, **Alan Ford,**

Arthur Chester, **Mick Langton**, Peter Worthington, **Dave Lennon.** John Tolson,

Clare Cook (QEC), Harry Arnold MBE, **Colin Greenhall,**

Oliver and Jen at PhotoFirstAid, Preston,

James MacKenzie, John Harrison (Railway Artist), **George Clarke,** Dave Aspinall,

David A Ingham, J Mercer Collection, **Paul Dyson**, P Norton Collection,

Peter Blackmore Collection, Barry Coomer, **DocBrown,**

Ernest Pyke, **J A Sommerfield Collection,** Val Seddon, **Ray Burgess,** Geoffrey Shrylane,

Wigan Observer, Ron Couchman, **D J & Mark Norton,** Brian and Ron at Wigan World,

The Wigan Courier, The Deeping St James Community,

The Widnes and Warrington Libraries, The Warrington Museum,

The Liverpool Daily Post and Echo, The Llanidloes Library,

The National Union of Railwaymen, The Stamford Mercury,

and **Andrew Gardiner** for providing materials and information, Richard H N Hardy, **Bob Hynds,**

Gary Steele, **Tony Donoghue,** Jimmy Hill, **R W L Jones (Big Bob),** Randy Fitzpatrick,

Dave Gosling, and Bill Paxford for information given.

My sincere gratitude to **Dave Holcroft**, for the many hours of hard work and encouragement he gave, also to **Charlie Andrews, Alan Young, Terry Callaghan, H.G. and Stephen Carnes** for their invaluable help.

Not forgetting my old box lad and fellow author

Dave Borshik.

Special thanks to **Jan Glasscock,** and my son **Tony,** who skilfully piloted the aircraft **with me as his co-pilot (!)** on which my good friend **Joe Gerrard** took the aerial photographs at Edge Hill, Liverpool and Runcorn, and **Martin Peers**, who took the aerial photographs in Warrington from his helicopter.

Finally, my sincere thanks to my dear wife **Elizabeth,** who just let me get on with it.

This book is dedicated to the following people:

My workmate **Roy Hamilton,** who went to a football match along with 95 others and never came home.

R.I.P. my friend.
'YOU'LL NEVER WALK ALONE'.

Signalman Dougie Doughty – my mate for over 60 years.

Signalman Sidney Clare of Deeping St James.

D J Norton - Railway Photographer: Rest in Peace.

My son **Tony -** who died in a tragic motorcycle accident in 2004.
R.I.P. 'Cookie'.

And all **Signalmen / Women** past and present.

Tony Cook. Railway Signalman

The 8D Association

The 8D Association was formed in late 2010 by a group of six like-minded enthusiasts. The aim of the group was to build up a historical record of the rail network within a ten-mile radius of the steam shed 8D at Widnes. The association undertakes walks, study tours, site visits and presentations throughout the year. We produce a quarterly journal with news updates and features contributed by our membership. A website is also maintained with pages on all the main lines, stations and signal boxes within the ten-mile radius of 8D. From the initial six, the membership has grown to nearly 70 by 2015.

Our major site visit for 2015 was the Wapping Tunnel, as guests of the Friends Williamson's Tunnels in Liverpool. The tunnel was a world's first: the first main line railway tunnel constructed between 1826 and 1829. It gave us not only the chance to see the interior of the tunnel, but also to record it with the pictures going into our ever-expanding archive.

The archiving of both written and photographic material has also become very important for the group, with our archivist and group members holding several important documents and artefacts. Contributions of photographic collections have increased significantly as the association has become well-established; these are then digitized so further degradation of images is avoided.

The association also provides reference for modellers, historians and authors, such as the writer of this book, Anthony Cook. Following an exchange of e-mails regarding his book we were able to supply and/or gain permission for the use of several of the images reproduced in this work.

It has been a pleasure to help Tony, and the 8D Association wish him the very best of luck with his book.

Members of the 8D Association on a visit to Rainford Junction in 2015.

SIGNAL BOX DIAGRAMS, BY THE AUTHOR

SIGNAL BOX DIAGRAMS (CONTINUED)

The 'Merseyside Express' at Wigan. Courtesy of Wigan World.

For every copy that is sold of
'JOURNEY OF A RAILWAY SIGNALMAN'
the author wishes to make a donation to these charities:

THE ALZHEIMER'S CHARITY,
in memory of D J Norton, Railway Photographer

and

SAVE OUR SIGNAL BOX CAMPAIGN
at Deeping St James, Lincolnshire

FINALE.

In 2002, I had the misfortune of having a leg amputated, and was fitted with one of these modern, black metal, single pole legs.

During a visit from one of my Great Grandchildren aged 4 in January 2016, he came over to my chair and enquired "Was I a pirate?" I replied "Yes!" adding "I was also a Captain." He then asked "Where was my parrot?"

The following week he went to school, and told his mates.

"His Granddad was a pirate, named Captain Cook, and his parrot made the tea in the kitchen?"

"FAME AT LAST".

T.C.